The Low Fat
Cook's Companion

The Low Fat
Cook's Companion

OVER 300 DELICIOUS RECIPES
FOR HEALTHY EATING

HERMES
HOUSE

This edition published in 1999 by Hermes House

© Anness Publishing Limited 1998, 1999

Hermes House is an imprint of
Anness Publishing Limited
Hermes House
88–89 Blackfriars Road
London SE1 8HA

Published in the United States by Hermes House
Anness Publishing Inc., 27 West 20th Street
New York, NY 10011; (800) 354-9657

ISBN 1 84038 279 1

A CIP catalogue record for this book is available from the British Library

Publisher: Joanna Lorenz
Senior Cookbook Editor: Linda Fraser
Project Editor: Sarah Ainley
Photographers: James Duncan, Michelle Garrett, Ferguson Hill,
David Jordan, Don Last, Peter Reilly
Recipes: Catherine Atkinson, Christine France, Silvana Franco,
Shehzad Husain, Sue Maggs, Annie Nichols, Anne Sheasby, Liz Trigg
Jacket Design: Bobbie Colgate Stone
Nutritionalist: Helen Daniels

The material in this book previously appeared as individual titles in the *Step-by-Step* series.

Printed and bound in Indonesia

1 3 5 7 9 10 8 6 4 2

CONTENTS

INTRODUCTION

Many changes to our diet and to our lifestyle can help us reduce the risk of coronary heart disease (CHD). There are three main things we can do to improve our health:

We can become more active—exercise for 30 minutes five times a week; we can give up smoking—see a doctor or call one of the helplines for advice; and we can learn to cope with stress.

If we also improve our diet, we will enhance these changes and in addition will help control the other major risk factors of CHD, which are: high cholesterol, high blood pressure and obesity (or being overweight).

Eating for a healthy heart isn't difficult. As a first step, eat at least five portions of vegetables and/or fruit a day, and make sure that at least half your meals consist of starchy foods like bread, pasta, rice and potatoes, without too much added fat. Even simple changes in eating habits can make a considerable difference. Cooking our own food puts us in control and makes it easy to limit the amount of fat (particularly saturated fat), salt and sugar we consume. The recipes in this collection prove just how delicious a well-balanced diet can be, and there are numerous techniques and suggestions for eliminating the less desirable elements in our food while retaining—and even enhancing—the flavor.

So, change to a healthier lifestyle and follow the food recommendations in this book, then relax and enjoy life—it'll do your heart good.

Do we need fat in our diet?

We only need 10 g fat in our daily diet for our bodies to function properly. A totally fat-free diet would be almost impossible to achieve, since some fat is present in virtually every food.

A certain amount of essential fatty acids are necessary in our diet to help our bodies absorb vitamins A, D, E and K as they are fat-soluble and cannot be made by the body. Fat is also needed to make hormones. Recent research has proved that we all eat far too much fat. Doctors now recommend that we limit our fat intake to no more than 30% of our total daily calorie intake, even as low as 25% for a really healthy diet. Some fats in the diet are a contributory factor in heart disease and breast, prostate and colon cancers.

Types of fat in foods
Saturated fats are hard fats found in meat, most dairy products, such as butter, cream, margarine, cheeses and animal fats. Palm and coconut oil are also high in saturated fats. Saturated fats can raise the blood cholesterol level and clog up the arteries. The way we prepare and cook foods can limit the amount of saturated fat that we consume.

Polyunsaturated fats are soft fats such as sunflower, safflower, and corn oils, and fish such as mackerel, salmon or herring and nuts, seeds, cereals, lean meats and green vegetables. These fats may help to reduce our cholesterol levels.

Mono-unsaturated fats should make up most of the fat in our diet. They appear to have a protective effect and help lower cholesterol levels. Olive oil, peanut oil and avocados are all rich sources of mono-unsaturated fats.

A selection of foods containing the three main types of fat found in foods.

Eating a healthy low-fat diet

Eat a good variety of different foods every day to make sure you get all the nutrients you need.

1 Skim milk contains the same amount of calcium, protein and B vitamins as whole milk, but a fraction of the fat.
2 Low-fat yogurt, cottage cheese and ricotta cheese are all high in calcium and protein, and are good substitutes for cream.
3 Starchy foods such as rice, bread, potatoes, cereals and pasta should be eaten at every meal. These foods provide energy and some vitamins, minerals and dietary fiber.
4 Vegetables, salads and fruits should form a major part of the diet, and about 1 lb should be eaten each day.
5 Eat meat in moderation but eat plenty of fish, particularly oily fish such as mackerel, salmon, tuna, herring and sardines.

A few simple changes to a normal diet can reduce fat intake considerably. The following tips are designed to make the change to a healthier diet as easy as possible.

Meat and poultry
Red meats such as lamb, pork and beef are high in saturated fats, but chicken and turkey contain far less fat. Remove the skin before cooking and trim off any visible fat. Avoid sausages, burgers, pâtés, bacon and minced beef. Buy lean cuts of meat and skim any fat from the surface of stocks and stews.

Dairy products
Replace whole milk with skim or 1% milk and use low-fat yogurt, low-fat sour cream or ricotta cheese instead of cream. Use cream, cream cheese and hard cheeses in moderation. There are reduced-fat cheeses on the market with 14% fat content which is half the fat content of full fat cheese. Use these wherever possible.

Spreads, oils and dressings
Use butter, margarine and low-fat spreads sparingly. Try to avoid using fat and oil for cooking. If you have to use oil, choose olive, corn, sunflower, canola and peanut oils, which are low in saturates. Look out for oil-free dressings and reduced-fat mayonnaise.

Hidden fats
Muffins, cakes, pastries, snacks, chips, and processed meals all contain high proportions of fat. Get into the habit of reading food labels carefully and looking for a low-fat option.

Cooking methods
Grill, poach and steam foods whenever possible. If you do fry foods, use as little fat as possible and pat off the excess after browning, with paper towels. Make sauces and stews by first cooking the onions and garlic in a small quantity of stock, rather than frying in oil.

A selection of foods for a healthy low-fat diet.

The Fat and Calorie Contents of Food

This chart shows the weight of fat and the energy content of 4 oz (115g) of various foods.

FRUIT AND NUTS	Fat	Energy
Apples	0.1 g	47 Kcals/197 kJ
Avocados	19.5 g	190 Kcals/795 kJ
Bananas	0.3 g	95 Kcals/397 kJ
Dried mixed fruit	1.6 g	227 Kcals/950 kJ
Grapefruit	0.1 g	30 Kcals/125 kJ
Oranges	0.1 g	37 Kcals/155 kJ
Peaches	0.1 g	33 Kcals/138 kJ
Almonds	55.8 g	612 Kcals/2560 kJ
Brazil nuts	68.2 g	682 Kcals/2853 kJ
Peanut butter, smooth	53.7 g	623 Kcals/2606 kJ
Pine nuts	68.6 g	688 Kcals/2878 kJ

DAIRY PRODUCE, FATS AND OILS	Fat	Energy
Cream, heavy	48.0 g	449 Kcals/1897 kJ
Cream, light	19.1 g	198 Kcals/828 kJ
Cream, whipping	39.3 g	373 Kcals/1560 kJ
Milk, skim	0.1 g	33 Kcals/130 kJ
Milk, whole	3.9 g	66 Kcals/276 kJ
Cheddar cheese	34.4 g	412 Kcals/1724 kJ
Cheddar-type, reduced-fat	15.0 g	261 Kcals/1092 kJ
Cream cheese	47.4 g	439 Kcals/1837 kJ
Brie	26.9 g	319 Kcals/1335kJ
Edam cheese	25.4 g	333 Kcals/1393 kJ
Feta cheese	20.2 g	250 Kcals/1046 kJ
Parmesan cheese	32.7 g	452 Kcals/1891 kJ
Plain yogurt	9.1 g	115 Kcals/481 kJ
Low fat yogurt, natural	0.8 g	56 Kcals/234 kJ
Butter	81.7 g	737 Kcals/308 kJ
Lard	99.0 g	891 Kcals/3730 kJ
Low fat spread	40.5 g	390 Kcals/1632 kJ
Margarine	81.6 g	739 Kcals/3092 kJ
Coconut oil	99.9 g	899 Kcals/3761 kJ
Corn oil	99.9 g	899 Kcals/3761 kJ
Olive oil	99.9 g	899 Kcals/3761 kJ
Safflower oil	99.9 g	899 Kcals/3761 kJ
Eggs (2)	10.9 g	147 Kcals/615 kJ
Egg white	Trace	36 Kcals/150 kJ
Egg yolk	30.5 g	339 Kcals/1418 kJ

OTHER FOODS	Fat	Energy
Sugar	0	94 Kcals/648 kJ
Chocolate, milk	30.3 g	529 Kcals/2213 kJ
Honey	0	88 Kcals/1205 kJ
Jam	0	61 Kcals/1092 kJ
Marmalade	0	61 Kcals/1092 kJ
Lemon curd	5.1 g	283 Kcals/1184 kJ

The Lowdown on Low Fat

Reduce your fat intake simply by switching to lower fat foods.

0.2 g fat
1 tsp whole milk
scant 1 cup skim milk

1.0 g fat
½ cup low fat plain yogurt
½ oz strained whole yogurt
1 thin slice (⅟₂₀th) avocado pear
3 bananas
9 apples, apricots, peaches, pears, oranges or small bunches of grapes

2.5 g fat
1 small slice bacon
8 slices turkey bacon

10 g fat
½ cup reduced fat cocoa powder
¼ cup cocoa powder

12 g fat
½ oz butter
1 oz low fat spread

15 g fat
2 oz Cheddar cheese
2½ oz Edam cheese
3 oz feta cheese
4 oz reduced fat cheddar
7 oz cottage cheese

WEIGHING NOTE

The weights given here have been rounded slightly up or down to make measuring portions easier.

Choosing Foods

The amount of fat, particularly saturated fat, is affected by two main factors – the type of foods we eat most often and the way in which we prepare and cook them.

Low fat doesn't mean no fat. It's misleading to start thinking simply of 'good' and 'bad' foods, it's really how much we eat of them that matters.

If you are going to cut down your fat intake, you'll need to make other alterations to your diet to compensate. High-fiber fruit, vegetables and cereals will help fill the gap. You should aim to increase your intake of carbohydrate foods to provide more than half your energy requirements. This will not only make your diet healthier, but you will also gradually lose weight, if you need to.

Fresh Foods and Ingredients

Fresh Beans and Peas

There are many varieties of fresh beans and peas available, including peas, fava beans and Italian green beans and more unusual ones such as Chinese long beans, black-eyed peas and lima beans.

Fresh corn on the cob and baby corn are also popular, as are snow peas, sugar-snap peas and green beans.

All are good sources of dietary fiber and contain other nutrients, including vitamins and minerals. Beans and peas are very versatile and can be used in many dishes including salads, stir-fries, casseroles, pasta sauces, soups and curries. Some varieties, such as sugar-snap peas and snow peas, can be eaten either raw or cooked.

Fresh Fruit

Fresh fruit plays an important part in a healthy, balanced, high-fiber diet. Choose fruits that contain useful amounts of fiber, such as apples, pears and bananas, berries such as raspberries, blackberries and gooseberries, and guava, mangoes, oranges, peaches and pears.

Fruits are very versatile and can be enjoyed raw or cooked, on their own or as part of a recipe. They are also good sources of vitamins and minerals, particularly vitamin C. A piece of fresh fruit makes a quick and easy nutritious snack at any time of the day. Try topping whole-wheat breakfast cereals with some fruit, such as raspberries, for a tasty and nutritious start to the day.

Fresh Herbs

In cooking, herbs are used mainly for their flavoring and seasoning properties, as well as for adding color and texture. They have a great deal to offer: by simply adding a single herb or a combination of herbs to foods, everyday dishes can be transformed into delicious meals.

Herbs are also very low in fat and calories, and those such as parsley provide a useful balance of vitamins and minerals. Many people grow their own herbs; a wide selection is also available in supermarkets, vegetable markets and local groceries.

Potatoes

Potatoes are one of the most commonly eaten vegetables in the world and are valuable in terms of nutrition. They are high in carbohydrate, low in fat and contain some vitamin C and dietary fiber. Potatoes contain more dietary fiber when eaten with their skins on. Wash old and new potatoes thoroughly and cook them with their skins on – for example, baked, boiled and roasted. The flavor will be just as delicious, and you will be getting extra fiber.

Potatoes are very versatile and are used in many dishes. Mashed potatoes (with their skins left on, of course!) make an ideal topping for savory pies and casseroles. For roast potatoes, use a minimum amount

of oil, and if you need to make french fries, leave the skins on and cut the slices thickly using a knife. With baked and mashed potatoes, avoid adding high-fat butter, sour cream or cheese and instead use skim milk, low-fat hard cheese and herbs to add flavor.

Fresh Vegetables

Fresh vegetables, like fresh fruit, play an important part in a healthy, balanced diet. We are now encouraged to eat at least five portions of fruit and vegetables each day for a healthy diet. Vegetables are nutritious and are valuable sources of vitamins and minerals, some being especially rich in vitamins A, C and E. Vegetables also contain some dietary fiber; those that are particularly good sources include broccoli, Brussels sprouts, cabbage, carrots, fennel, okra, parsnips, spinach, chard, collards and corn.

Vegetables are also very versatile, and many can be eaten either raw or cooked. Add vegetables to dishes such as soups, stews, casseroles, stir-fries, salads, hamburgers and meat loaves, or simply serve them on their own, raw or lightly cooked and tossed in a little lemon juice.

Whole-wheat Baked Goods

Baked goods such as whole-wheat pita breads, scones, muffins and cupcakes make a good high-fiber snack or treat. Choose whole-wheat or whole-grain varieties whenever possible, or bake your own at home using whole-wheat flour and adding extra dried fruit. Serve bagels, scones or muffins plain or with a little low-fat

spread, honey or reduced-sugar jam for a delicious, filling snack.

Whole-wheat Bread

Bread has been an important part of the diet in many countries for thousands of years, and nowadays continues to contribute to a healthy, balanced diet. Bread is available in many varieties and is a good source of carbohydrates as well as being low in fat. It also contains some calcium, iron and B vitamins, and whole-wheat varieties are high in fiber.

Make delicious sandwiches and toasted sandwiches using whole-wheat bread and low-fat fillings. Use whole-wheat bread crumbs in recipes for stuffings, coatings and toppings, and serve thick slices of whole-wheat bread at mealtimes for a filling, healthy and high-fiber accompaniment to many dishes.

Equipment

There are only a few essentials for low fat recipes –
accurate measuring and weighing equipment and a
non-stick frying pan. There are, however, many
gadgets which make cooking with the minimum of fat
a lot easier.

non-stick baking paper

non-stick baking tins

Baking sheet
A flat, rigid, non-stick baking
sheet ensures even cooking.

Baking tray
A shallow-sided non-stick tray
that won't buckle at high
temperatures is ideal for
roasting.

Bowls
A set of bowls is useful for
mixing, whisking and soaking. A
non-porous material such as
glass or stainless steel is
essential when whisking egg
whites.

Cutting board
A hygienic nylon board is
recommended for chopping and
cutting.

Colander
This is useful for draining
cooked pasta and vegetables
quickly.

Chef's knife
A large all-purpose cook's knife
is essential for chopping, dicing
and slicing.

Filleting knife
A thin, flexible-bladed knife is
useful for filleting fish.

Frying pan
A non-stick surface is vital for
'frying' and browning meat and
vegetables.

Large spoon
Use this for folding in, stirring
and basting.

**Measuring cups or
weighing scales**
Use these for accurately
measuring both dry and wet
ingredients.

Measuring spoons
Essential for measuring small
quantities accurately.

Non-stick coated fabric sheet
This re-usable non-stick
material can be cut to size, and
used to line cake pans, baking
sheets or frying pans. Heat
resistant up to 550°F and
microwave-safe, it will last up to
5 years.

Non-stick baking paper
Ideal for lining cake pans and
baking sheets without the need
for greasing.

Non-stick baking tins
For easy removal of low fat
bakes and sponge cakes.

Perforated spoon
Useful for lifting cooked food
out of cooking liquid.

Ridged grill pan
For giving broiled meat and
vegetables characteristic
"grill marks."

Sieve
For sifting dry ingredients and
draining yogurt.

Small grater
For finely grating fresh Parmesan
cheese and nutmeg.

Vegetable peeler
For preparing fruit and
vegetables.

Whisk
Essential for whisking egg
whites and for thorough mixing.

ridged grill pan

non-stick baking tins

non-stick coated
fabric sheet

sieve

large spoon

baking sheet

chopping boards

measuring cups

vegetable peeler

Healthy Cooking Techniques

The goals of cooking for a healthy heart are to avoid adding fat to food, to reduce the saturated fat content of the ingredients where possible, to use techniques that retain vitamins and minerals and, of course, to ensure that the food is delicious by preserving or enhancing its flavor, color and texture.

STIR-FRYING

This method means that food cooks quickly to retain maximum nutritional value, color and texture.

Slivers of meat can be marinated in savory mixtures of, for example, soy sauce, fruit juice, tomato paste and vinegar, or similar sauces before cooking to tenderize them and add flavor.

Foods need to be cut into small pieces so they cook quickly and evenly.

2 Add garlic to flavor a stir-fry for a few seconds, then add the meat.

1 Preheat the wok, then drizzle 1–2 tsp oil around the rim. Cut meat into thin slivers or cubes to minimize cooking time.

3 Once the meat is almost cooked, add the other ingredients.

STEAMING

Food is cooked over boiling liquid (usually water) but it does not touch the liquid. As a result, most of the vitamins and minerals are retained.

Browning is not part of the process, so fat never needs to be added.

Steaming preserved the texture of foods and is a good cooking method for those who prefer their vegetables with a bit of bite. It is also very useful for fish, poultry and some desserts.

1 Prepare ingredients as for stir-frying. Expandable steamers will fit a range of saucepan sizes. Add food to the steamer and cover.

2 If using a bamboo steamer over either a wok or pan of boiling liquid, place the food in a bowl first, then cover.

MICROWAVING

This is a quick and useful way of cooking vegetables, fruit and fish.

Naturally moist foods are cooked without additional liquid, and only a small amount of liquid is added to other foods. As a result, vitamins and minerals do not leach out into cooking water, which is then thrown away.

Fat is not required for cooking, and microwaved food can be seasoned with fresh chopped herbs instead of salt. The flavor can be sharpened by adding a little lemon juice.

CASSEROLING

One-pot meals are good for stress-free entertaining. They also have the advantage that vitamins and minerals are retained in the stock, which is served alongside the other ingredients.

Use only the minimum amount of fat for cooking and make the casserole a day ahead, then cool and chill it. Any fat will solidify on the surface and can easily be lifted off before the casserole is re-heated.

PRESSURE COOKING

This method cuts cooking time dramatically, which encourages the frequent consumption of beneficial low-fat foods (brown rice cooks in 7 minutes, potatoes in 6). Like steaming, pressure cooking retains more nutrients because the food is not in contact with the cooking water.

1 Place the food in a microwave-proof dish. Refer to the manufacturer's handbook for information on power levels and cooking times.

1 Trim visible fat from meat or remove skin from poultry.

GRILLING

There is no need to add fat when broiling meat, fish or vegetables. Use a rack, and any fat that runs from the meat can be easily be drained. Brush the rack with oil before cooking to prevent the food from sticking. Cook under the preheated broiler and baste with lemon juice, if desired.

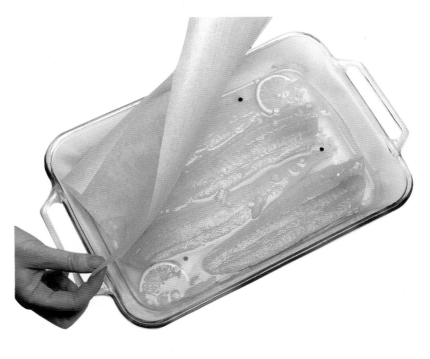

POACHING

This is an excellent way of cooking delicate white fish (plaice) or whole oily fish (mackerel, salmon, trout). Fish steaks, particularly cod, halibut, salmon and tuna also cook well by either method and there is no need to add any fat.

Poaching can be done either in the oven or on top of the stove.

1 To oven-poach fish, pour in boiling liquid to barely cover the fish, add any flavorings and cover with buttered waxed paper. Cook in an oven preheated to 350°F.

2 To poach on top of the stove suspend the fish in the poaching liquid on a rack. Cover with liquid, bring to a boil and simmer gently until cooked.

Puréeing Soup

1 Allow the cooked soup to cool slightly, then ladle it into a blender or food processor.

2 Process the mixture until smooth. If there is a large quantity of soup, blend or purée it in a couple of batches.

3 Rinse the saucepan, then pour the blended soup back into it. Adjust the seasoning and reheat the soup gently before serving.

Peeling Tomatoes

1 Using a sharp knife, cut a small cross in the base of each tomato.

2 Place the tomatoes in a bowl and cover them with boiling water. Leave them for 30 seconds, then using a slotted spoon, transfer them to a bowl of cold water.

3 Remove the tomatoes from the water and peel off the skins. Slice or chop the tomatoes and use as required in the recipe.

Chicken Stock

This classic, flavorful stock forms the base for many soups and sauces.

Makes 6¼ cups

INGREDIENTS
2¼ lb chicken wings or thighs
1 onion
2 whole cloves
1 bay leaf
1 sprig of thyme
3–4 sprigs of parsley
10 black peppercorns

Vegetable Stock

A vegetarian version of the basic stock.

Makes 6¼ cups

INGREDIENTS
2 carrots
2 celery stalks
2 onions
2 tomatoes
10 mushroom stems
2 bay leaves
1 sprig of thyme
3–4 sprigs of parsley
10 black peppercorns

1 Cut the chicken into pieces and put into a large, heavy-based saucepan. Peel the onion and stick with the cloves. Tie the bay leaf, thyme, parsley and peppercorns in a piece of muslin and add to the saucepan together with the onion.

2 Pour in 7½ cups of cold water. Slowly bring to simmering point, skimming off any scum which rises to the surface with a slotted spoon. Continue to simmer very gently, uncovered, for 1½ hours.

1 Roughly chop the carrots, celery, onions, tomatoes and mushroom stems. Place them in a large heavy-based saucepan. Tie the bay leaves, thyme, parsley and peppercorns in a piece of cheesecloth and add to the pan.

2 Pour in 7½ cups cold water. Slowly bring to simmering point. Continue to simmer very gently, uncovered, for 1½ hours.

3 Strain the stock through a sieve into a large bowl and leave until cold. Remove any fat from the surface with a slotted spoon. Keep chilled in the refrigerator until required, or freeze in usable amounts.

3 Strain through a sieve into a large bowl and leave until cold. Keep chilled in the refrigerator until required, or freeze in usable amounts.

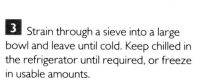

Sautéed Onions

Fried onions form the basis of many savory recipes. This is a fat free version.

INGREDIENTS
2 medium onions, sliced
¾ cup chicken or vegetable
    stock
1 tbsp dry red or white wine or wine
    vinegar

Whipped 'Cream'

Serve this sweet 'cream' instead of whipped heavy cream. It isn't suitable for cooking, but freezes very well.

Makes ²⁄₃ cup

INGREDIENTS
½ tsp powdered gelatin
¼ cup non fat milk
    powder
1 tbsp superfine sugar
1 tbsp lemon juice

1 Put the onions and stock into a non-stick frying pan. Cover and bring to the boil. Simmer for 1 minute.

2 Uncover and boil for about 5 minutes, or until the stock has reduced entirely. Lower the heat and stir the onions until just beginning to color.

1 Sprinkle the gelatin over 1 tbsp cold water in a small bowl and leave to 'sponge' for 5 minutes. Place the bowl over a saucepan of hot water and stir until dissolved. Leave to cool.

2 Whisk the skim milk powder, superfine sugar, lemon juice and 4 tbsp cold water until frothy. Add the dissolved gelatin and whisk for a few seconds more. Chill in the refrigerator for 30 minutes.

3 Add the wine or vinegar and continue to cook until the onions are dry and lightly browned.

3 Whisk the chilled mixture again until very thick and frothy. Serve within 30 minutes of making.

Making Whole-wheat Pastry

I Put flour and salt in a bowl and add shortening. Rub shortening into the flour with your fingertips until the mixture resembles bread crumbs.

2 Using a round-bladed knife, keep stirring in small amounts of cold water until the mixture begins to stick together in lumps.

3 Collect the dough together and knead lightly to form a smooth, soft ball. Wrap in waxed paper or foil and let rest in the refrigerator for 30 minutes before rolling out and using as required.

Preventing Fruit Discoloration

Use this method for bananas, apples and pears.

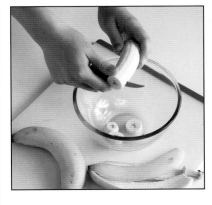

I Choose firm, ripe fruit (bananas in this instance). Peel, slice and put the fruit into a bowl.

2 Sprinkle lemon juice liberally all over the fruit.

3 Remove the fruit from the bowl using a slotted spoon to drain off any excess lemon juice and use as required, as soon as possible. Discard any remaining lemon juice.

Soups & Appetizers

Melon and Basil Soup

A deliciously refreshing, chilled fruit soup, just right for a hot summer's day.

Serves 4–6

INGREDIENTS
2 Charentais melons
⅓ cup superfine sugar
¾ cup water
finely grated zest and juice of 1 lime
3 tbsp shredded fresh basil
fresh basil leaves, to garnish

basil

superfine sugar

lime

Charentais melon

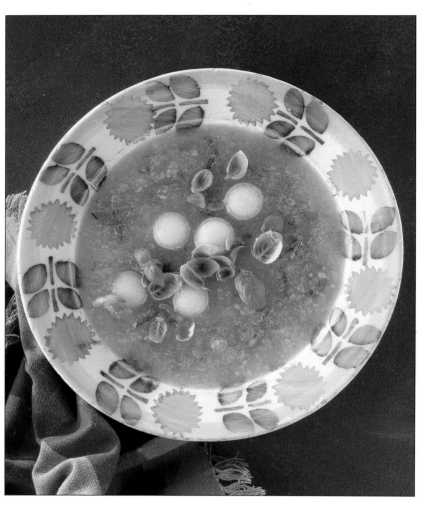

1 Cut the melons in half across the middle. Scrape out the seeds and discard. Using a melon baller, scoop out 20–24 balls and set aside for the garnish. Scoop out the remaining flesh and place in a blender or food processor.

2 Place the sugar water and lime zest in a small pan over low heat. Stir until dissolved, bring to a boil and simmer for 2–3 minutes. Remove from the heat and leave to cool slightly. Pour half the mixture into the blender or food processor with the melon flesh. Blend until smooth, adding the remaining syrup and lime juice to taste.

COOK'S TIP

Add the syrup in two stages, as the amount of sugar needed will depend on the sweetness of the melon.

3 Pour the mixture into a bowl, stir in the basil and chill. Serve garnished with basil leaves and melon balls.

NUTRITIONAL NOTES

PER PORTION:

ENERGY 63 Kcals **ENERGY** 0.28 g
FAT 0.09 g **SATURATED FAT** 0 g
CARBOHYDRATE 16 g
FIBER 0.25 g **SUGAR** 0.25 g
SODIUM 17.3 mg

Leek, Parsnip and Ginger Soup

A flavorful winter soup, with the added spiciness of fresh ginger.

INGREDIENTS
2 tbsp olive oil
8 oz leeks, sliced
1 oz fresh ginger, finely
   chopped
1¼ cups dry white wine
5 cups vegetable stock or water
salt and freshly ground black pepper
low-fat sour cream, to garnish
paprika, to garnish

ginger

parsnips

vegetable stock

leek

1 Heat the oil in a large pan and add the leeks and ginger. Cook gently for 2–3 minutes, until the leeks start to soften.

2 Add the parsnips and cook for a further 7–8 minutes.

NUTRITIONAL NOTES
PER PORTION:

ENERGY 165 Kcals PROTEIN 3.4 g
FAT 6.5 g SATURATED FAT 0.99 g
CARBOHYDRATE 16.4 g
FIBER 6 g SUGAR 8.2 g
SODIUM 17 mg

3 Pour in the wine and stock or water and bring to the boil. Reduce the heat and simmer for 20–30 minutes or until the parsnips are tender.

4 Purée in a blender until smooth. Season to taste. Reheat and garnish with a swirl of sour cream and a light dusting of paprika.

Broccoli and Almond Soup

The creaminess of the toasted almonds combines perfectly with the slight bitterness of the taste of broccoli.

Serves 4–6

INGREDIENTS
⅔ cup ground almonds
1½ lb broccoli
3¾ cups vegetable stock or water
1¼ cups skim milk
salt and freshly ground black pepper

ground almonds

skim milk

broccoli

NUTRITIONAL NOTES
PER PORTION:

ENERGY 104 Kcals PROTEIN 8.36 g
FAT 5.7 g SATURATED FAT 0.66 g
CARBOHYDRATE 5.1 g
FIBER 3.5 g SUGAR 4.5 g
SODIUM 37.2 mg

1 Preheat the oven to 350°F. Spread the ground almonds evenly on a baking sheet and toast for about 10 minutes or until golden. Reserve ¼ of the almonds and set aside for the garnish.

2 Cut the broccoli into small florets and steam for 6–7 minutes or until tender.

3 Place the remaining toasted almonds, broccoli, stock or water and milk in a blender and blend until smooth. Season to taste.

4 Reheat the soup and serve sprinkled with the reserved toasted almonds.

Pea, Leek and Broccoli Soup

A delicious and nutritious soup, ideal for warming those chilly winter evenings.

Serves 4–6

INGREDIENTS
1 onion, chopped
2 cups trimmed, sliced leeks
8 ounces unpeeled potatoes, diced
3¾ cups vegetable stock or
   vegetable bouillon cube and water
1 bay leaf
2 cups broccoli florets
1½ cups frozen peas
2–3 tablespoons chopped
   fresh parsley, plus leaves
   to garnish
salt and ground black pepper

onion

leeks

potatoes

vegetable stock

bay leaf

broccoli

peas

parsley

salt

black pepper

NUTRITIONAL NOTES

PER PORTION:

CALORIES 125 PROTEIN 8.11g
FAT 1.92g SATURATED FAT 0.26g
CARBOHYDRATE 19.94g
FIBER 6.31g ADDED SUGAR 0.04g
SODIUM 0.52g

1 Put the onion, leeks, potatoes, stock and bay leaf in a large saucepan and mix together. Cover, bring to the boil and simmer for 10 minutes, stirring.

2 Add the broccoli and peas, cover, return to the boil and simmer for a further 10 minutes, stirring occasionally.

COOK'S TIP
If you prefer, cut the vegetables finely and leave the cooked soup chunky rather than puréeing it.

3 Set aside to cool slightly and remove and discard the bay leaf. Purée in a blender or food processor until smooth.

4 Add the parsley, season to taste and process briefly. Return to the saucepan and reheat gently until piping hot. Ladle into soup bowls and garnish with parsley leaves.

Italian Vegetable Soup

The success of this clear soup depends on the quality of the stock, so use homemade vegetable stock rather than bouillon cubes.

Serves 4

INGREDIENTS
1 small carrot
1 baby leek
1 celery stalk
2 oz green cabbage
3¾ cups vegetable
    stock
1 bay leaf
1 cup cooked cannellini beans, rinsed
    and drained
⅓ cup soup pasta, such as tiny shells,
    bows, stars or elbows
salt and freshly ground black pepper
snipped fresh chives, to garnish

stock

cabbage

bay leaf

chives

baby leek

celery

carrot

pasta

1 Cut the carrot, leek and celery into 2 in long julienne strips. Slice the cabbage very finely.

2 Put the stock and bay leaf into a large saucepan and bring to the boil. Add the carrot, leek and celery, cover and simmer for 6 minutes.

NUTRITIONAL NOTES
Per portion:

CALORIES 126
FAT 2.2 g **SATURATED FAT** 0.6 g
CHOLESTEROL 19 mg

3 Add the cabbage, beans and pasta shapes. Stir, then simmer uncovered for a further 4-5 minutes, or until the vegetables and pasta are tender.

4 Remove the bay leaf and season to taste. Ladle into four soup bowls and garnish with snipped chives. Serve immediately.

Corn and Chicken Soup

This popular classic Chinese soup is very easy to make.

Serves 4-6

INGREDIENTS
1 chicken breast fillet,
  about 4 oz, cubed
2 tsp light soy sauce
1 tbsp Chinese rice wine
1 tsp cornstarch
4 tbsp cold water
1 tsp sesame oil
2 tbsp peanut oil
1 tsp fresh ginger,
  finely grated
4 cups chicken stock, or
  bouillon cube and water
15-oz can cream-style corn
8-oz can corn kernels
2 eggs, beaten
2-3 scallions, green parts only,
  cut into tiny rounds
salt and ground black pepper

NUTRITIONAL NOTES
PER PORTION:
CALORIES 163
FAT 4.6 g **SATURATED FAT** 1.0 g
CHOLESTEROL 72.4 mg

1 Grind the chicken in a food processor, taking care not to over-process. Transfer the chicken to a bowl and stir in the soy sauce, rice wine, cornstarch, water, sesame oil and seasoning. Cover and leave for about 15 minutes to absorb the flavors.

cornstarch

chicken stock

cream-style corn

chicken

corn kernels

egg

Chinese rice wine

sesame oil

ginger

2 Heat a wok over medium heat. Add the peanut oil and swirl it around. Add the ginger and stir-fry for a few seconds. Add the stock, creamed corn and corn kernels. Bring to just below boiling point.

3 Spoon about 6 tbsp of the hot liquid into the chicken mixture and stir until it forms a smooth paste. Return this to the wok. Slowly bring to a boil, stirring constantly, then simmer for 2–3 minutes until the chicken is cooked.

4 Pour the beaten eggs into the soup in a slow steady stream, using a fork or chopsticks to stir the top of the soup in a figure-eight pattern. The egg should set in lacy shreds. Serve immediately with the scallions sprinkled over.

Red Onion and Beet Soup

This beautiful vivid ruby-red soup will look stunning at any dinner party.

Serves 4–6

INGREDIENTS
1 tbsp olive oil
12 oz red onions, sliced
2 garlic cloves, crushed
10 oz cooked beets, cut into
   thin sticks
5 cups fresh vegetable stock or water
1 cup cooked soup pasta
2 tbsp raspberry vinegar
salt and freshly ground black pepper
low-fat yogurt or ricotta cheese, to
   garnish
snipped chives, to garnish

garlic

red onion

beets

pasta

chives

COOK'S TIP
Try substituting cooked barley for the pasta to give extra nuttiness.

NUTRITIONAL NOTES
PER PORTION:

ENERGY 104 Kcals **FAT** 1.4 g
SATURATED FAT 0.1 g

1 Heat the olive oil and add the onions and garlic.

2 Cook gently for about 20 minutes or until soft and tender.

3 Add the beets, stock or water, cooked pasta shapes and vinegar and heat through. Season to taste.

4 Ladle into bowls. Top each one with a spoonful of yogurt or ricotta cheese and sprinkle with chives.

Cauliflower, Flageolet and Fennel Seed Soup

The sweet, anise-licorice flavor of the fennel seeds gives a delicious edge to this hearty soup.

Serves 4–6

INGREDIENTS
1 tbsp olive oil
1 garlic clove, crushed
1 onion, chopped
2 tsp fennel seeds
1 cauliflower, cut into small florets
2 × 14 oz cans flageolet beans,
    drained and rinsed
5 cups fresh vegetable stock or water
salt and freshly ground black pepper
chopped fresh parsley, to garnish
toasted slices of French bread, to
    serve

flageolet beans

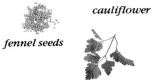
French bread

onion

garlic

cauliflower

fennel seeds

parsley

1 Heat the olive oil. Add the garlic, onion and fennel seeds and cook gently for 5 minutes or until softened.

2 Add the cauliflower, half of the beans and the stock or water.

NUTRITIONAL NOTES
PER PORTION:

ENERGY 169 Kcals **FAT** 3.9 g
SATURATED FAT 0.7 g

3 Bring to the boil. Reduce the heat and simmer for 10 minutes or until the cauliflower is tender.

4 Pour the soup into a blender and blend until smooth. Stir in the remaining beans and season to taste. Reheat and pour into bowls. Sprinkle with chopped parsley and serve with toasted slices of French bread.

Spicy Chick-pea and Bacon Soup

This is a tasty mixture of chick-peas and bacon flavored with a subtle mix of spices.

NUTRITIONAL NOTES
PER PORTION:

CALORIES 207 PROTEIN 15.56g
FAT 7.28g SATURATED FAT 1.43g
CARBOHYDRATE 22.40g
FIBER 4.82g ADDED SUGAR 0.02g
SODIUM 1.17g

Serves 4–6

INGREDIENTS
2 teaspoons sunflower oil
1 onion, chopped
2 garlic cloves, crushed
1 teaspoon each garam masala and
 ground coriander, cumin
 and turmeric
½ teaspoon chili powder
2 tablespoons all-purpose
 whole-wheat flour
2½ cups vegetable stock
1 can (14 ounces) chopped tomatoes
1 can (14 ounces) chickpeas, rinsed
 and drained
6 slices smoked Canadian bacon
salt and ground black pepper
cilantro sprigs, to garnish

1 Heat the oil in a large saucepan. Add the onion and garlic and cook for 5 minutes, stirring occasionally.

2 Add the spices and flour and cook for 1 minute, stirring.

3 Gradually add the stock, stirring constantly, then add the tomatoes and chick-peas.

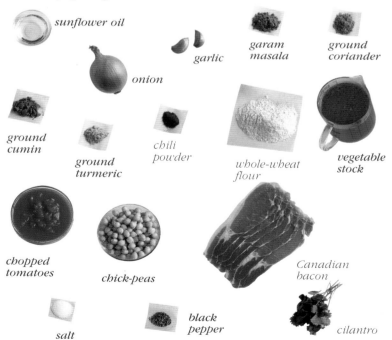

sunflower oil

garlic

garam masala

ground coriander

onion

ground cumin

ground turmeric

chili powder

whole-wheat flour

vegetable stock

chopped tomatoes

chick-peas

Canadian bacon

salt

black pepper

cilantro

4 Bring to the boil, stirring, then cover and simmer for 25 minutes, stirring occasionally.

COOK'S TIP
Use other canned beans such as red kidney beans or flageolet beans in place of the chick-peas.

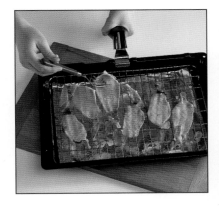

5 Meanwhile, broil the bacon for 2–3 minutes on each side.

6 Dice the bacon, then stir into the soup. Season to taste, reheat gently until piping hot and ladle into soup bowls to serve. Garnish each with a cilantro sprig and serve immediately.

Fresh Tomato, Lentil and Onion Soup

This wholesome soup is delicious served with thick slices of whole-wheat or multigrain bread.

Serves 4–6

INGREDIENTS
2 teaspoons sunflower oil
1 large onion, chopped
2 stalks celery, chopped
1 cup split red lentils
2 large tomatoes, peeled and
    coarsely chopped
4 cups vegetable stock
2 teaspoons dried *herbes
    de Provence*
salt and ground black pepper
chopped fresh parsley, to garnish

sunflower oil

onion

celery

split red
lentils

tomatoes

herbes de
Provence

vegetable
stock   salt

black pepper

NUTRITIONAL NOTES
PER PORTION:

CALORIES 202 PROTEIN 12.40g
FAT 3.07g SATURATED FAT 0.38g
CARBOHYDRATE 33.34g
FIBER 4.27g ADDED SUGAR 0.04g
SODIUM 0.54g

1 Heat the oil in a large saucepan. Add the onion and celery and cook for 5 minutes, stirring occasionally. Add the lentils and cook for 1 minute.

2 Stir in the tomatoes, stock, herbs and seasoning. Cover, bring to the boil and simmer for about 20 minutes, stirring occasionally.

3 When the lentils are cooked and tender, set the soup aside to cool slightly.

4 Purée in a blender or food processor until smooth. Adjust the seasoning, return to the saucepan and reheat gently until piping hot. Ladle into soup bowls to serve and garnish each with chopped parsley.

Chilled Fresh Tomato Soup

This effortless uncooked soup can be made in minutes.

Serves 4–6

INGREDIENTS
3–3½ lb ripe tomatoes, peeled and
    roughly chopped
4 garlic cloves
2 tbsp balsamic vinegar
freshly ground black pepper
4 slices whole-wheat bread
low fat sour cream, to garnish

whole-wheat bread

garlic

*low fat
sour cream*

peppercorns

tomato

COOK'S TIP

For the best flavor, it is important
to use only fully ripened, flavorful
tomatoes in this soup.

1 Place the tomatoes in a blender with
the garlic and olive oil if using. Blend until
smooth.

2 Pass the mixture through a sieve to
remove the seeds. Stir in the balsamic
vinegar and season to taste with pepper.
Set in the refrigerator to chill.

NUTRITIONAL NOTES
Per portion:

ENERGY 104 Kcals **PROTEIN** 5.42 g
FAT 1. 4g **SATURATED FAT** 0.1 g
CARBOHYDRATE 19.22 g
FIBER 3.9 g **SUGAR** 3.97 g
SODIUM 160.33 mg

3 Toast the bread lightly on both sides.
Whilst still hot, cut off the crusts and slice
in half horizontally. Place the toast on a
board with the uncooked sides facing
down and, using a circular motion, rub to
remove any doughy pieces of bread.

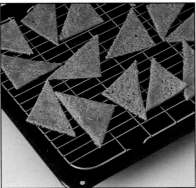

4 Cut each slice into 4 triangles. Place
on a broiler pan and toast the uncooked
sides until lightly golden. Garnish each
bowl or soup with a spoonful of sour
cream, and serve with the toast.

Curried Celery Soup

An unusual combination of flavors, this warming soup is excellent served with warm whole-wheat bread rolls or whole-wheat pita bread.

NUTRITIONAL NOTES
PER PORTION:

CALORIES 102 PROTEIN 3.72g
FAT 2.93g SATURATED FAT 0.25g
CARBOHYDRATE 16.11g
FIBER 4.44g ADDED SUGAR 0.04g
SODIUM 0.62g

Serves 4–6

INGREDIENTS
2 teaspoons olive oil
1 onion, chopped
1 leek, washed and sliced
1½ pounds celery, chopped,
  leaves reserved
1 tablespoon curry powder
8 ounces unpeeled potatoes,
  washed and diced
4 cups vegetable stock or vegetable
  bouillon cube and water
1 bouquet garni
2 tablespoons chopped fresh
  mixed herbs
salt
celery seeds and leaves, to garnish

olive oil

onion

leek

celery

curry powder

potatoes

vegetable stock

bouquet garni

fresh mixed herbs

salt

celery seeds

1 Heat the oil in a large saucepan. Add the onion, leek and celery, cover and cook gently for 10 minutes, stirring occasionally.

2 Add the curry powder and cook for 2 minutes, stirring occasionally.

3 Add the potatoes, stock and bouquet garni, cover, and bring to the boil. Simmer for 20 minutes, until the vegetables are tender

4 Remove and discard the bouquet garni and set the soup aside to cool slightly.

5 Purée in a blender or food processor until smooth.

6 Add the mixed herbs, season to taste and process briefly. Return to the saucepan and reheat gently until piping hot. Ladle into soup bowls and garnish each with a sprinkling of celery seeds and some celery leaves.

COOK'S TIP
For a tasty change, use celeriac and sweet potatoes in place of celery and standard potatoes.

Consommé with Agnolotti

Serves 4–6

INGREDIENTS
3 ounces cooked peeled shrimp
3 ounces canned crab meat, drained
1 teaspoon fresh ginger, peeled and
   finely grated
1 tablespoon fresh white bread
   crumbs
1 teaspoon light soy sauce
1 scallion, finely chopped
1 garlic clove, crushed
1 recipe basic pasta dough
egg white, beaten
14 ounce can chicken or
   fish consommé
2 tablespoons sherry or vermouth
salt and ground black pepper
2 ounces cooked, peeled shrimp
   and fresh cilantro leaves,
   to garnish

fresh
ginger

crab meat

shrimp

scallion

fresh
cilantro

garlic

chicken
consommé

flour

fresh white
bread crumbs

basic pasta
dough

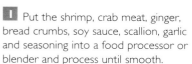 Put the shrimp, crab meat, ginger, bread crumbs, soy sauce, scallion, garlic and seasoning into a food processor or blender and process until smooth.

 **2** Roll the pasta into thin sheets. Cut out 32 rounds 2 inches in diameter, with a fluted pastry cutter.

 **3** Place a small teaspoon of the filling in the center of half the pasta rounds. Brush the edges of each round with egg white and place a second round on top of the filling. Pinch the edges together firmly to stop the filling from escaping.

 **4** Cook the pasta in a large pan of boiling, salted water for 5 minutes (cook in batches to stop them sticking together). Remove and drop into a bowl of cold water for 5 seconds before placing on a tray. (You can make these pasta shapes a day in advance. Cover with plastic wrap and store in the fridge.)

 **5** Heat the chicken or fish consommé in a pan with the sherry or vermouth. When piping hot, add the cooked pasta shapes and simmer for 1–2 minutes.

6 Serve in a shallow soup bowl. Garnish with extra peeled shrimp and fresh cilantro leaves.

NUTRITIONAL NOTES
PER PORTION:

ENERGY 300 calories **FAT** 4.6g
SATURATED FAT 1.1g **CHOLESTEROL** 148mg
CARBOHYDRATE 43g **FIBER** 1.7g

Chicken Stellette Soup

Serves 4–6

INGREDIENTS
3¾ cups chicken stock
1 bay leaf
4 scallions, sliced
2 ounces stellette
8 ounces button
    mushrooms, sliced
1 cooked chicken breast
⅔ cup dry white wine
1 tablespoon chopped parsley
salt and ground black pepper

stellette   *white wine*

stock

*cooked
chicken
breast*
                     scallions

parsley   *bay leaf*

       mushrooms

1 Put the stock and bay leaf into a pan and bring to the boil.

2 Add the scallions and mushrooms to the stock.

NUTRITIONAL NOTES
PER PORTION:

ENERGY 126 calories **FAT** 2.2g
SATURATED FAT 0.6g **CHOLESTEROL** 19mg
CARBOHYDRATE 11g **FIBER** 1.3g

3 Remove the skin from the chicken and slice thinly. Transfer to a plate and set aside.

4 Add the pasta to the pan, cover and simmer for 7–8 minutes. Just before serving, add the chicken, wine and parsley, heat through for 2–3 minutes.

Vegetable Minestrone with Anellini

Serves 6–8

INGREDIENTS
large pinch of saffron strands
1 onion, chopped
1 leek, sliced
1 stick celery, sliced
2 carrots, diced
2–3 garlic cloves, crushed
2½ cups chicken stock
2 x 14-ounce cans
    chopped tomatoes
½ cup frozen peas
2 ounces soup pasta (anellini)
1 teaspoon caster sugar
1 tablespoon chopped fresh parsley
1 tablespoon chopped fresh basil
salt and ground black pepper

anellini *frozen peas* *onion*

saffron strands *basil* *stock*

parsley *chopped tomatoes*

carrot *celery*

garlic *leek*

1 Soak the pinch of saffron strands in 1 tablespoon boiling water. Let stand for 10 minutes.

2 Meanwhile, put the prepared onion, leek, celery, carrots and garlic into a pan. Add the chicken stock, bring to the boil, cover and simmer for 10 minutes.

NUTRITIONAL NOTES
PER PORTION:

ENERGY 87 calories **FAT** 0.7g
SATURATED FAT 0.1g **CHOLESTEROL** 0mg
CARBOHYDRATE 17g **FIBER** 3.3g

3 Add the canned tomatoes, the saffron with its liquid, and the peas. Bring back to the boil and add the anellini. Simmer for 10 minutes until tender.

4 Season with salt, pepper and sugar to taste. Stir in the chopped herbs just before serving.

Beet Soup with Ravioli

Serves 4–6

INGREDIENTS
1 recipe basic pasta dough
egg white, beaten, for brushing
flour, for dusting
1 small onion or shallot,
    finely chopped
2 garlic cloves, crushed
1 teaspoon fennel seeds
2½ cups chicken or vegetable stock
8 ounces cooked beets
2 tablespoons fresh orange juice
fennel or dill leaves, to garnish
crusty bread, to serve

FOR THE FILLING
4 ounces mushrooms,
    finely chopped
1 shallot or small onion,
    finely chopped
1–2 garlic cloves, crushed
1 teaspoon fresh thyme
1 tablespoon fresh parsley
6 tablespoons fresh white
    bread crumbs
large pinch ground nutmeg
salt and ground black pepper

onion   orange

mushrooms

shallot   cooked beets

thyme   parsley

garlic   fennel seeds   stock

nutmeg

basic pasta dough   bread crumbs

dill

1 Process all the filling ingredients in a food processor or blender.

2 Roll the pasta into thin sheets. Lay one piece over a ravioli tray and put a teaspoonful of the filling into each depression. Brush around the edges of each ravioli with egg white. Cover with another sheet of pasta and press the edges well together to seal. Transfer to a floured dish towel and rest for 1 hour before cooking.

3 Cook the ravioli in a large pan of boiling, salted water for 2 minutes. (Cook in batches to stop them from sticking together.) Remove and drop into a bowl of cold water for 5 seconds before placing on a tray. (You can make these pasta shapes a day in advance. Cover with clear film and store in the fridge.) Put the onion, garlic and fennel seeds into a pan with ⅔ cup of the stock. Bring to a boil, cover and simmer for 5 minutes until tender. Peel and finely dice the beets. (Reserve 4 tbsp for the garnish.) Add the rest to the soup with the remaining stock and bring to a boil.

4 Add the orange juice and cooked ravioli and simmer for 2 minutes. Serve in shallow soup bowls, garnished with the reserved diced beets and fennel or dill leaves. Serve hot, with some crusty bread.

NUTRITIONAL NOTES
PER PORTION:

ENERGY 358 calories **FAT** 4.9g
SATURATED FAT 1.0g **CHOLESTEROL** 110mg
CARBOHYDRATE 67g **FIBER** 4.3g

Corn Chowder with Conchigliette

Serves 6–8

INGREDIENTS

1 small green bell pepper
1 pound potatoes, peeled
    and diced
2 cups canned or frozen corn
1 onion, chopped
1 stick celery, chopped
bouquet garni (bay leaf, parsley and
    thyme)
2½ cups chicken stock
1¼ cups skim milk
2 ounces small pasta shells
    (conchigliette)
5 ounces smoked turkey
    bacon, diced
bread sticks, to serve
salt and ground black pepper

1 Halve the green pepper, remove the stalk and seeds. Cut the flesh into small dice, cover with boiling water and stand for 2 minutes. Drain and rinse.

2 Put the potatoes into a saucepan with the corn, onion, celery, green pepper, bouquet garni and stock. Bring to a boil, cover and simmer for 20 minutes until tender.

3 Add the milk, and season with salt and pepper. Process half of the soup in a food processor or blender and return to the pan with the conchigliette. Simmer for 10 minutes.

4 Fry the turkey bacon quickly in a non-stick frying pan for 2–3 minutes. Stir into the soup. Serve with bread sticks.

smoked turkey bacon   *corn*

potatoes

small pasta shells   *stock*

onion   *parsley*   *green pepper*

celery

skim milk

bay leaf   *thyme*

NUTRITIONAL NOTES

PER PORTION:

ENERGY 215 calories **FAT** 1.6g
SATURATED FAT 0.3g **CHOLESTEROL** 13mg
CARBOHYDRATE 41g **FIBER** 2.8g

Tsatziki

Serve this classic Greek dip with strips of toasted pitta bread.

Serves 4

INGREDIENTS
1 mini cucumber
4 scallions
1 garlic clove
scant 1 cup plain
  yogurt
3 tbsp chopped fresh mint
fresh mint sprig, to garnish (optional)
salt and pepper

*mini
cucumber*

scallions

garlic

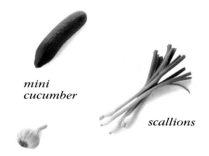

*plain
yogurt*

mint

1 Trim the ends from the cucumber, then cut it into ¼-in dice.

2 Trim the scallions and garlic, then chop both very finely.

3 Beat the yogurt until smooth, if necessary, then gently stir in the cucumber, onions, garlic and mint.

4 Transfer the mixture to a serving bowl and add salt and plenty of freshly ground black pepper to taste. Chill until ready to serve and then garnish with a small mint sprig, if you like.

COOK'S TIP
Choose Greek-style yogurt for this dip – it has a higher fat content than most yogurts, but this gives it a deliciously rich, creamy texture.

NUTRITIONAL NOTES
PER PORTION:

CALORIES 65 **FAT** 4.7 g
SATURATED FAT 2.9 g **PROTEIN** 3.9 g
CARBOHYDRATE 2.1 g **FIBER** 0.3 g

Spiced Carrot Dip

This is a delicious low-fat dip with a sweet and spicy flavour. Serve wheat crackers or fiery tortilla chips as accompaniments for dipping.

Serves 4

INGREDIENTS
1 onion
3 carrots, plus extra, to garnish
grated rind and juice of 2 oranges
1 tbsp hot curry paste
⅔ cup low-fat plain yogurt
handful of fresh basil leaves
1–2 tbsp fresh lemon juice,
   to taste
red Tabasco sauce, to taste
salt and pepper

NUTRITIONAL NOTES
PER PORTION:

ENERGY 67 Kcals **FAT** 1.5 g
SATURATED FAT 1 g

VARIATION
Sour cream may be used in place of the plain yogurt to make a richer, creamy dip.

onion   *carrots*

orange rind and juice   *curry paste*

basil   *lemon juice*

low-fat plain yogurt   *red Tabasco sauce*

1 Finely chop the onion. Peel and grate the carrots. Place the onion, carrots, orange rind and juice and curry paste in a small saucepan. Bring to the boil, cover and simmer for 10 minutes, until tender.

2 Process the mixture in a blender or food processor until smooth. Leave to cool completely.

3 Stir in the yogurt, then tear the basil leaves into small pieces and stir them into the carrot mixture.

4 Add the lemon juice, Tabasco, salt and pepper to taste. Serve within a few hours at room temperature. Garnish with grated carrot.

Garlic and Chili Dip

Plainly cooked fish can sometimes be rather bland.
This sauce will spice it up.

Serves 4

INGREDIENTS
1 small red chile
1-in piece fresh ginger
2 garlic cloves
1 tsp mustard powder
1 tbsp chili sauce
2 tbsp olive oil
2 tbsp light soy sauce
juice of two limes
2 tbsp chopped fresh parsley
salt and pepper

parsley

*mustard
powder*   *red chile*

ginger

*light soy
sauce*

limes

chili sauce

garlic

1 Halve the chilli, remove the seeds,
stalk and membrane, and chop finely.
Peel and roughly chop the ginger.

2 Crush the chilli, ginger, garlic and
mustard powder to a paste, using a
pestle and mortar.

3 In a bowl, mix together all the
remaining ingredients, except the parsley
Add the paste and blend it in. Cover
and chill for 24 hours.

4 Stir in the parsley and season to
taste. It is best to serve in small
individual bowls for dipping.

COOK'S TIP

Large shrimps are ideal served
with this sauce. Remove the shell
but leave the tails intact so there
is something to hold on to for
dipping.

NUTRITIONAL NOTES

PER PORTION:

CALORIES 41 **FAT** 3.3 g
SATURATED FAT 0.4 g **PROTEIN** 1.2 g
CARBOHYDRATE 1.8 g **FIBER** 0.4 g

Asian Hoisin Dip

This speedy Asian dip needs no cooking and can be made in just a few minutes – it tastes great with mini spring rolls or shrimp crackers.

Serves 4

INGREDIENTS
4 scallions
1½-in piece ginger
2 red chilies
2 garlic cloves
¼ cup hoisin sauce
½ cup passata
1 tsp sesame oil (optional)

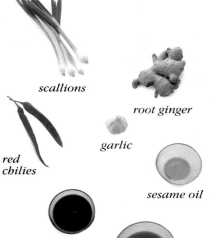

scallions

root ginger

garlic

red
chilies

sesame oil

hoisin sauce

passata

1 Trim off and discard the green ends of the scallions. Slice the remainder very thinly.

2 Peel the ginger with a swivel-bladed vegetable peeler, then chop it finely.

3 Halve the chilies lengthwise and remove their seeds. Finely slice the flesh horizontally into tiny strips. Finely chop the garlic.

4 Stir together the hoisin sauce, passata, scallions, ginger, chili, garlic and sesame oil, if using, and serve within 1 hour.

COOK'S TIP
Hoisin sauce makes an excellent base for full-flavor dips, especially when combining crunchy vegetables and other Asian seasonings.

NUTRITIONAL NOTES
PER PORTION:

CALORIES 33 **FAT** 0.9 g
SATURATED FAT 0.1 g **PROTEIN** 1.3 g
CARBOHYDRATE 5.3 g **FIBER** 0.4 g

Fat-free Saffron Dip

Serve this mild dip with fresh vegetable crudités -
it is particularly good with florets of cauliflower.

Serves 4

INGREDIENTS
1 tbsp boiling water
small pinch of saffron strands
scant 1 cup fat-free
    cottage cheese
10 fresh chives
10 fresh basil leaves
salt and pepper

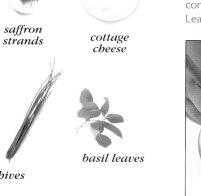

*saffron
strands*   *cottage
                  cheese*

basil leaves

chives

1 Pour the boiling water into a small
container and add the saffron strands.
Leave to infuse for 3 minutes.

2 Beat the cottage cheese until
smooth, then stir in the infused saffron
liquid.

3 Use a pair of scissors to snip the
chives into the dip. Tear the basil leaves
into small pieces and stir them in.

4 Add salt and pepper to taste. Serve
immediately.

VARIATION
Leave out the saffron and add a
squeeze of lemon or lime juice
instead.

NUTRITIONAL NOTES
PER PORTION:

ENERGY 30 Kcals **FAT** 0.1 g
SATURATED FAT 0.05 g

Guacamole with Crudités

This fresh-tasting spicy dip is made using peas instead of the traditional avocados.

Serves 4–6

INGREDIENTS
2¼ cups frozen peas, defrosted
1 garlic clove, crushed
2 scallions, trimmed and chopped
1 tsp finely grated zest and juice of
    1 lime
½ tsp ground cumin
dash of Tabasco sauce
1 tbsp reduced calorie mayonnaise
2 tbsp chopped fresh cilantro
salt and freshly ground black pepper
pinch of paprika and lime slices,
    to garnish

FOR THE CRUDITÉS
6 cups carrots
2 celery stalks
1 red apple
1 pear
1 tbsp lemon or lime juice
6 baby corn

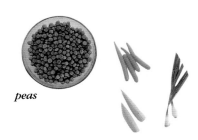

peas

vegetables

NUTRITIONAL NOTES
Per portion:

ENERGY 266 Kcals **PROTEIN** 27 g
FAT 2.1 g **SATURATED FAT** 0.4 g
CARBOHYDRATE 32g
FIBER 3.43 g **SUGAR** 3.36 g
SODIUM 289.7 mg

1 Put the peas, garlic and scallions, lime zest and juice, cumin, Tabasco sauce, mayonnaise and salt and freshly ground pepper in a food processor or blend for a few minutes and process until smooth.

2 Add the chopped cilantro and process for a few more seconds. Spoon into a serving bowl, cover with the plastic wrap and chill for 30 minutes, to let the flavors develop.

3 For the crudités. trim and peel the carrots. Halve the celery stalks lengthwise and trim into sticks, the same length as the carrots. Quarter, core and thickly slice the apple and pear, then dip into the lemon or lime juice. Arrange with the baby corn on a platter.

4 Sprinkle the paprika over the guacamole and garnish with lime slices.

Minted Melon and Grapefruit Cocktail

Melon is always a popular starter. Here the flavor is complemented by the refreshing taste of citrus fruit and a simple dressing.

Serves 4

INGREDIENTS
1 small cantaloupe, weighing about
   2¼ lb
2 pink grapefruits
1 yellow grapefruit
1 tsp Dijon mustard
1 tsp raspberry or sherry vinegar
1 tsp honey
1 tbsp chopped fresh mint
sprigs of fresh mint, to garnish

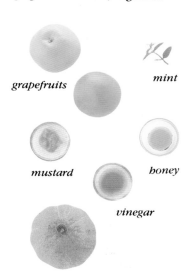

grapefruits   *mint*

mustard   *honey*

vinegar

melon

NUTRITIONAL NOTES

Per serving:

CALORIES 97 **PROTEIN** 2.22 g
FAT 0.63 g **SATURATED FAT** 0.00 g
CARBOHYDRATE 22.45 g **FIBER** 3.05 g
ADDED SUGAR 0.96 g **SODIUM** 0.24 g

1 Halve the melon and remove the seeds with a teaspoon. With a melon baller, carefully scoop the flesh into balls.

2 With a sharp knife, peel the grapefruit and remove all the white pith. Remove the segments by cutting between the membranes, holding the fruit over a small bowl to catch any juices.

3 Whisk the mustard, vinegar, honey, chopped mint and grapefruit juices together in a mixing bowl. Add the melon balls together with the grapefruit and mix well. Chill for 30 minutes.

4 Ladle into four dishes and serve garnished with a sprig of fresh mint.

Melon and Prosciutto Salad with Strawberry Salsa

Sections of cool fragrant melon wrapped with slices of prosciutto make a delicious appetizer. If strawberries are in season, serve with a savory-sweet strawberry salsa and watch it disappear.

Serves 6

INGREDIENTS
1 large melon, cantaloupe, Spanish or
  charentais
6 oz prosciutto, thinly sliced

SALSA
½ lb strawberries
1 tsp superfine sugar
1 tbsp sunflower oil
1 tbsp orange juice
½ tsp finely grated orange zest
½ tsp finely grated fresh ginger
salt and black pepper

2 To make the salsa, hull the strawberries and cut them into large dice. Place in a small mixing bowl with the sugar and crush lightly to release the juices. Add the oil, orange juice, zest and ginger. Season with salt and a generous twist of black pepper.

3 Arrange the melon on a serving plate, lay the ham over the top and serve with a bowl of salsa.

1 Halve the melon and take the seeds out with a spoon. Cut the rind away with a paring knife, then slice the melon thickly. Chill until ready to serve.

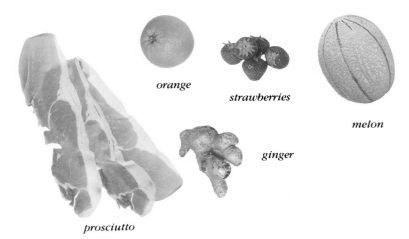

orange

strawberries

melon

ginger

prosciutto

NUTRITIONAL NOTES
PER PORTION:

ENERGY 87 Kcals FAT 3.5 g
SATURATED FAT 0.8 g

Mushroom and Bean Pâté

A light and tasty pâté, delicious served on whole-wheat bread or toast for an appetizer or a suppertime snack.

Serves 12

INGREDIENTS
6 cups mushrooms, sliced
1 onion, chopped
2 garlic cloves, crushed
1 red bell pepper, seeded and diced
2 tablespoons vegetable stock
2 tablespoons dry white wine
1 can (14 ounces) red kidney
  beans, rinsed and drained
1 egg, beaten
1 cup fresh whole-wheat
  bread crumbs
1 tablespoon chopped fresh thyme
1 tablespoon chopped fresh
  rosemary
salt and ground black pepper
lettuce and tomatoes, to garnish

mushrooms
onion
garlic
red pepper
vegetable stock
dry white wine
red kidney beans
egg
fresh whole-wheat bread crumbs
fresh thyme
fresh rosemary
salt
black pepper

1 Preheat the oven to 350°F. Lightly grease and line a nonstick loaf pan. Put the mushrooms, onion, garlic, pepper, stock and wine in a saucepan. Cover and cook for 10 minutes, stirring occasionally.

2 Set aside to cool slightly, then purée the mixture with the kidney beans in a blender or food processor until smooth.

3 Transfer the mixture to a bowl, add the egg, breadcrumbs and herbs and mix thoroughly. Season to taste.

NUTRITIONAL NOTES

PER PORTION:

CALORIES 53 PROTEIN 3.42g
FAT 1.04g SATURATED FAT 0.26g
CARBOHYDRATE 7.65g FIBER 2.33g
ADDED SUGAR 0.00g SODIUM 0.11g

4 Spoon into the prepared tin and level the surface. Bake for 45–60 minutes, until lightly set and browned on top. Place on a wire rack and allow the pâté to cool completely in the tin. Once cool, cover and refrigerate for several hours. Turn out of the tin and serve in slices. Garnish with lettuce and tomatoes.

Cannellini Bean Pureé with Grilled Radicchio

The slightly bitter flavors of the radicchio and chicory make a wonderful marriage with the creamy citrus flavored bean purée.

Serves 4

INGREDIENTS
14 oz can cannellini beans
3 tbsp low-fat ricotta cheese
finely grated rind and juice of 1
    large orange
1 tbsp finely chopped fresh rosemary
4 heads of chicory
2 medium radicchio
1 tbsp walnut oil

chicory

ricotta cheese

cannellini beans

rosemary

radicchio

orange

1 Drain the beans, rinse, and drain again. Purée the beans in a blender or food processor with the ricotta cheese, orange juice and rosemary. Set aside.

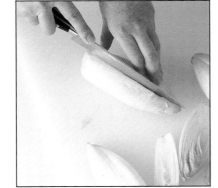

2 Cut the chicory in half lengthwise.

3 Cut each radicchio into 8 wedges

4 Lay out the chicory and radicchio on a baking tray and brush with walnut oil. Grill for 2–3 minutes. Serve with the puree and scatter over the orange rind.

COOK'S TIP
Other suitable beans to use are navy, mung or broad beans.

NUTRITIONAL NOTES
PER PORTION:

ENERGY 121 Kcals **FAT** 3.6 g
SATURATED FAT 0.4 g

Eggplant, Roast Garlic and Red Bell Pepper Pâté

This is a simple pâté of smoky baked eggplant, sweet pink peppercorns and red bell peppers, with more than a hint of garlic!

Serves 4

INGREDIENTS
3 medium eggplants
2 red bell peppers
5 whole garlic cloves
1½ tsp pink peppercorns in brine,
    drained and crushed
2 tbsp chopped fresh cilantro

eggplant

garlic

cilantro

pink peppercorns

red bell pepper

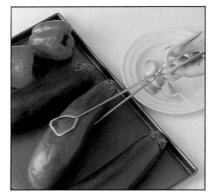

1 Preheat the oven to 400°F. Arrange the whole eggplants, peppers and garlic cloves on a cookie sheet and place in the oven. After 10 minutes remove the garlic cloves and turn over the eggplants and peppers.

2 Peel the garlic cloves and place in the bowl of a blender.

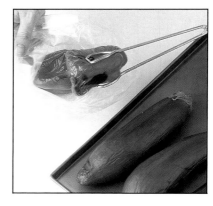

3 After a further 20 minutes remove the blistered and charred peppers from the oven and place in a plastic bag. Leave to cool.

4 After another 10 minutes remove the eggplants from the oven. Split in half and scoop the flesh into a sieve placed over a bowl. Press the flesh with a spoon to remove the bitter juices.

5 Add the mixture to the garlic in the blender and blend until smooth. Place in a large mixing bowl.

6 Peel and chop the red bell peppers and stir into the eggplant mixture. Mix in the peppercorns and cilantro and serve at once.

Crunchy Baked Mushrooms with Dill Dip

These crispy-coated bites are ideal as an informal appetizer or served with drinks.

NUTRITIONAL NOTES

PER SERVING:

CALORIES 173 PROTEIN 11.88 g
FAT 6.04 g SATURATED FAT 3.24 g
CARBOHYDRATE 19.23 g FIBER 1.99 g
ADDED SUGAR 0 SODIUM 0.91 g

Serves 4–6

INGREDIENTS
2 cups fresh fine white bread
   crumbs
1½ tbsp finely grated sharp Cheddar
   cheese
1 tsp paprika
8 oz button mushrooms
2 egg whites

FOR THE TOMATO AND DILL DIP
4 ripe tomatoes
½ cup cottage cheese
4 tbsp natural low fat yogurt
1 garlic clove, crushed
2 tbsp chopped fresh dill
salt and freshly ground black pepper
sprig of fresh dill, to garnish

paprika

mushrooms

dill

tomatoes

breadcrumbs

cottage cheese

1 Preheat the oven to 375°F. Mix together the bread crumbs, cheese and paprika in a bowl.

2 Wipe the mushrooms clean and trim the stalks, if necessary. Lightly whisk the egg whites with a fork, until frothy.

3 Dip each mushroom into the egg whites, then into the breadcrumb mixture. Repeat until all the mushrooms are coated.

4 Put the mushrooms on a non-stick baking sheet. Bake in the pre-heated oven for 15 minutes, or until tender and the coating has turned golden and crunchy.

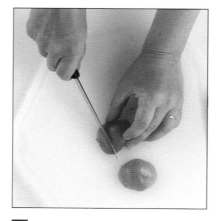

5 Meanwhile, to make the dip, plunge the tomatoes into a saucepan of boiling water for 1 minute, then into a saucepan of cold water. Slip off the skins. Halve, remove the seeds and cores and roughly chop the flesh.

6 Put the cottage cheese, yogurt, garlic clove and dill into a mixing bowl and combine well. Season to taste. Stir in the chopped tomatoes. Spoon the mixture into a serving dish and garnish with a sprig of fresh dill. Serve the mushrooms hot, together with the dip.

Pasta Bonbons

Serves 4–6

INGREDIENTS
1 quantity basic pasta dough
flour, for dusting
egg white, beaten
salt and pepper

FOR THE FILLING
1 small onion, finely chopped
1 garlic clove, crushed
$^2/_3$ cup chicken stock
8 ounces ground turkey meat
2–3 fresh sage leaves, chopped
2 canned anchovy fillets, drained

FOR THE SAUCE
$^2/_3$ cup chicken stock
7 ounces low-fat cream cheese
1 tablespoon lemon juice
1 teaspoon caster sugar
2 tomatoes, peeled, seeded and
   finely diced
$^1/_2$ purple onion, finely chopped
6 small cornichons, sliced

1 To make the filling, put the onion, garlic and stock into a pan. Bring to a boil, cover and simmer for 5 minutes until tender. Uncover and boil for about 5 minutes or until the stock is reduced to 2 tablespoons.

2 Add the ground turkey, and stir over the heat until no longer pink in color. Add the sage and anchovy fillets and season with salt and pepper. Cook uncovered for 5 minutes until all the liquid has been absorbed. Let cool.

3 Divide the pasta dough in half. Roll into thin sheets and cut into rectangles measuring $3^1/_2 \times 2^1/_2$ inches. Lay on a lightly floured dish towel and repeat with the remaining dough.

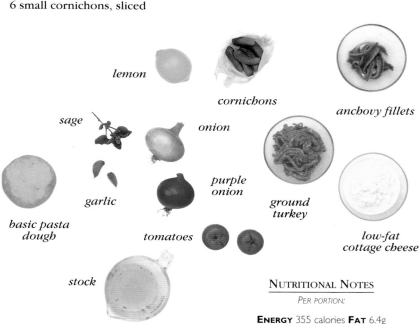

lemon

cornichons

anchovy fillets

sage

onion

garlic

purple
onion

ground
turkey

basic pasta
dough

tomatoes

low-fat
cottage cheese

stock

NUTRITIONAL NOTES
PER PORTION:

ENERGY 355 calories **FAT** 6.4g
SATURATED FAT 1.4g **CHOLESTEROL** 150mg
CARBOHYDRATE 46g **FIBER** 2.6g

4 Place a heaped teaspoon of the filling on the center of each rectangle, brush around the meat with beaten egg white and roll up the pasta, pinching in the ends. Set it aside onto a floured dish towel for 1 hour before cooking.

5 To make the sauce, put the stock, cream cheese, lemon juice and sugar into a pan. Heat gently and whisk until smooth. Add the diced tomatoes, onion and cornichons.

6 Cook the pasta in a large pan of boiling, salted water for 5 minutes. (Cook in batches to stop them sticking together). Remove with a slotted spoon, drain well and drop into the sauce. Repeat until all the bonbons are cooked. Simmer for 2–3 minutes. Serve in pasta bowls or soup plates and spoon over a little sauce.

Onions in Toast Cups

Fill crisp bread cups with tender pearl onions tossed in a mustardy glaze.

Serves 4–6

INGREDIENTS
8 oz pearl onions
   or shallots
⅔ cup vegetable stock
1 tbsp dry white wine or
   dry sherry
2 pieces turkey bacon, cut into
   thin strips
2 tsp Worcestershire sauce
1 tsp tomato paste
¼ tsp prepared English mustard
salt and freshly ground black pepper
sprigs of Italian parsley, to garnish

pearl onions

stock

white bread

parsley

turkey bacon

NUTRITIONAL NOTES

PER SERVING:

CALORIES 178 **PROTEIN** 9.42 g
FAT 1.57 g **SATURATED FAT** 0.30 g
CARBOHYDRATE 33.26 g **FIBER** 1.82 g
ADDED SUGAR 0 **SODIUM** 1.23 g

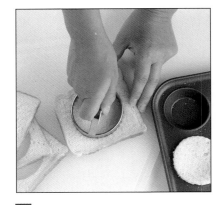

1 Preheat the oven to 400°F. Stamp out the bread into rounds with a 3 in fluted cookie cutter and use to line a twelve-cup cupcake pan.

2 Cover each bread case with non-stick baking paper, and fill with baking beans or rice. Bake 'blind' for 5 minutes in the pre-heated oven. Remove the paper and beans and continue to bake for a further 5 minutes, until lightly browned and crisp.

3 Meanwhile, put the pearl onions in a bowl and cover with boiling water. Leave for 3 minutes, then drain and rinse under cold water. Trim off their top and root ends and slip them out of their skins.

4 Simmer the onions and stock in a covered saucepan for 5 minutes. Uncover and cook, stirring occasionally until the stock has reduced entirely. Add all the remaining ingredients, except the parsley. Cook for 2-3 minutes. Fill the toast cups with the deviled onions. Serve hot, garnished with sprigs of Italian parsley.

Grilled Green Mussels with Cumin

Large green shelled mussels have a more distinctive flavor than the more common small black variety. If you can't find these the black mussels are also delicious prepared this way.

Serves 4

INGREDIENTS
3 tbsp fresh parsley
3 tbsp fresh cilantro
1 garlic clove, crushed
pinch of ground cumin
1 tbsp low-fat spread
3 tbsp brown bread crumbs
freshly ground black pepper
12 green mussels or 24 small mussels on the half-shell
chopped fresh parsley, to garnish

parsley

butter

garlic

bread

cilantro

mussels

1 Chop the herbs finely.

2 Beat the garlic, herbs, cumin and butter together with a wooden spoon.

NUTRITIONAL NOTES
PER PORTION:

ENERGY 63 Kcals **FAT** 3.6 g
SATURATED FAT 0.8 g

3 Stir in the breadcrumbs and freshly ground black pepper.

4 Spoon a little of the mixture onto each mussel and broil for 2 minutes. Serve with chopped fresh parsley.

Lemon and Ginger Spicy Beans

An extremely quick delicious meal, made with canned beans for speed. You probably won't need extra salt as canned beans tend to be already salted.

Serves 4

INGREDIENTS
2 tbsp roughly chopped fresh ginger
3 garlic cloves, roughly chopped
1 cup cold water
1 tbsp sunflower oil
1 large onion, thinly sliced
1 fresh red chile, seeded and
   finely chopped
¼ tsp cayenne pepper
2 tsp ground cumin
1 tsp ground coriander
½ tsp ground tumeric
2 tbsp lemon juice
⅓ cup chopped fresh cilantro
14-oz can black-eyed peas, drained
   and rinsed
14-oz can adzuki beans, drained
   and rinsed
14-oz can navy beans, drained
   and rinsed
freshly ground pepper

1 Place the ginger, garlic and 60 ml/ 4 tbsp of the cold water in a blender and mix until smooth.

NUTRITIONAL NOTES
PER PORTION:

ENERGY 373 Kcals **FAT** 4.4 g
SATURATED FAT 0.9 g

2 Heat the oil in a pan. Add the onion and chile and cook gently for 5 minutes until softened.

3 Add the cayenne pepper, cumin, ground coriander and turmeric and stir-fry for 1 minute.

4 Stir in the ginger and garlic paste from the blender and cook for another minute.

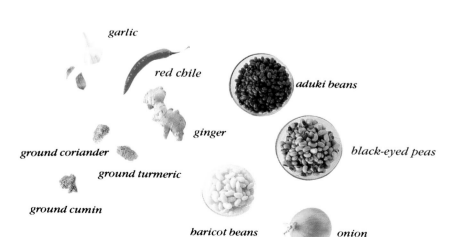

garlic

red chile

aduki beans

ginger

ground coriander

ground turmeric

black-eyed peas

ground cumin

haricot beans

onion

5 Add the remaining water, lemon juice and fresh cilantro, stir well and bring to a boil. Cover the pan tightly and cook for 5 minutes.

6 Add all the beans and cook for a further 5–10 minutes. Season with pepper and serve.

Red Bell Pepper and Watercress Phyllo Parcels

Peppery watercress combines well with sweet red bell peppers in these crisp little parcels.

Makes 8

INGREDIENTS
3 red bell peppers
6 oz watercress
1 cup ricotta cheese
¼ cup blanched almonds, toasted and chopped
salt and freshiy ground black pepper
8 sheets of phyllo pastry
2 tbsp olive oil

ricotta

red bell pepper

watercress

almonds

phyllo pastry

NUTRITIONAL NOTES
PER PORTION:
ENERGY 151 Kcals FAT 10.2 g
SATURATED FAT 3 g

1 Preheat the oven to 375°F. Place the peppers under a hot broiler until blistered and charred. Place in a paper bag. When cool enough to handle peel, seed and pat dry on paper towels.

2 Place the peppers and watercress in a food processor and pulse until coarsely chopped. Spoon into a bowl.

3 Mix in the ricotta and almonds, and season to taste.

4 Working with 1 sheet of phyllo pastry at a time, cut out 2 × 7-in and 2 × 2-in squares from each sheet. Brush 1 large square with a little olive oil and place a second large square at an angle of 90 degrees to form a star shape.

5 Place 1 of the small squares in the centre of the star shape, brush lightly with oil and top with a second small square.

6 Top with ⅛ of the red pepper mixture. Bring the edges together to form a purse shape and twist to seal. Place on a lightly greased baking sheet and cook for 25–30 minutes until golden.

Steamed Spiced Pork and Water Chestnut Wontons

Ginger and Chinese five-spice powder flavor this version of steamed open dumplings – a favorite snack in many teahouses.

Makes about 36

INGREDIENTS
2 large Chinese cabbage leaves, plus extra for lining the steamer
2 scallions, finely chopped
½-in piece fresh ginger, finely chopped
2 oz canned water chestnuts (drained weight), rinsed and finely chopped
8oz ground pork
½ tsp Chinese five-spice powder
1 tbsp cornstarch
1 tbsp light soy sauce
1 tbsp Chinese rice wine
2 tsp sesame oil
generous pinch of sugar
about 36 wonton wrappers, each 3 in square
light soy sauce and hot chili oil, for dipping

caster sugar

Chinese cabbage

cornstarch

scallions

water chestnuts

pork

Chinese rice wine

ginger

light soy sauce

sesame oil

wonton wrappers

Chinese five-spice powder

NUTRITIONAL NOTES
PER WONTON:

ENERGY 32 Kcals FAT 1.25 g
SATURATED FAT 0.7 g

VARIATION

These can also be deep fried, in which case fold the edges over the filling to enclose it completely. Press well to seal. Deep fry in batches in hot oil for about 2 minutes.

1 Place the Chinese cabbage leaves one on top of another. Cut them lengthways into quarters and then across into thin shreds.

2 Place the shredded Chinese cabbage leaves in a bowl. Add the scallions, ginger, water chestnuts, pork, five-spice powder, cornstarch, soy sauce, rice wine, sesame oil and sugar; mix well.

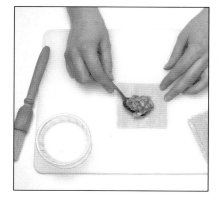

3 Set one wonton wrapper on a work surface. Place a heaped teaspoon of the filling in the center of the wrapper, then lightly dampen the edges with water.

4 Lift the wrapper up around the filling, gathering to form a purse. Squeeze the wrapper firmly around the middle, then tap on the bottom to make a flat base. The top should be open. Place the wonton on a tray and cover with a damp dish towel.

5 Line the steamer with cabbage leaves and steam the dumplings for 12–15 minutes or until tender. Remove each batch from the steamer as soon as they are cooked, cover with foil and keep warm. Serve hot with soy sauce and chili oil for dipping.

Creamy Raspberry Dressing with Asparagus

Raspberry vinegar gives this quick low fat dressing a refreshing, tangy flavor – the perfect accompaniment to asparagus.

Serves 4

INGREDIENTS
1½ pounds thin asparagus spears
2 tablespoons raspberry vinegar
½ teaspoon salt
1 teaspoon Dijon-style mustard
4 tablespoons half fat crème fraîche
  or natural low fat yogurt
ground white pepper
4 ounces fresh raspberries

asparagus spears

raspberry vinegar

Dijon-style mustard

half fat crème fraîche

fresh raspberries

NUTRITIONAL NOTES

PER PORTION:

CALORIES 60 **FAT** 1.3 g
SATURATED FAT 0.1 g **PROTEIN** 6.2 g
CARBOHYDRATE 6.0 g **FIBER** 3.6 g

1 Fill a large wide frying pan, or wok, with water about 4 inches deep and bring to a boil.

2 Trim the tough ends of the asparagus spears. If desired, remove the "scales" using a vegetable peeler.

3 Tie the asparagus spears into two bundles. Lower the bundles into the boiling water and cook for 3–5 minutes, or until just tender.

4 Carefully remove the asparagus bundles from the boiling water using a slotted spoon and immerse them in cold water to stop the cooking. Drain and untie the bundles. Pat dry with kitchen paper. Chill the asparagus for at least 1 hour.

5 Mix together the vinegar and salt in a bowl and stir with a fork until dissolved. Stir in the mustard. Gradually stir in the crème fraîche or yogurt until blended. Add pepper to taste. To serve, place the asparagus on individual plates and drizzle the dressing across the middle of the spears. Garnish with the fresh raspberries and serve at once.

Thai Fish Cakes

Bursting with the flavors of chilies, lime and lemongrass, these little fish cakes make a wonderful appetizer.

Serves 4

INGREDIENTS
1 lb white fish fillets, such as
    cod or haddock
3 scallions, sliced
2 tbsp chopped fresh cilantro
2 tbsp Thai red curry paste
1 fresh green chili,
    seeded and chopped
2 tsp grated lime rind
1 tbsp lime juice
2 tbsp peanut oil
salt, to taste
crisp lettuce leaves,
    shredded scallions,
    fresh red chili slices,
    cilantro sprigs and
    lime wedges, to serve

lettuce *white fish fillets*

lime *scallions*

peanut oil

cilantro

red chili

green chili *Thai red curry paste*

NUTRITIONAL NOTES
PER PORTION:

ENERGY 154 Kcals **FAT** 7.2 g
SATURATED FAT 1.5 g

1 Cut the fish into chunks, then place in a blender or food processor.

2 Add the scallions, cilantro, red curry paste, green chili, lime rind and juice to the fish. Season with salt. Process until finely ground.

3 Using lightly floured hands, divide the mixture into 16 pieces and shape each one into a small cake about 1½ in across. Place the fish cakes on a plate, cover with plastic wrap and chill for about 2 hours, until firm. Heat the wok over high heat until hot. Add the oil and swirl it around.

4 Fry the fish cakes, a few at a time, for 6–8 minutes, turning them carefully until evenly browned. Drain each batch on paper towels and keep hot while cooking the remainder. Serve on a bed of crisp lettuce leaves with shredded scallions, red chili slices, cilantro sprigs and lime wedges.

Shrimp Salad with Curry Dressing

Curry spices add an unexpected twist to this salad. Warm flavors combine especially well with sweet shrimp and grated apple.

Serves 4

INGREDIENTS
1 ripe tomato
½ iceberg lettuce, shredded
1 small onion
1 small bunch fresh cilantro
1 tbsp lemon juice
salt
1 lb cooked peeled shrimp
1 apple, peeled

DRESSING
5 tbsp low-fat mayonnaise
1 tsp mild curry paste
1 tbsp ketchup

TO DECORATE
8 whole shrimp
8 lemon wedges
4 sprigs fresh cilantro

1 To peel the tomato, pierce the skin with a knife and immerse in boiling water for 20 seconds. Drain and cool under running water. Peel off the skin. Halve the tomato, push the seeds out with your thumb and discard them. Cut the flesh into large dice.

2 Finely shred the lettuce, onion, and cilantro. Add the tomato, toss with lemon juice, and season with salt.

3 To make the dressing, combine the mayonnaise, curry paste, and tomato ketchup in a small bowl. Add 2 tbsp water to thin the dressing and season to taste with salt.

4 Combine the shrimp with the dressing. Quarter and core the apple, and grate into the mixture.

shrimp

cilantro

tomato

apple

lemon

onion

COOK'S TIP

Fresh cilantro is inclined to wilt if kept out of water. Keep it in a jar of water in the refrigerator covered with a plastic bag and it will stay fresh for several days.

NUTRITIONAL NOTES

PER PORTION:

ENERGY 133 Kcals **FAT** 4.5 g
SATURATED FAT 0.2 g

5 Distribute the shredded lettuce mixture between 4 plates or bowls. Pile the shrimp mixture in the center of each and decorate with 2 whole shrimp, 2 lemon wedges, and a sprig of cilantro.

Chicken Tikka

The red food coloring gives this dish its traditional bright color. Serve with lemon wedges and a crisp mixed salad.

Serves 4

INGREDIENTS
1 × 3½ lb chicken
mixed salad leaves, e.g. frisée and
   oakleaf lettuce or radicchio,
   to serve

FOR THE MARINADE
⅔ cup plain low fat yogurt
1 tsp ground paprika
2 tsp grated fresh ginger root
1 garlic clove, crushed
2 tsp garam masala
½ tsp salt
red food coloring (optional)
juice of 1 lemon

lemon

chicken

salt

yogurt

paprika

ginger

garlic

garam masala

1 Joint the chicken and cut it into eight pieces, using a sharp knife.

2 Mix all the marinade ingredients in a container large enough to hold the chicken pieces. Add the chicken, coat well and chill for 4 hours or overnight to allow the flavors to penetrate the flesh.

NUTRITIONAL NOTES

PER PORTION:

CALORIES 131
FAT 4.5 g **SATURATED FAT** 1.4 g
CHOLESTEROL 55.4 mg

3 Preheat the oven to 400°F. Remove the chicken pieces from the marinade and arrange them in a single layer in a large ovenproof dish. Bake for 30–40 minutes or until tender.

4 Baste with a little of the marinade while cooking. Arrange on a bed of salad leaves and serve hot or cold.

Sesame Seed Chicken Bites

Best served warm, these crunchy bites are delicious accompanied by a glass of chilled dry white wine.

Makes 20

INGREDIENTS
6 oz raw chicken breast
2 cloves garlic, crushed
1 in piece ginger root, peeled
   and grated
1 medium egg white
1 tsp cornstarch
¼ cup shelled pistachios, roughly
   chopped
4 tbsp sesame seeds
2 tbsp grapeseed oil
salt and freshly ground black pepper

FOR THE SAUCE
¼ cup hoisin sauce
1 tbsp sweet chili sauce

TO GARNISH
ginger root, finely shredded
pistachios, roughly chopped
fresh dill sprigs

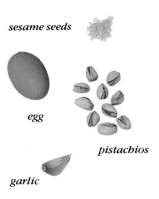

sesame seeds

egg

pistachios

garlic

ginger

1 Place the chicken, garlic, grated ginger, egg white and cornstarch into the food processor and process them to a smooth paste.

2 Stir in the pistachios and season well with salt and pepper.

NUTRITIONAL NOTES
PER PORTION:

CALORIES 53
FAT 4.1 g **SATURATED FAT** 0.2 g
CHOLESTEROL 3.8 mg

3 Roll into 20 balls and coat with sesame seeds. Heat the wok and add the oil. When the oil is hot, stir-fry the chicken bites in batches, turning regularly until golden. Drain on kitchen towels.

4 Make the sauce by mixing together the hoisin and chili sauces in a bowl. Garnish the bites with shredded ginger, pistachios and dill, then serve hot, with a dish of sauce for dipping.

Grilled Jumbo Shrimp Bhoona

The unusual and delicious flavor of this dish is achieved by grilling the shrimp to give them a smoky taste and then adding them to fried onions and bell peppers.

Serves 4

INGREDIENTS
3 tbsp low fat plain yogurt
1 tsp paprika
1 tsp minced ginger
12–14 cooked and peeled
    jumbo shrimp
1 tbsp corn oil
3 medium onions, sliced
½ tsp fennel seeds, crushed
1-in piece cinnamon stick
1 tsp minced garlic
1 tsp chili powder
1 medium yellow bell pepper,
    seeded and roughly chopped
1 medium red bell pepper,
    seeded and roughly chopped
salt
1 tbsp fresh cilantro leaves,
    to garnish

1 Blend together the yogurt, paprika, ginger, and salt to taste. Pour this mixture over the shrimp and marinate for 30–45 minutes.

fennel seeds   paprika

chili powder   minced ginger

minced garlic

king prawns

jumbo shrimp

yogurt

fresh cilantro

onions

red bell pepper   yellow bell pepper

COOK'S TIP
Although dried cilantro is available, the fresh herb is much better for garnishes.

2 Meanwhile, heat the oil in a non-stick wok or frying pan and fry the onions with the fennel seeds and the cinnamon stick.

3 Lower the heat and add the garlic and chili powder.

4 Add the peppers and stir-fry gently for 3–5 minutes.

NUTRITIONAL NOTES

PER PORTION:

ENERGY 132 Kcals **PROTEIN** 9.97 g
FAT 3.94 g **SATURATED FAT** 0.58 g
CARBOHYDRATE 15.93 g **FIBER** 3.11 g
ADDED SUGAR 0.02 g
SALT 0.79 g

5 Remove from heat and transfer to a serving dish, discarding the cinnamon stick.

6 Preheat the broiler and turn the heat to medium. Put the shrimp in a broiler pan or flameproof dish and place under the broiler to darken their tops and achieve a smoky effect. Add the shrimp to the onion mixture, garnish with the cilantro and serve.

Raw Salmon Sushi

A quite complicated starter which needs to be made
with very fresh fish. Try to buy green wasabi powder
to mix with water and serve with the soy sauce and
pickled ginger. It will give a very authentic taste.

Serves 4

INGREDIENTS

1½ cups short grain rice
3¼ in piece of konbu seaweed
1 tbsp of sake or dry white wine
12 oz salmon fillet, skinned
1 cucumber, peeled
5 sheets of nori
2 tsp sliced pickled (optional)
    ginger
1 small jar of salmon roe
2½ tbsp rice vinegar
1 tbsp sugar
salt and freshly ground black pepper
wasabi, for dipping
soy sauce, for dipping

NUTRITIONAL NOTES

PER PORTION:

ENERGY 323 Kcals **FAT** 8.7 g
SATURATED FAT 1.7 g

1 Wash the rice in cold running water until clear. Place in a large heavy-based saucepan with 1½ cups cold water, the konbu and the sake or dry white wine. Cover and bring to a boil. Remove the konbu and replace the lid. Turn the heat down and allow the rice to cook for a further 10–15 minutes. Using a wooden spoon, carefully mix the rice to fluff it up.

2 Transfer the rice to a shallow bowl. Leave to cool slightly. Cover with a damp dish towel to prevent the rice from drying.

3 Cut the salmon and cucumber into long strips. Lay the nori out flat on a dry dish towel.

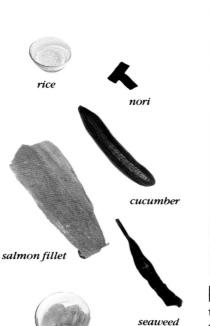

rice

nori

cucumber

salmon fillet

seaweed

pickled ginger

4 Spoon a thin line of sushi rice across the width of the nori, leaving 2 in of the nori clear. Then lay a line of the salmon, cucumber, pickled ginger, salmon roe and vinegar, sugar and seasoning across the top. Top with more sushi rice.

5 Fold over the end of the nori, then using the dish towel, roll tightly. Leave for 10 minutes, unwrap, then cut into 1¼ in lengths. Repeat with the remaining ingredients. Serve with wasabi and soy sauce.

Meat
Dishes

Deviled Ham and Pineapple Salad

Serves 4

INGREDIENTS
8 ounces whole wheat penne
²/₃ cup low-fat yogurt
1 tablespoon cider vinegar
1 teaspoon wholegrain mustard
large pinch of sugar
2 tablespoons hot mango chutney
4 ounces cooked lean ham, cubed
7 ounce can pineapple chunks
2 sticks celery, chopped
¹/₂ green bell pepper, seeded
    and diced
1 tablespoon toasted slivered
    almonds, chopped roughly
salt and ground black pepper
crusty bread, to serve

celery

green pepper

wholewheat penne

hot mango chutney

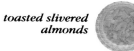

pineapple chunks *low-fat yogurt* *lean ham*

toasted slivered almonds

Cook the pasta in a large pan of boiling, salted water until *al dente*. Drain and rinse thoroughly. Leave to cool.

2 To make the dressing, mix the yogurt, vinegar, mustard, sugar and mango chutney together. Season, add the pasta and toss lightly together.

3 Transfer the pasta to a serving dish. Scatter over the ham, pineapple, celery and pepper.

4 Sprinkle the top with toasted almonds. Serve with crusty bread.

NUTRITIONAL NOTES
PER PORTION:

ENERGY 303 calories **FAT** 5.4g
SATURATED FAT 0.9g **CHOLESTEROL** 18.5mg
CARBOHYDRATE 51g **FIBER** 6g

Stir-fried Pork with Lychees

Lychees have a very pretty pink skin which, when peeled, reveals a soft fleshy berry with a hard shiny stone. If you cannot buy fresh lychees, this dish can be made with drained canned lychees.

Serves 4

INGREDIENTS
1 lb lean pork, diced
2 tbsp hoisin sauce
4 scallions, sliced
6 oz lychees, peeled, pitted and cut
    into slivers
salt and freshly ground pepper
fresh lychees and fresh parsley sprigs,
    to garnish

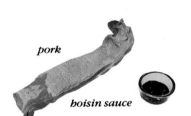
pork

hoisin sauce

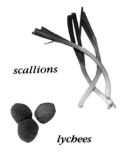
scallions

lychees

1 Cut the pork into bite-size pieces.

2 Pour the hoisin sauce over the pork and marinate for 30 minutes.

3 Heat the wok, then add the pork and stir-fry for 5 minutes until crisp and golden. Add the scallions and stir-fry for a further 2 minutes.

4 Scatter the lychee slivers over the pork, and season well with salt and pepper. Garnish with fresh lychees and fresh parsley, and serve.

NUTRITIONAL NOTES
PER PORTION:
ENERGY 171 Kcals **FAT** 4.6 g
SATURATED FAT 1.6 g

Pork and Vegetable Stir-fry

A quick and easy stir-fry of pork and vegetables.

Serves 4

INGREDIENTS
1 can (8 ounces) pineapple cubes
1 tablespoon cornstarch
2 tablespoons light soy sauce
1 tablespoon each dry sherry,
  brown sugar and wine vinegar
1 teaspoon five-spice powder
2 teaspoons olive oil
1 red onion, sliced
1 garlic clove, crushed
1 fresh seeded red chili, chopped
1-inch piece fresh ginger
12 ounces lean pork tenderloin,
  cut into thin strips
6 ounces carrots
1 red bell pepper, seeded
  and sliced
6 ounces snow peas, halved
½ cup bean sprouts
1 can (7 ounces) corn kernels
2 tablespoons chopped cilantro
salt
1 tablespoon toasted sesame seeds,
  to garnish

pineapple cubes *light soy sauce* *dry sherry* *wine vinegar* *five-spice powder* *olive oil* *red onion* *garlic* *red chili* *ginger* *carrots* *red pepper* *snow peas* *pork tenderloin* *corn kernels* *cilantro* *bean sprouts*

1 Drain the pineapple, reserving the juice. In a small bowl, blend the cornstarch with the pineapple juice. Add the soy sauce, sherry, sugar, vinegar and spice, stir to mix and set aside.

2 Heat the oil in a large nonstick frying pan or wok. Add the onion, garlic, chili and ginger and stir-fry for 30 seconds. Add the pork and stir-fry for 2–3 minutes.

NUTRITIONAL NOTES
PER PORTION:

CALORIES 327 PROTEIN 24.95g
FAT 7.90g SATURATED FAT 1.89g
CARBOHYDRATE 40.81g FIBER 4.77g
ADDED SUGAR 5.38g SODIUM 0.73g

3 Cut the carrots into matchstick strips. Add to the wok with the pepper and stir-fry for 2–3 minutes. Add the snow peas, bean sprouts and corn and stir-fry for 1–2 minutes.

4 Pour in the sauce mixture and the reserved pineapple and stir-fry until the sauce thickens. Reduce the heat and stir-fry for another 1–2 minutes. Stir in the cilantro and season to taste. Sprinkle with sesame seeds and serve immediately.

Sage and Orange Sauce with Pork Fillet

Sage is often partnered with pork – there seems to be a natural affinity – and the addition of orange to the sauce balances the flavor.

Serves 4

INGREDIENTS
2 pork fillets, about 12 ounces each
2 teaspoons butter
½ cup dry sherry
¾ cup chicken broth
2 garlic cloves, very finely chopped
grated rind and juice of
  1 unwaxed orange
3 or 4 sage leaves, finely chopped
2 teaspoons cornstarch
salt and pepper
orange wedges and sage leaves,
  to garnish

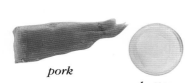

pork

butter

dry sherry

chicken stock

garlic cloves

orange

sage leaves

cornstarch

NUTRITIONAL NOTES
PER PORTION:

CALORIES 330 **FAT** 14.6 g
SATURATED FAT 5.8 g **PROTEIN** 36.8 g
CARBOHYDRATE 4.4 g **FIBER** 0.1 g

1 Season the pork fillets lightly with salt and pepper. Melt the butter in a heavy flameproof casserole over a medium-high heat, then add the meat and cook for 5–6 minutes, turning to brown all sides evenly.

2 Add the sherry, boil for about 1 minute, then add the broth, garlic, orange rind and sage. Bring to a boil and reduce the heat to low, then cover and simmer for 20 minutes, turning once. The meat is cooked if the juices run clear when the meat is pierced with a knife or a meat thermometer inserted into the thickest part of the meat registers 150°F.

3 Transfer the pork to a warmed platter and cover to keep warm.

4 Bring the sauce to a boil. Blend the cornstarch and orange juice and stir into the sauce, then boil gently over medium heat for a few minutes, stirring frequently, until the sauce is slightly thickened. Strain into a gravy cup or serving pitcher.

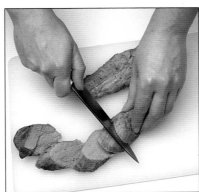

5 Slice the pork diagonally and pour the meat juices into the sauce. Spoon a little sauce over the pork and garnish with orange wedges and sage leaves. Serve the remaining sauce separately.

Hot and Sour Pork

Chinese five-spice powder is made from a mixture of ground star anise, Szechuan pepper, cassia, cloves and fennel seed and has a flavor similar to licorice. If you can't find any, use allspice instead.

NUTRITIONAL NOTES
PER SERVING:

CALORIES 196 **PROTEIN** 19.78 g
FAT 7.29 g **SATURATED FAT** 2.37 g
CARBOHYDRATE 13.63 g **FIBER** 1.16 g
ADDED SUGAR 0 **SODIUM** 0.77 g

Serves 4

INGREDIENTS
12 oz pork fillet
1 tsp sunflower oil
1 in piece ginger root, grated
1-in piece ginger, grated
1 red chile, seeded and finely chopped
1 tsp Chinese five-spice powder
1 tbsp sherry vinegar
1 tbsp soy sauce
8-oz can pineapple chunks in
    natural juice
4 tsp cornstarch
1 small green bell pepper, seeded and
    sliced
4 oz baby corn, halved
salt and freshly ground black pepper
sprig of Italian parsley, to garnish
boiled rice, to serve

pineapple chunks

pork fillet

chile

cornstarch

pepper

soy sauce

baby corn

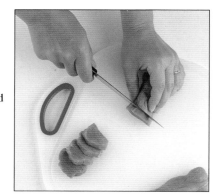

1 Preheat the oven to 325°F. Trim away any visible fat from the pork and cut into ½ in thick slices.

2 Brush the sunflower oil over the base of a flameproof casserole. Heat over a medium flame, then fry the meat for about 2 minutes on each side or until lightly browned.

3 Blend together the ginger, chile, five-spice powder, vinegar and soy sauce.

4 Drain the pineapple chunks, reserving the juice. Make the stock up to 1¼ cups with the reserved juice, mix together with the spices and pour over the pork.

5 Slowly bring to a boil. Blend the cornstarch with 1 tbsp of cold water and gradually stir into the pork. Add the vegetables and season to taste.

6 Cover and cook in the oven for 30 minutes. Stir in the pineapple and cook for another 5 minutes. Garnish with Italian parsley and served with boiled rice.

Honey-roasted Pork with Thyme and Rosemary

Herbs and honey add flavor and sweetness to tenderloin—the leanest cut of pork.

NUTRITIONAL NOTES
Per portion:

ENERGY 248.75 Kcals **PROTEIN** 26.15 g
FAT 8.12 g **SATURATED FAT** 2.63 g
CARBOHYDRATE 16.42 g
FIBER 0.87 g **SUGAR** 14.54 g
SODIUM 284.5 mg

Serves 4

INGREDIENTS
1 lb pork tenderloin
2 tbsp honey
2 tbsp Dijon mustard
1 tsp chopped fresh rosemary
½ tsp chopped fresh thyme
¼ tsp whole tropical peppercorns
sprigs of fresh rosemary and thyme,
   to garnish
potato gratin and cauliflower,
   to serve

FOR THE RED ONION CONFIT
4 red onions
1½ cups vegetable stock
1 tbsp red wine vinegar
1 tbsp superfine sugar
1 garlic clove, crushed
2 tbsp ruby port
pinch of salt

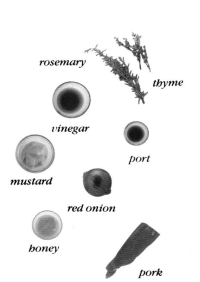

rosemary

thyme

vinegar

port

mustard

red onion

honey

pork

1 Preheat the oven to 350°F. Trim off any visible fat from the port. Put the honey, mustard, rosemary and thyme in a small bowl and combine them well.

2 Crush the peppercorns using a mortar and pestle. Spread the honey mixture over the pork and sprinkle with the crushed peppercorns. Place in a non-stick roasting pan and cook in the pre-heated oven for 35–45 minutes.

3 For the red onion confit, slice the onions into rings and put them into a heavy-based saucepan.

4 Add the stock, vinegar, sugar and garlic clove to the saucepan. Bring to the boil, then reduce the heat. Cover and simmer for 15 minutes.

5 Uncover and pour in the port and continue to simmer, stirring occasionally, until the onions are soft and the juices thick and syrupy. Season to taste with salt.

6 Cut the pork into slices and arrange on four warmed plates. Serve garnished with rosemary and thyme and accompanied by the red onion confit, potato gratin and cucumber.

Tagliatelle with Milanese Sauce

Serves 4

INGREDIENTS

1 onion, finely chopped
1 stalk celery, finely chopped
1 red bell pepper, seeded and diced
1–2 garlic cloves, crushed
²/₃ cup vegetable stock
14 ounce can tomatoes
1 tbsp tomato paste
2 teaspoons sugar
1 teaspoon mixed dried herbs
12 ounces tagliatelle
4 ounces button mushrooms, sliced
4 tablespoons white wine
4 ounces lean cooked ham, diced
salt and ground black pepper
1 tablespoon chopped fresh parsley,
   to garnish

garlic

celery

tagliatelle

red pepper

onion

lean cooked ham

button mushrooms

parsley

tomato paste

vegetable stock

tomatoes

white wine

1 Put the chopped onion, celery, pepper and garlic into a non-stick pan. Add the stock, bring to the boil and cook for 5 minutes or until tender.

2 Add the tomatoes, tomato paste, sugar and herbs. Season with salt and pepper. Bring to a boil, simmer for 30 minutes until thick. Stir occasionally.

3 Cook the pasta in a large pan of boiling, salted water until *al dente*. Drain thoroughly.

4 Put the mushrooms into a pan with the white wine, cover and cook for 3–4 minutes until tender and all the wine has been absorbed.

5 Add the mushrooms and diced ham to the tomato sauce. Reheat gently.

6 Transfer the pasta to a warmed serving dish and spoon on the sauce. Garnish with parsley.

NUTRITIONAL NOTES

PER PORTION:

ENERGY 405 calories **FAT** 3.5g
SATURATED FAT 0.8g **CHOLESTEROL** 17mg
CARBOHYDRATE 77g **FIBER** 4.5g

Ham-filled Paprika Ravioli

Serves 4

INGREDIENTS
8 ounces cooked smoked ham
4 tablespoons mango chutney
1 recipe basic pasta dough, with
   1 teaspoon ground paprika
   added
egg white, beaten
flour, for dusting
1–2 garlic cloves, crushed
1 stick celery, sliced
2 ounces sun-dried tomatoes
1 red chili, seeded and chopped
2/3 cup red wine
14-ounce can chopped tomatoes
1 teaspoons chopped fresh thyme,
   plus extra to garnish
2 teaspoons sugar
salt and ground black pepper

garlic

celery   *red chili*   *smoked ham*

thyme   *red wine*

sun-dried tomatoes

chopped tomatoes

mango chutney

basic pasta dough   *paprika*

1 Remove all traces of fat from the ham, place it with the mango chutney in a food processor or blender and mince the mixture finely.

2 Roll the pasta into thin sheets and lay one piece over a ravioli tray. Put a teaspoonful of the ham filling into each of the depressions.

3 Brush around the edges of each ravioli with egg white. Cover with another sheet of pasta and press the edges well together to seal.

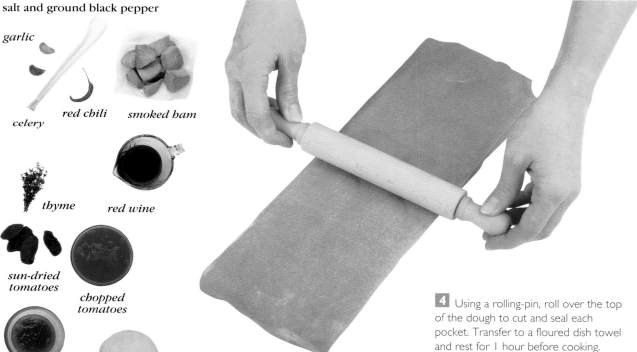

4 Using a rolling-pin, roll over the top of the dough to cut and seal each pocket. Transfer to a floured dish towel and rest for 1 hour before cooking.

5 Put the garlic, celery, sun-dried tomatoes, chili, wine, canned tomatoes and thyme into a pan. Cover and cook for 15–20 minutes. Season with salt, pepper and sugar.

6 Cook the ravioli in a large pan of boiling, salted water for 4–5 minutes. Drain thoroughly. Spoon a little of the sauce on to a serving plate and arrange the ravioli on top. Sprinkle with fresh thyme and serve at once.

NUTRITIONAL NOTES
PER PORTION:

ENERGY 380 calories **FAT** 7.6g
SATURATED FAT 2.1g **CHOLESTEROL** 152mg
CARBOHYDRATE 52g **FIBER** 2.4g

Bean and Ham Lasagne

Serve this tasty lasagne with a salad and bread.

Serves 6

INGREDIENTS
2 teaspoons olive oil
3 cups sliced leeks
1 garlic clove, crushed
3 cups mushrooms, sliced
2 zucchini, sliced
12 ounces baby fava beans
2 cups diced lean smoked ham
5 tablespoons chopped fresh
　parsley
2 tablespoons chopped fresh chives
4 tablespoons reduced-fat spread
½ cup whole-wheat flour
2½ cups skim milk
1¼ cups vegetable stock, cooled
6 ounces low-fat cheese
1 teaspoon smooth mustard
8 ounces instant no-boil
　whole-wheat lasagne
½ cup fresh whole-wheat
　bread crumbs
1 tablespoon grated Parmesan
salt and ground black pepper
fresh herb sprigs, to garnish

zucchini

baby fava
beans

smoked ham

olive
oil

leeks

garlic

mushrooms

fresh parsley

fresh
chives

reduced-
fat spread

whole-wheat
flour

skim milk

vegetable
stock

mustard

low fat
cheese

wholewheat lasagne

Parmesan
cheese

fresh whole-
wheat bread
crumbs

salt

black
pepper

1 Preheat the oven to 350°F. Heat the oil in a saucepan, add the leeks and garlic and cook, stirring, for 3 minutes. Add the mushrooms and zucchini and cook, stirring, for 5 minutes.

2 Remove the pan from the heat and stir in the fava beans, ham and herbs. Set aside.

3 Make the cheese sauce. Put the reduced-fat spread, flour, milk and stock in a saucepan and heat gently, whisking constantly, until the sauce comes to a boil and thickens. Simmer gently for 3 minutes, stirring. Grate the cheese.

4 Remove the pan from the heat, add the mustard and grated cheese and stir until the cheese has melted and is well blended. Season to taste. Reserve ½ cup of cheese sauce and set aside. Mix the remaining sauce with the ham and vegetables.

5 Spoon half the ham mixture over the base of a shallow ovenproof dish or baking tin. Cover this with half the pasta. Repeat these layers with the remaining ham mixture and pasta, then pour the reserved cheese sauce over the pasta to cover it completely.

6 Mix together the breadcrumbs and Parmesan cheese and sprinkle over the lasagne. Bake for 45–60 minutes, until cooked and golden brown on top. Garnish with fresh herb sprigs and serve immediately.

NUTRITIONAL NOTES
PER PORTION:

CALORIES 448 PROTEIN 38.45g
FAT 13.05g SATURATED FAT 5.07g
CARBOHYDRATE 46.16g FIBER 10.86g
ADDED SUGAR 0.02g SODIUM 0.50g

Veal Cutlets with Artichokes

Artichokes are very hard to prepare fresh, so use canned artichoke hearts instead—they have an excellent flavor and are simple to use.

Serves 4

INGREDIENTS
1 lb veal cutlets
1 shallot
4 oz lean turkey bacon, finely chopped
14-oz can of artichoke hearts in brine, drained and quartered
⅔ cup veal stock
3 fresh rosemary sprigs
4 tbsp low fat crème fraiche
salt and freshly ground black pepper
fresh rosemary sprigs to garnish

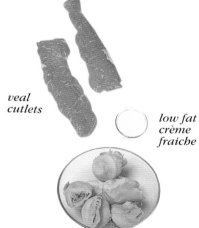

veal cutlets

low fat crème fraiche

artichoke hearts

1 Cut the veal into thin slices.

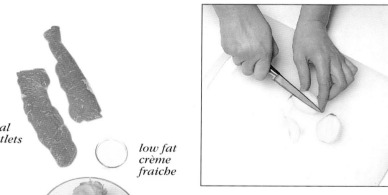

2 Using a sharp knife, cut the shallot into thin slices.

NUTRITIONAL NOTES
PER PORTION:

ENERGY 33.2 Kcals **FAT** 11.3
SATURATED FAT 5.9 g

3 Heat the wok, then add the bacon. Stir-fry for 2 minutes. When the fat is released, add the veal and shallot and stir-fry for 3–4 minutes.

4 Add the artichokes and stir-fry for 1 minute. Stir in the stock and rosemary and simmer for 2 minutes. Stir in the crème fraiche, season with salt and pepper and serve immediately, garnished with sprigs of fresh rosemary.

Stir-fried Beef and Broccoli

This spicy beef may be served with noodles or on a bed of boiled rice for a speedy and low calorie Chinese meal.

Serves 4

INGREDIENTS
12 oz sirloin or lean London
    broil steak
1 tbsp cornstarch
1 tsp sesame oil
12 oz broccoli, cut into small
    florets
4 scallions, sliced on the diagonal
1 carrot, cut into matchstick strips
1 garlic clove, crushed
1 in piece ginger root, cut into very
    fine strips
½ cup low fat beef stock
2 tbsp soy sauce
2 tbsp dry sherry
2 tsp light brown sugar
scallion tassels, to garnish
noodles or rice, to serve

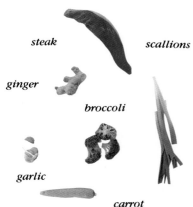

steak   scallions

ginger

broccoli

garlic

carrot

NUTRITIONAL NOTES

PER SERVING:

CALORIES 195 **PROTEIN** 22.84 g
FAT 6.21 g **SATURATED FAT** 1.81 g
CARBOHYDRATE 10.35 g **FIBER** 2.87 g
ADDED SUGAR 2.67 g **SODIUM** 1.36 g

1 Trim the beef and cut into thin slices across the grain. Cut each slice into thin strips. Toss in the cornstarch to coat thoroughly.

2 Heat the sesame oil in a large non-stick frying pan or wok. Add the beef strips and stir-fry over a brisk heat for 3 minutes. Remove and set aside.

COOK'S TIP

To make scallion tassels, trim the bulb base then cut the green shoot so that the onion is 3 in long. Shred to within 1 in of the base and put into iced water for 1 hour.

3 Add the broccoli, scallions, carrot, garlic clove, ginger and stock to the frying pan or wok. Cover and simmer for 3 minutes. Uncover and cook, stirring until all the stock has reduced entirely.

4 Mix the soy sauce, sherry and brown sugar together. Add to the frying pan or wok with the beef. Cook for 2–3 minutes stirring continuously. Spoon into a warm serving dish and garnish with scallion tassels. Serve on a bed of noodles or rice.

Sukiyaki-style Beef

This Japanese dish is a meal in itself; the recipe incorporates all the traditional elements—meat, vegetables, noodles and tofu. If you want to do it properly, eat the meal with chopsticks, and a use of spoon to collect the juices.

Serves 4

INGREDIENTS
1 lb thick rump steak
9 oz Japanese rice noodles
1 tbsp peanut oil
7 oz fine tofu, cut
   into cubes
8 shiitake mushrooms, trimmed
2 medium leeks, sliced into 1-in
   lengths
3½ oz baby spinach, well washed,
   to serve

FOR THE STOCK
1 tbsp superfine sugar
6 tbsp rice wine
3 tbsp dark soy sauce
½ cup water

rice noodles

leek

baby spinach

shiitake mushrooms

rump steak

1 Cut the beef into thin slices.

2 Blanch the noodles in boiling water for 2 minutes. Strain well.

3 Mix together all the stock ingredients in a bowl.

4 Heat the wok, then add the oil. When the oil is hot, stir-fry the beef for about 2–3 minutes, until it is cooked but still pink in color.

5 Pour the stock over the beef.

Nutritional Notes

Per portion:

Energy 406 Kcals **Fat** 10.9 g
Saturated Fat 2.6 g

6 Add the remaining ingredients and cook for 4 minutes, until the leeks are tender. Serve a selection of the different ingredients, with a few baby spinach leaves, to each person.

Asian Beef

This sumptuously rich beef melts in the mouth, and is perfectly complemented by the cool, crunchy relish.

Serves 4

INGREDIENTS
1 lb rump steak

FOR THE MARINADE
1 tbsp sunflower oil
2 cloves garlic, crushed
4 tbsp dark soy sauce
2 tbsp dry sherry
2 tsp soft dark brown sugar

FOR THE RELISH
6 radishes
4 in piece cucumber
1 piece preserved ginger
4 whole radishes, to garnish

rump steak

brown sugar

soy sauce

garlic

radish

1 Cut the beef into thin strips. Place in a bowl.

2 To make the marinade, mix together the garlic, soy sauce, sherry and sugar in a bowl. Pour it over the beef and leave to marinate overnight.

NUTRITIONAL NOTES
PER PORTION:

ENERGY 110 Kcals **FAT** 4.9 g
SATURATED FAT 1.49 g

3 To make the relish, chop the radishes and cucumber into matchsticks and the ginger into small matchsticks. Mix well together in a bowl.

4 Heat the wok, then add the oil. When the oil is hot, add the meat and marinade and stir-fry for 3–4 minutes. Serve with the relish, and garnish with a whole radish on each plate.

Chili over Pasta

Serves 6

INGREDIENTS

1 pound extra lean ground beef
    or turkey
1 onion, finely chopped
2–3 garlic cloves, crushed
1–2 red chiles, seeded and
    finely chopped
14-ounce can chopped tomatoes
3 tablespoons tomato paste
1 teaspoon mixed dried herbs
1¾ cups water
1 pound pipe rigati
14-ounce can red kidney beans,
    drained
salt and ground black pepper

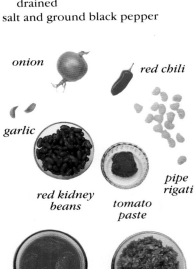

onion

red chili

garlic

red kidney beans

tomato paste

pipe rigati

chopped tomatoes

ground beef

1 Cook the ground beef or turkey in a non-stick saucepan, breaking up any large pieces with a wooden spoon until browned all over.

2 Add the onion, garlic and chilies, cover with a lid and cook gently for 5 minutes.

NUTRITIONAL NOTES

PER PORTION:

ENERGY 425 calories **FAT** 5.4g
SATURATED FAT 1.4g **CHOLESTEROL** 44mg
CARBOHYDRATE 70g **FIBER** 6.1g

3 Add the tomatoes, tomato paste, herbs, water and seasoning. Bring to a boil and simmer for 1½ hours. Leave to cool slightly.

4 Cook the pasta in a large pan of boiling, salted water until *al dente*. Drain thoroughly. Skim off any fat from the surface of the mince. Add the red kidney beans and heat for 5–10 minutes. Pour over the cooked pasta, and serve.

Herbed Beef Salad

Serves 6

INGREDIENTS
1 pound beef fillet
1 pound fresh tagliatelle with
    sun-dried tomatoes and herbs
4 ounces cherry tomatoes
½ cucumber

FOR THE MARINADE
1 tablespoon soy sauce
1 tablespoon sherry
1 tablespoon fresh ginger, grated
1 garlic clove, crushed

FOR THE HERB DRESSING
2–3 tablespoons horseradish
⅔ cup low-fat yogurt
1 garlic clove, crushed
2–3 tablespoons chopped fresh
    herbs (chives, parsley, thyme)
salt and ground black pepper

cherry tomatoes

cucumber

fillet beef

root ginger

garlic

tagliatelle

thyme

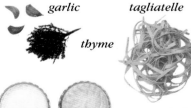

low-fat yogurt *horseradish sauce*

parsley

soy sauce

chives

1 Mix all the marinade ingredients together in a shallow dish, put the beef in and turn it over to coat it. Cover with clear film and leave for 30 minutes to allow the flavours to penetrate the meat.

2 Preheat the grill. Lift the fillet out of the marinade and pat it dry with paper towels. Place on a broiler rack and broil for 8 minutes on each side, basting with the marinade during cooking.

3 Transfer to a plate, cover with foil and leave to stand for 20 minutes.

4 Put all the dressing ingredients into a bowl and mix thoroughly together. Cook the pasta according to the directions on the packet, drain thoroughly, rinse under cold water and leave to dry.

5 Cut the cherry tomatoes in half. Cut the cucumber in half lengthways, scoop out the seeds with a teaspoon and slice thinly into crescents.

6 Put the pasta, cherry tomatoes, cucumber and dressing into a bowl and toss to coat. Slice the beef thinly and arrange on a plate with the pasta salad.

NUTRITIONAL NOTES
PER PORTION:

ENERGY 374 calories **FAT** 5.7g
SATURATED FAT 1.7g **CHOLESTEROL** 46mg
CARBOHYDRATE 57g **FIBER** 2.9g

Lasagne

Serves 6—8

INGREDIENTS
1 large onion, chopped
2 garlic cloves, crushed
1¼ lb ground turkey meat
1 pound tomato sauce
1 teaspoon mixed dried herbs
8 ounces frozen spinach,
  defrosted
7 ounces lasagne verde
7 ounces low fat cottage cheese

FOR THE SAUCE
¼ cup low fat margarine
⅛ cup flour
1¼ cups skim milk
¼ teaspoon ground nutmeg
2 tbsp grated Parmesan cheese
salt and ground black pepper
mixed greens, to serve

ground turkey

spinach

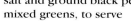
garlic

nutmeg

Parmesan cheese

lasagne verdi

flour

skim milk

low fat margarine

low fat cottage cheese

tomato sauce

1 Put the onion, garlic and ground turkey into a non-stick saucepan. Brown quickly for 5 minutes, stirring with a wooden spoon to separate the pieces.

2 Add the tomato sauce, herbs and seasoning. Bring to a boil, cover and simmer for 30 minutes.

3 For the sauce: put all the sauce ingredients, except the Parmesan cheese, into a saucepan. Heat to thicken, whisking constantly until bubbling and smooth. Adjust the seasoning, add the cheese to the sauce and stir.

4 Preheat the oven to 375°F. Lay the spinach leaves on paper towels and pat dry.

5 Layer the turkey mixture, dried lasagne, cottage cheese and spinach in a 8-cup ovenproof dish, starting and ending with a layer of turkey.

6 Spoon the sauce over the top to cover and bake for 45-50 minutes or until bubbling. Serve with a mixed salad.

NUTRITIONAL NOTES
PER PORTION:

ENERGY 351 calories **FAT** 6.0g
SATURATED FAT 1.7g **CHOLESTEROL** 52mg
CARBOHYDRATE 40g **FIBER** 3g

Cannelloni

Serves 4

INGREDIENTS
2 garlic cloves, crushed
2 x 14 ounce cans
   chopped tomatoes
2 teaspoons brown sugar
1 tablespoon fresh basil
1 tablespoon fresh marjoram
1 pound chopped frozen spinach
large pinch ground nutmeg
4 ounces cooked, ground lean ham
7 ounces low-fat cottage cheese
12–14 cannelloni tubes
2 ounces low-fat mozzarella
   cheese, diced
1 ounce sharp Cheddar
   cheese, grated
1 ounce fresh white bread crumbs
salt and ground black pepper
flat-leaf parsley, to garnish

1 To make the sauce put the garlic, canned tomatoes, sugar and herbs into a pan, bring to the boil and cook, uncovered, for 30 minutes, stirring occasionally, until fairly thick.

2 To make the filling put the spinach into a pan, cover and cook slowly until defrosted. Break up with a fork, then increase the heat to drive off any water. Season with salt, pepper and nutmeg. Turn the spinach into a bowl, cool slightly, then add the minced ham and cottage cheese.

3 Pipe the filling into each tube of uncooked cannelloni. It is easiest to hold them upright with one end flat on a chopping board, while piping from the other end.

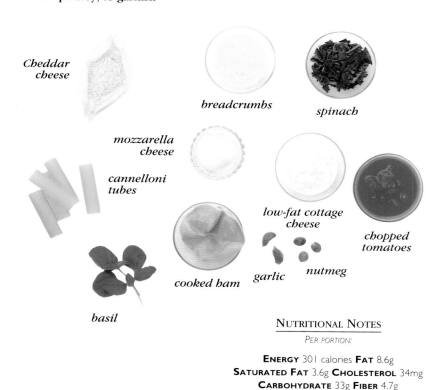

Cheddar cheese

breadcrumbs   spinach

mozzarella cheese

cannelloni tubes

low-fat cottage cheese

chopped tomatoes

basil   cooked ham   garlic   nutmeg

NUTRITIONAL NOTES

PER PORTION:

ENERGY 301 calories **FAT** 8.6g
SATURATED FAT 3.6g **CHOLESTEROL** 34mg
CARBOHYDRATE 33g **FIBER** 4.7g

4 Preheat the oven to 350°F. Spoon half of the tomato sauce into the bottom of an 8-inch square ovenproof dish. Lay two rows of filled cannelloni on top of the sauce.

5 Scatter over the diced mozzarella and cover with the rest of the sauce.

6 Sprinkle with the Cheddar cheese and bread crumbs. Bake in a preheated oven for 30–40 minutes. Place under broiler to brown, if necessary. Garnish with flat-leaf parsley.

Ravioli (with Bolognese Sauce)

Serves 6

INGREDIENTS

8 ounces low-fat cottage cheese
2 tablespoons grated Parmesan cheese, plus extra for serving
1 egg white, beaten, including extra for brushing
$\frac{1}{4}$ teaspoon ground nutmeg
1 recipe pasta dough
flour, for dusting
1 medium onion, finely chopped
1 garlic clove, crushed
$\frac{2}{3}$ cup beef stock
12 ounces extra lean ground beef
$\frac{1}{2}$ cup red wine
2 tablespoons tomato paste
14 ounce can chopped tomatoes
$\frac{1}{2}$ tsp chopped fresh rosemary
$\frac{1}{4}$ tsp ground allspice
salt and ground black pepper

nutmeg

onion *ground beef* *stock*

tomato purée *low-fat cottage cheese* *red wine*

Parmesan cheese *chopped tomatoes*

egg *rosemary*
garlic

1 To make the filling mix the cottage cheese, grated Parmesan, egg white, seasoning and nutmeg together thoroughly.

2 Roll the pasta into thin sheets and place a small teaspoon of filling along the pasta in rows 2 inches apart.

3 Moisten between the filling with beaten egg white. Lay a second sheet of pasta lightly over the top and press between each pocket to remove any air and seal firmly.

4 Cut into rounds with a fluted ravioli or pastry cutter. Transfer to a floured cloth and rest for at least 30 minutes before cooking.

5 To make the Bolognese sauce cook the onion and garlic in the stock for 5 minutes or until all the stock is reduced. Add the beef and cook quickly to brown, breaking up the meat with a fork. Add the wine, tomato paste, chopped tomatoes, rosemary and allspice, bring to a boil and simmer for 1 hour. Adjust the seasoning to taste.

6 Cook the ravioli in a large pan of boiling, salted water for 4–5 minutes. (Cook in batches to stop them sticking together). Drain thoroughly. Serve topped with Bolognese sauce. Serve grated Parmesan cheese separately.

NUTRITIONAL NOTES

PER PORTION:

ENERGY 321 calories **FAT** 8.8g
SATURATED FAT 3g **CHOLESTEROL** 158mg
CARBOHYDRATE 32g **FIBER** 2g

Spaghetti alla Carbonara

Serves 4

INGREDIENTS

5 ounces smoked turkey bacon
1 medium onion, chopped
1–2 garlic cloves, crushed
$^2\!/_3$ cup chicken stock
$^2\!/_3$ cup dry white wine
7 ounces low-fat cream cheese
1 pound chili and garlic-
   flavored spaghetti
2 tablespoons chopped
   fresh parsley
salt and ground black pepper
shavings of Parmesan cheese,
   to serve

1 Cut the turkey bacon into $^1\!/_2$-inch strips. Fry quickly in a non-stick pan for 2–3 minutes. Add the onion, garlic and stock to the pan. Bring to a boil, cover and simmer for 5 minutes until tender.

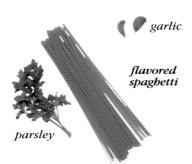

garlic

flavored spaghetti

parsley

2 Add the wine and boil rapidly until reduced by half. Whisk in the cream cheese until smooth.

smoked turkey bacon   **low-fat cream cheese**

onion

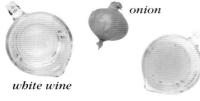

white wine

stock

NUTRITIONAL NOTES

PER PORTION:

ENERGY 500 calories **FAT** 3.3g
SATURATED FAT 0.5g **CHOLESTEROL** 21mg
CARBOHYDRATE 89g **FIBER** 4g

3 Meanwhile cook the spaghetti in a large pan of boiling, salted water for 10–12 minutes. Drain thoroughly.

4 Return to the pan with the sauce and parsley, toss well and serve immediately with shavings of Parmesan cheese.

Spaghetti Bolognese

Serves 8

INGREDIENTS

1 medium onion, chopped
2–3 garlic cloves, crushed
1¼ cups beef or chicken stock
1 lb extra lean ground turkey
    or beef
2 x 14 ounce cans chopped
    tomatoes
1 teaspoon dried basil
1 teaspoon dried oregano
4 tablespoons concentrated
    tomato paste
1 pound button mushrooms,
    quartered or sliced
⅔ cup red wine
1 pound spaghetti
salt and ground black pepper

garlic

mushrooms

stock

spaghetti

onion

ground turkey

red wine

chopped tomatoes

tomato paste

1 Put the chopped onion and garlic into a non-stick pan with half of the stock. Bring to the boil and cook for 5 minutes until the onions are tender and the stock has reduced completely.

2 Add the turkey or beef and cook for 5 minutes breaking the meat up with a fork. Add the tomatoes, herbs and tomato paste, bring to the boil, cover and simmer for about 1 hour.

NUTRITIONAL NOTES

PER PORTION:

ENERGY 321 calories **FAT** 4.1g
SATURATED FAT 1.3g **CHOLESTEROL** 33mg
CARBOHYDRATE 49g **FIBER** 3.7g

3 Meanwhile put the mushrooms into a non-stick pan with the wine, bring to the boil and cook for 5 minutes or until the wine has evaporated. Add the mushrooms to the meat.

4 Cook the pasta in a large pan of boiling, salted water for 8–10 minutes until tender. Drain thoroughly. Serve topped with meat sauce.

Spiced Lamb and Vegetable Couscous

A delicious stew of tender lamb and vegetables served with couscous.

Serves 6

INGREDIENTS

12 ounces lean lamb, cut
    into ¾-inch cubes
2 tablespoons whole-wheat
    flour, seasoned
2 teaspoons sunflower oil
1 onion, chopped
2 garlic cloves, crushed
1 red bell pepper, seeded and dic
1 teaspoon ground coriander
1 teaspoon ground cumin
1 teaspoon ground allspice
½ teaspoon chili powder
1 cup lamb or beef stock
1 can (14 ounces) chopped tomatoes
8 ounces carrots, sliced
6 ounces parsnips, sliced
6 ounces zucchini, sliced
6 ounces small mushrooms,
    quartered
8 ounces fava beans
⅔ cup golden raisins
1 pound quick-cooking couscous
salt and ground black pepper
cilantro, to garnish

1 Toss the lamb in the flour. Heat the oil in a large saucepan and add the lamb, onion, garlic and pepper. Cook for 5 minutes, stirring frequently.

2 Add any remaining flour and the spices and cook for 1 minute, stirring.

lamb

whole-wheat flour

sunflower oil

onion

garlic

red pepper

ground coriander

ground cumin

ground allspice

chili powder

lamb stock

chopped tomatoes

carrots

parsnips

zucchini

mushrooms

fava beans

golden raisins

couscous

3 Gradually add the stock, stirring continuously, then add the tomatoes, carrots and parsnips and mix well.

4 Bring to the boil, stirring, then cover and simmer for 30 minutes, stirring occasionally.

NUTRITIONAL NOTES

PER PORTION:

CALORIES 439 PROTEIN 23.29g
FAT 8.15g SATURATED FAT 2.57g
CARBOHYDRATE 72.98g FIBER 7.34g
ADDED SUGAR 0.00g SODIUM 0.18g

COOK'S TIP

For a tasty alternative, serve the lamb and vegetable stew on a bed of cooked bulgur wheat or brown rice.

5 Add the zucchini, mushrooms, fava beans and golden raisins. Cover, return to a boil and simmer for another 20–30 minutes, stirring occasionally, until the lamb and vegetables are tender. Season to taste.

6 Meanwhile, soak the couscous and steam in a lined colander over a pan of boiling water for about 20 minutes, until cooked, or prepare according to the package instructions. Pile the cooked couscous on a warmed serving platter or individual plates and top with the lamb and vegetable stew. Garnish with cilantro and serve immediately.

Paper-thin Lamb with Scallions

Scallions lend a delicious flavor to the lamb in this simple supper dish.

Serves 3–4

INGREDIENTS

1 lb lamb
2 tbsp Chinese rice wine
2 tsp light soy sauce
½ tsp roasted and ground
  Szechuan peppercorns
½ tsp salt
½ tsp dark brown sugar
4 tsp dark soy sauce
1 tbsp sesame oil
2 tbsp peanut oil
2 garlic cloves, thinly sliced
2 bunches scallions, cut
  into 3-in lengths,
  then shredded
2 tbsp chopped
  fresh cilantro

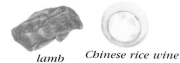

scallions

lamb   *Chinese rice wine*

sesame oil
              salt

dark soy sauce
              cilantro

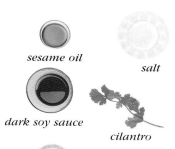

brown sugar   *garlic*

1 Wrap the lamb and place in the freezer for about 1 hour, until just frozen. Cut the meat across the grain into paper-thin slices. Put the lamb slices in a bowl, add 2 tsp of the rice wine, the light soy sauce and ground Szechuan peppercorns. Mix well and allow to marinate for 15–30 minutes.

2 Make the sauce: in a bowl mix together the remaining rice wine, the salt, brown sugar, dark soy sauce and 2 tsp of the sesame oil. Set aside.

3 Heat a wok until hot, add the oil and swirl it around. Add the garlic and let it sizzle for a few seconds, then add the lamb. Stir-fry for about 1 minute until the lamb is no longer pink. Pour in the sauce and stir briefly.

4 Add the scallions and cilantro and stir-fry for 15–20 seconds until the scallions just wilt. The finished dish should be slightly dry in appearance. Serve at once, sprinkled with the remaining sesame oil.

Spring Lamb Chops

It is best to marinate the chops overnight as this makes them very tender and also helps them to absorb the maximum amount of flavor. Serve with a crisp salad.

Serves 4

INGREDIENTS
8 small lean lamb chops
1 large red chile, seeded
2 tbsp chopped fresh cilantro
1 tbsp chopped fresh mint
1 tsp salt
1 tsp brown sugar
1 tsp garam masala
1 tsp minced garlic
1 tsp minced ginger
⅔ cup low fat plain yogurt
2 tsp corn oil

minced garlic

garam masala

lamb chops

minced ginger

mint

fresh cilantro

salt

red chile   yogurt   brown sugar

NUTRITIONAL NOTES
PER PORTION:

ENERGY 207 Kcals **PROTEIN** 23.15 g
FAT 10.29 g **SATURATED FAT** 4.26 g
CARBOHYDRATE 5.62 g **FIBER** 0.27 g
ADDED SUGAR 1.01 g
SALT 0.6 g

1 Trim the lamb chops to remove any excess fat. Place them in a large bowl.

2 Finely chop the chile, then mix the cilantro, mint, salt, brown sugar, garam masala, garlic and ginger.

COOK'S TIP
These chops can also be grilled.

3 Pour the yogurt into the herb mixture and, using a small whisk or a fork, mix thoroughly. Pour this mixture over the top of the chops and turn them with your fingers to make sure that they are completely covered. Leave to marinate overnight in the fridge.

4 Heat the oil in a large, non-stick wok or frying pan and add the chops. Lower the heat and allow to cook over a medium heat. Turn the chops over and continue frying until they are cooked right through—about 20 minutes—turning again if needed.

Mini Koftas in Onion Sauce

This kofta curry is very popular in most Indian homes. It is also extremely easy to make. Serve with pilaf rice.

Serves 4

INGREDIENTS
8 oz lean ground lamb
2 tsp poppy seeds
1 medium onion, chopped
1 tsp minced ginger
1 tsp minced garlic
1 tsp salt
1 tsp chili powder
1½ tsp ground coriander
2 tbsp fresh cilantro
1 small egg

FOR THE SAUCE
⅔ cup low fat plain yogurt
2 tbsp tomato paste
1 tsp chili powder
1 tsp salt
1 tsp minced garlic
1 tsp minced ginger
1 tsp garam masala
2 tsp corn oil
1-in piece cinnamon stick
1⅔ cups water

ground coriander

onion

minced garlic

minced ginger

salt

cinnamon stick

fresh cilantro

lamb

poppy seeds

yogurt

garam masala

tomato paste

chili powder

1 Place the lamb in a food processor and grind for about 1 minute. Remove from the processor, put in a bowl, add the poppy seeds and set aside.

2 Place the onion in the food processor, together with the ginger, garlic, salt, chili powder, ground coriander and half the fresh cilantro. Grind the mixture for about 30 seconds, then blend it into the ground lamb.

3 Whisk the egg and thoroughly mix it into the ground lamb. Let stand for about 1 hour.

4 For the sauce, whisk together the yogurt, tomato paste, chili powder, salt, garlic, ginger and garam masala.

5 Heat the oil with the cinnamon stick in a non-stick wok or frying pan for about 1 minute, then pour in the sauce. Lower the heat and cook for about 1 minute. Remove the wok or frying pan from heat and set aside.

NUTRITIONAL NOTES

PER PORTION:

ENERGY 155 Kcals **PROTEIN** 14.74 g
FAT 9.24 g **SATURATED FAT** 2.79 g
CARBOHYDRATE 7.56 g **FIBER** 1.16 g
ADDED SUGAR 0
SALT 1.07 g

COOK'S TIP

This curry is also absolutely delicious served with warm, freshly made chapatis.

6 Break off small balls of the mixture and make the koftas using your hands. When all the koftas are ready, return the sauce to the heat and add the water. Place the remaining fresh cilantro on top, cover with a lid and cook for 7–10 minutes, stirring gently occasionally to turn the koftas around. Serve hot.

Lamb with Peas and Potatoes

Fresh mint leaves are used in this dish, but if they are obtainable, use ready-minted frozen peas to bring an added freshness. Serve with rice.

Serves 4

INGREDIENTS
8 oz lean lamb
½ cup low fat plain yogurt
1 cinnamon stick
2 green cardamom pods
3 black peppercorns
1 tsp minced garlic
1 tsp minced ginger
1 tsp chili powder
1 tsp garam masala
1 tsp salt
2 tbsp roughly chopped
    fresh mint
3 tbsp corn oil
2 medium onions, sliced
1¼ cups water
4 oz frozen peas
1 large potato, diced
1 firm tomato, skinned, seeded
    and diced

minced garlic *potato* *lamb* *garam masala* *onions* *salt* *cardamom* *cinnamon stick* *peppercorns* *minced ginger* *mint* *peas* *chili powder* *tomato* *yogurt*

1 Using a sharp knife, cut the lamb into strips, then place it in a bowl.

2 Add the yogurt, cinnamon, cardamoms, peppercorns, garlic, ginger, chili powder, garam masala, salt and half the mint. Marinate for about 2 hours.

3 Heat the oil in a non-stick wok or frying pan and fry the onions until golden brown. Stir in the lamb and the marinade and stir-fry for about 3 minutes.

4 Pour in the water, lower the heat and cook until the meat is cooked right through, about 15 minutes, depending on the age of the lamb. Meanwhile cook the potato in boiling water until just soft, but not mushy.

5 Add the peas and potato to the lamb and stir to mix gently.

NUTRITIONAL NOTES
Per portion:

ENERGY 231 Kcals **PROTEIN** 17.54 g
FAT 8.47 g **SATURATED FAT** 2.79 g
CARBOHYDRATE 22.72 g **FIBER** 3.73 g
ADDED SUGAR 0
SALT 0.57 g

COOK'S TIP
You can cook this dish in advance and keep it in the refrigerator. In fact, this will improve the flavor.

6 Finally, add the remaining mint and the tomato and cook for another 5 minutes, before serving.

Stir-fried Lamb with Baby Onions and Bell Peppers

The baby onions are used whole in this recipe. Serve with rice or lentils.

NUTRITIONAL NOTES
Per portion:
ENERGY 155 K Cals **PROTEIN** 12.75g
FAT 9.48g **SATURATED FAT** 2.82g
CARBOHYDRATE 5.74g **FIBER** 1.49g
ADDED SUGAR 0
SALT 0.55g

Serves 4

INGREDIENTS
1 tablespoon corn oil
8 baby onions
8 ounces boned lean lamb, cut into strips
1 teaspoon ground cumin
1 teaspoon ground coriander
1 tablespoon tomato paste
1 teaspoon chili powder
1 teaspoon salt
1 tablespoon lemon juice
½ teaspoon onion seeds
4 curry leaves
1¼ cups water
1 small red bell pepper, seeded and roughly sliced
1 small green bell pepper, seeded and roughly sliced
1 tablespoon chopped fresh cilantro
1 tablespoon chopped fresh mint

onions

bell peppers   lamb

onion seeds

lemon juice

mint   curry leaves   fresh cilantro

ground cumin   ground coriander   chili powder

tomato paste   salt

1 Heat the oil in a nonstick wok or frying pan and stir-fry the whole baby onions for about 3 minutes. Using a slotted spoon, remove the onions from the wok and set aside to drain.

2 Mix together the lamb, cumin, ground coriander, tomato paste, chili powder, salt and lemon juice in a bowl and set aside.

3 Reheat the oil and stir-fry the onion seeds and curry leaves for 2–3 minutes.

4 Add the lamb and spice mixture and stir-fry for about 5 minutes, then pour in the water, lower the heat and cook gently for about 10 minutes, until the lamb is cooked through.

5 Add the peppers and half the fresh cilantro and mint. Stir-fry for a further 2 minutes.

6 Finally, add the baby onions and the remaining fresh cilantro and chopped mint and serve.

COOK'S TIP

This dish benefits from being cooked a day in advance and kept in the fridge.

Lamb with Cauliflower

Cauliflower and lamb go beautifully together. This curry is given a final tarka of cumin seeds and curry leaves, which enhances the flavor.

Serves 4

INGREDIENTS
2 tsp corn oil
2 medium onions, sliced
1 tsp minced ginger
1 tsp chili powder
1 tsp minced garlic
½ tsp ground tumeric
½ tsp ground coriander
2 tbsp fresh fenugreek leaves
10 oz lean lamb, cut into strips
1 small cauliflower, cut into
    small florets
1¼ cups water
2 tbsp fresh cilantro leaves
½ red bell pepper, seeded, sliced
1 tbsp lemon slice

FOR THE TARKA
2 tsp corn oil
½ tsp white cumin seeds
4–6 curry leaves

ground coriander

cumin seeds

lemon juice

lamb

curry leaves

fenugreek

cauliflower

fresh cilantro

onions

red bell pepper

ground turmeric

chili powder

minced ginger

minced garlic

COOK'S TIP
If you wish, you may use a good-quality olive oil for the tarka.

1 Heat the oil in a non-stick wok or frying pan and fry the onions until golden brown. Lower the heat and add the ginger, chili powder, garlic, tumeric and ground coriander, followed by the fenugreek.

2 Add the lamb strips to the wok and stir-fry until the lamb is completely coated with the spices. Add half the cauliflower florets and stir the mixture well.

3 Pour in the water, cover the wok, lower the heat and cook for 5–7 minutes until the cauliflower and lamb are almost cooked through.

4 Add the remaining cauliflower, half of the fresh cilantro, the red bell pepper and lemon juice and stir-fry for about 5 minutes, making sure that the sauce does not catch on the bottom of the wok.

NUTRITIONAL NOTES

Per portion:

ENERGY 202 Kcals **PROTEIN** 18.42 g
FAT 9.88 g **SATURATED FAT** 3.24 g
CARBOHYDRATE 10.86 g **FIBER** 2.88 g
ADDED SUGAR 0
SALT 0.07 g

5 Check that the lamb is completely cooked, then remove from the heat and set aside.

6 To make the tarka, heat the oil and fry the seeds and curry leaves for about 30 seconds. While it is still hot, pour the seasoned oil over the cauliflower and lamb and serve garnished with the remaining fresh cilantro leaves.

Zucchini with Lamb

Lamb is cooked with yogurt, and then the zucchini, which has already been broiled are added to the mixture.

Serves 4

INGREDIENTS
1 tbsp corn oil
2 medium onions, chopped
8 oz lean lamb, cut
   into strips
½ cup plain low fat yogurt
1 tsp garam marsala
1 tsp chili powder
1 tsp minced garlic
1 tsp minced ginger
½ tsp ground coriander
2 medium zucchini, sliced
1 tbsp chopped fresh cilantro
   to garnish

onions

zucchini

lamb

minced garlic

minced ginger

fresh cilantro

chili powder

ground coriander

garam masala

yogurt

NUTRITIONAL NOTES
PER PORTION:

ENERGY 178 Kcals **PROTEIN** 15.80 g
FAT 8.36 g **SATURATED FAT** 2.78 g
CARBOHYDRATE 10.83 g **FIBER** 1.99 g
ADDED SUGAR 0
SALT 0.08 g

1 Heat the oil in a non-stick wok or frying pan and fry the onions until they are golden brown.

2 Add the lamb strips and stir-fry for 1 minute to seal the meat.

3 Put the yogurt, garam masala, chili powder, garlic, ginger and ground coriander into a bowl. Whisk the mixture together.

4 Pour the yogurt mixture over the lamb and stir-fry for a further 2 minutes. Cover and cook over a medium to low heat for 12–15 minutes.

5 Put the zucchini in a flameproof dish and cook under the broiler for about 3 minutes, turning once.

6 Check that the lamb is cooked through and the sauce is quite thick, then add the zucchini and serve garnished with the fresh cilantro.

Chicken & Poultry Dishes

Warm Chicken Salad with Shallots and Snow Peas

Succulent cooked chicken pieces are combined with vegetables in a light chili dressing.

Serves 6

INGREDIENTS
2 ounces mixed lettuce leaves
2 ounces baby spinach leaves
2 ounces watercress
2 tablespoons chili sauce
2 tablespoons dry sherry
1 tablespoon light soy sauce
1 tablespoon ketchup
2 teaspoons olive oil
8 shallots, finely chopped
1 garlic clove, crushed
12 ounces skinless, boneless
  chicken breast, cut into thin strips
1 red bell pepper, sliced
6 ounces snow peas, trimmed
1 can (14 ounces) baby corn,
  drained and halved
1 cup brown rice
salt and ground black pepper
parsley sprig to garnish

1 Arrange the mixed salad leaves, tearing up any large ones, and the spinach leaves on a serving dish. Add the watercress and toss to mix.

2 In a small bowl, mix together the chili sauce, sherry, soy sauce and ketchup and set aside.

3 Heat the oil in a large non-stick frying pan or wok. Add the shallots and garlic and stir-fry over a medium heat for 1 minute.

4 Add the chicken and stir-fry for 3–4 minutes.

mixed salad leaves

spinach

watercress

chili sauce

dry sherry

light soy sauce

tomato ketchup

olive oil

shallots

garlic

chicken breasts

red bell pepper

snow peas

baby corn

brown rice

NUTRITIONAL NOTES
PER PORTION:

CALORIES 188 PROTEIN 19.22g
FAT 2.81g SATURATED FAT 0.52g
CARBOHYDRATE 21.39g FIBER 3.07g
ADDED SUGAR 0.71g SODIUM 1.07g

COOK'S TIP
Use other lean meat such as turkey breast, beef or pork in place of the chicken.

5 Add the pepper, snow peas, corn and rice and stir-fry for 2–3 minutes.

6 Pour in the chili sauce mixture and stir-fry for 2–3 minutes, until hot and bubbling. Season to taste. Spoon the chicken mixture over the salad leaves, toss together to mix and serve immediately, garnished with fresh parsley.

Grilled Chicken Salad with Lavender and Sweet Herbs

Lavender may seem like an odd salad ingredient, but its delightful scent has a natural affinity with sweet garlic, orange and other wild herbs. A serving of corn meal polenta makes this salad both filling and delicious.

Serves 4

INGREDIENTS
4 boneless chicken breasts
3¾ cups light chicken stock
1 cup fine polenta or cornmeal
2 oz butter
1 lb young spinach
6 oz lamb's lettuce
8 sprigs fresh lavender
8 small tomatoes, halved
salt and pepper

LAVENDER MARINADE
6 fresh lavender flowers
2 tsp finely grated orange zest
2 cloves garlic, crushed
2 tsp clear honey
salt
2 tbsp olive oil, French or Italian
2 tsp chopped fresh thyme
2 tsp chopped fresh marjoram

1 To make the marinade, strip the lavender flowers from the stems and combine with the orange zest, garlic, honey and salt. Add the olive oil and herbs. Slash the chicken deeply, spread the mixture over the chicken and leave to marinate in a cool place for at least 20 minutes.

polenta

orange

spinach

garlic

thyme

lavender   *chicken breasts*

2 To make the polenta, bring the chicken stock to a boil in a heavy saucepan. Add the cornmeal in a steady stream, stirring all the time until thick: this will take 2–3 minutes. Turn the cooked polenta out on to a 1-in-deep buttered tray and allow to cool.

3 Heat the broiler to a moderate temperature. (If using a barbecue, let the embers settle to a steady glow.) Broil the chicken for 15 minutes, turning once.

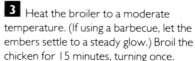

4 Cut the polenta into 1 in cubes with a wet knife. Heat the butter in a large skillet and fry the polenta until golden.

COOK'S TIP

Lavender marinade is a delicious flavoring for fish as well as chicken. Try it over broiled cod, haddock, halibut, sea bass, and bream.

NUTRITIONAL NOTES

PER PORTION:

CALORIES 352
FAT 9.4 g **SATURATED FAT** 2.1g
CHOLESTEROL 43.3 mg

5 Wash the salad leaves and spin dry, then divide between 4 large plates. Slice each chicken breast and lay over the salad. Place the polenta among the salad, decorate with sprigs of lavender and tomatoes, season and serve.

Lemon Chicken Stir-fry

It is essential to prepare all the ingredients before you begin so they are ready to cook. This dish is cooked in minutes.

Serves 4

INGREDIENTS
4 boned and skinned chicken breasts
1 tbsp light soy sauce
5 tbsp cornstarch
1 bunch scallions
1 lemon
1 garlic clove, crushed
1 tbsp superfine sugar
2 tbsp sherry
⅔ cup fresh or canned chicken stock
4 tbsp olive oil
salt and freshly ground black pepper

NUTRITIONAL NOTES
Per portion:

CALORIES 298
FAT 9.9 g **SATURATED FAT** 2.1 g
CHOLESTEROL 53.8 mg

superfine sugar

garlic

olive oil *scallions*

lemon

soy sauce

cornstarch

chicken breasts

1 Divide the chicken breasts into two natural fillets. Place each between two sheets of plastic wrap and flatten to a thickness of ¼ in with a rolling pin.

2 Cut into 1 in strips across the grain of the fillets. Put the chicken into a bowl with the soy sauce and toss to coat thoroughly, then sprinkle over 4 tbsp cornstarch to coat each piece.

3 Trim the roots off the scallions and cut diagonally into ½ in pieces. With a swivel peeler, remove the lemon rind in thin strips and cut into fine shreds. Reserve the lemon juice. Have ready the garlic clove, sugar, sherry, stock, lemon juice and the remaining cornstarch blended to a paste with cold water.

4 Heat the oil in a wok or large frying pan and cook the chicken very quickly in small batches for 3–4 minutes until lightly colored. Remove and keep warm while frying the rest of the chicken.

5 Add the scallions and garlic to the pan and cook for 2 minutes.

6 Add the remaining ingredients and bring to the boil, stirring until thickened. Add more sherry or stock if necessary and stir until the chicken is evenly covered with sauce. Reheat for 2 more minutes. Serve immediately.

Chicken and Bean Casserole

A delicious combination of chicken, fresh tarragon and mixed beans, topped with a layer of tender potatoes.

Serves 6

INGREDIENTS

2 pounds potatoes
½ cup reduced-fat aged
  Cheddar cheese, finely grated
2½ cups skim milk, plus
  2–3 tablespoons skim milk
2 tablespoons snipped
  fresh chives
2 leeks, washed and sliced
1 onion, sliced
2 tablespoons dry white wine
3 tablespoons low fat spread
¼ cup whole wheat flour
1¼ cups chicken broth, cooled
12 ounces cooked skinless
  chicken breast, diced
3 cups brown cap
  mushrooms, sliced
11-ounce can red
  kidney beans
14-ounce can lima beans
14-ounce can black-eyed peas
2–3 tablespoons chopped
  fresh tarragon
salt and ground black pepper

potatoes

reduced-fat aged Cheddar cheese

skim milk

fresh chives

leeks

onion

cooked chicken breasts

dry white wine

low fat spread

whole wheat flour

chicken broth

lima beans

black-eyed peas

brown cap mushrooms

red kidney beans

fresh tarragon

1 Preheat the oven to 400°F. Cut the potatoes into chunks and cook in lightly salted, boiling water for 15–20 minutes, until tender. Drain thoroughly and mash. Add the cheese, 2–3 tablespoons milk and chives, season to taste and mix well. Keep warm and set aside.

2 Meanwhile, put the leeks and onion in a saucepan with the wine. Cover and cook gently for 10 minutes, until the vegetables are just tender, stirring occasionally.

3 In the meantime, put the low fat spread, flour, remaining milk and broth in a saucepan. Heat gently, whisking continuously, until the sauce comes to a boil and thickens. Simmer gently for 3 minutes, stirring.

4 Remove the pan from the heat and add the leek mixture, chicken and mushrooms and mix well.

5 Add all the drained beans to the sauce and stir in with the tarragon and seasoning. Heat gently until the chicken mixture is piping hot, stirring.

COOK'S TIP

Sweet potatoes in place of standard potatoes work just as well in this recipe, and turkey or lean ham can be used in place of the chicken for a change.

6 Transfer it to an ovenproof dish and spoon or pipe the potato mixture over the top, to cover the chicken mixture completely. Bake for about 30 minutes, until the potato topping is crisp and golden brown. Serve immediately.

NUTRITIONAL NOTES
PER PORTION:

CALORIES 445
FAT 8.9 g **SATURATED FAT** 1.9 g
CHOLESTEROL 50.4 mg

Chicken and Apricot Phyllo Pie

Phyllo is the low fat cook's best friend, as it contains little fat and needs only a light brushing of melted butter to created a crisp crust.

Serves 6

INGREDIENTS
½ cup bulgur wheat
½ cup boiling water
2 tablespoons butter
1 onion, chopped
1 pound lean ground chicken
¼ cup dried apricots, finely chopped
¼ cup almonds, chopped
1 teaspoon ground cinnamon
½ teaspoon ground allspice
¼ cup low fat plain yogurt
1 tablespoon snipped fresh chives
2 tablespoons chopped fresh parsley
2 tablespoons chopped fresh parsley
10 sheets of phyllo pastry
salt and ground black pepper
chives, to garnish

bulgur wheat

onion

ground chicken

ground allspice

dried apricots

ground cinnamon

low fat plain yogurt

chives

phyllo pastry

1 Preheat the oven to 400°F. Put the bulgur wheat in a bowl and add the boiling water. Let soak for 5–10 minutes, until all the water is absorbed.

4 Melt the remaining butter. Cut the phyllo pastry into 10-inch rounds. Cover the rounds with a cloth.

2 Heat one tablespoon of the butter in a nonstick pan, and gently fry the onion and chicken until pale golden.

5 Line a 9-inch loose-based tart pan with three of the phyllo rounds, brushing each one lightly with butter as you layer them. Spoon in the chicken mixture, then cover with three more rounds, brushed with butter as before.

3 Stir in the apricots, almonds and bulgur. Cook for 2 more minutes. Remove from the heat and stir in the cinnamon, allspice, plain yogurt, chives and parsley. Season to taste with salt and pepper.

6 Crumple the remaining rounds and place them on top of the pie, then brush with melted butter. Bake for about 30 minutes, until golden brown and crisp. Serve the pie hot or cold, cut in wedges and garnished with chives.

NUTRITIONAL NOTES
Per portion:
CALORIES 239
FAT 6.3 g **SATURATED FAT** 1.6 g
CHOLESTEROL 43.0 mg

Chicken with Cashews

This hot and spicy Indian dish has a deliciously thick and nutty sauce, and is best served with plenty of plain boiled rice.

Serves 6

INGREDIENTS
2 onions
2 tablespoons tomato paste
½ cup cashews
1½ teaspoons garam masala
1 garlic clove, crushed
1 teaspoon chili powder
1 tablespoon lemon juice
¼ teaspoon ground turmeric
1 teaspoon salt
1 tablespoon low fat plain yogurt
1 tablespoon corn oil
1 tablespoon chopped fresh cilantro, plus extra to garnish
1 tablespoon golden raisins
1 pound boned and skinned chicken breasts, cubed
1½ cups button mushrooms, halved
1¼ cups water

1 Cut the onions into quarters and place in a food processor or blender. Process for about 1 minute.

2 Add the tomato paste, cashews, garam masala, garlic, chili powder, lemon juice, turmeric, salt and yogurt to the onions. Process for 1–1½ more minutes.

3 Heat the oil in a saucepan and fry the spice mixture over a medium heat for about 2 minutes, lowering the heat if necessary.

4 Add the cilantro, golden raisins and chicken and stir-fry for 1 minute more.

5 Add the mushrooms, pour in the water and bring to a simmer. Cover the pan and cook over a low heat for about 10 minutes.

6 After this time, check that the chicken is cooked through and the sauce is thick. Cook for a little longer if necessary. Garnish with chopped fresh cilantro and serve.

chili powder

lemon juice

button mushrooms

turmeric

plain yogurt

onion

garlic

garam masala

corn oil

fresh cilantro

cashew nuts

chicken

golden raisins

NUTRITIONAL NOTES
Per portion:

CALORIES 187
FAT 9.8 g **SATURATED FAT** 1.9 g
CHOLESTEROL 43.2 mg

Chicken in Spicy Yogurt

Plan this dish well in advance; the extra-long marinating time is necessary to develop a really mellow spicy flavor.

NUTRITIONAL NOTES

PER PORTION:

CALORIES 158
FAT 5.1 g **SATURATED FAT** 1.6 g
CHOLESTEROL 58 mg

Serves 6

INGREDIENTS
6 chicken pieces
juice of 1 lemon
1 teaspoon salt

FOR THE MARINADE
1 teaspoon coriander seeds
2 teaspoons cumin seeds
6 cloves
2 bay leaves
1 onion, quartered
2 garlic cloves
2-inch piece fresh ginger, peeled and coarsely chopped
½ teaspoon chili powder
1 teaspoon turmeric
⅔ cup plain yogurt
lemon or lime and cilantro, to garnish

lemon

yogurt   *coriander seeds*

ginger

onion

garlic   *bay leaves*

chili powder

turmeric

cloves   *cumin seeds*

1 Skin the chicken joints and make deep slashes in the fleshiest parts with a sharp knife. Sprinkle over the lemon and salt and rub in.

2 Spread the coriander and cumin seeds, cloves and bay leaves in the bottom of a large frying pan and dry-fry over a moderate heat until the bay leaves are crispy.

3 Cool the spices and grind coarsely with a pestle and mortar.

4 Finely mince the onion, garlic and ginger in a food processor or blender. Add the ground spices, chili, turmeric and yogurt, then strain in the lemon juice from the chicken.

5 Arrange the chicken in a single layer in a roasting tin. Pour over the marinade, then cover and chill for 24–36 hours.

6 Occasionally turn the chicken pieces in the marinade. Preheat the oven to 400°F. Cook the chicken for 45 minutes. Serve hot or cold, garnished with lemon or lime and cilantro leaves.

Grilled Chicken with Pica de Gallo Salsa

This dish originates from Mexico. Its hot fruity flavors form the essence of Tex-Mex Cooking.

NUTRITIONAL NOTES

Per portion:

CALORIES 197
FAT 7.1 g **SATURATED FAT** 1.7 g
CHOLESTEROL 53.8 mg

Serves 4

INGREDIENTS
4 chicken breasts
pinch of celery salt and cayenne
    pepper combined
2 tbsp vegetable oil
corn chips, to serve

FOR THE SALSA
10 oz watermelon
6 oz canteloupe
1 small red onion
1–2 green chiles
2 tbsp lime juice
4 tbsp chopped fresh cilantro
pinch of salt

1 Preheat the oven to 375°F. Slash the chicken breasts deeply to speed up the cooking time.

2 Season the chicken with celery salt and cayenne, brush with oil and broil for about 15 minutes.

3 To make the salsa, remove the rind and as many seeds as you can from the melons. Finely dice the flesh and put it into a bowl.

green chiles

chicken breasts

red onion

lime

cilantro

canteloupe

watermelon

4 Finely chop the onion, split the chiles (discarding the seeds, which contain most of the heat) and chop. Take care not to touch sensitive skin areas when handling cut chiles. Mix with the melon.

5 Add the lime juice and chopped cilantro, and season with a pinch of salt. Transfer the salsa to a small bowl.

6 Arrange the grilled chicken on a plate and serve with the salsa and a handful of corn chips.

Chicken in Orange and Black Pepper Sauce

Use virtually fat-free fromage frais to give this sauce a rich, creamy flavor.

Serves 4

INGREDIENTS
8 oz low fat fromage frais
¼ cup low fat plain yogurt
½ cup orange juice
1½ tsp minced ginger
1 tsp minced garlic
1 tsp freshly ground
    black pepper
1 tsp salt
1 tsp ground coriander
1 baby chicken, about 1½ lb,
    skinned and cut into 8 pieces
1 tbsp corn oil
1 bay leaf
1 large onion, chopped
1 tbsp fresh mint leaves
1 green chile, seeded and chopped

orange juice

minced ginger

onion

chicken

mint

green chile

minced garlic

fromage frais

bay leaf

NUTRITIONAL NOTES
PER PORTION:

ENERGY 199 Kcals **PROTEIN** 26.07 g
FAT 5.11 g **SATURATED FAT** 1.06 g
CARBOHYDRATE 13.20 g **FIBER** 1.02 g
ADDED SUGAR 1.20 g **SALT** 0.6 g

1 In a bowl, whisk together the fromage frais, yogurt, orange juice, ginger, garlic, pepper, salt and coriander.

2 Pour this over the chicken and set aside for 3–4 hours.

COOK'S TIP
If you prefer the taste of curry leaves, you can use them instead of the bay leaf, but you need to double the quantity.

3 Heat the oil with the bay leaf in a non-stick wok or frying pan and fry the onion until soft.

4 Pour in the chicken mixture and stir-fry for 3–5 minutes over medium heat. Lower the heat, cover with a lid and cook for 7–10 minutes, adding a little water in the sauce if too thick. Finally add the fresh mint and chile and serve.

Chicken in a Thick Creamy Coconut Sauce

If you like the flavor of coconut, you will really love this curry.

Serves 4

INGREDIENTS
1 tbsp ground almonds
1 tbsp unsweetened, shredded coconut
⅔ cup coconut milk
⅔ cup fromage frais
1½ tsp ground coriander
1 tsp chili powder
1 tsp minced garlic
1½ tsp minced ginger
1 tsp salt
1 tbsp corn oil
8 oz skinned chicken, cubed
3 green cardamom pods
1 bay leaf
1 dried red chile, crushed
2 tbsp chopped fresh cilantro

almonds
chili powder
fresh cilantro
chicken
minced garlic
bay leaf
cardamom
red chile
salt
coconut
fromage frais
coconut milk
minced ginger
ground coriander

NUTRITIONAL NOTES
PER PORTION:

ENERGY 166 Kcals **PROTEIN** 18.58 g
FAT 8.30 g **SATURATED FAT** 2.84 g
CARBOHYDRATE 5.52 g **FIBER** 0.95 g
ADDED SUGAR 0.86 g
SALT 0.57 g

1 Using a heavy saucepan, dry-roast the ground almonds and coconut until they turn a shade darker. Transfer to a mixing bowl.

2 Add the coconut milk, fromage frais, ground coriander, chili powder, garlic, ginger and salt to the mixing bowl.

COOK'S TIP
Cut the chicken into small, equal-sized cubes for quick and even cooking.

3 Heat the oil in a non-stick wok or frying pan and add the chicken cubes, cardamoms and bay leaf. Stir-fry for about 2 minutes to brown the chicken.

4 Pour in the coconut milk mixture and blend everything. Lower the heat, add the chile and fresh cilantro, cover and cook for 10–12 minutes, stirring occasionally. Uncover then stir and cook for another 2 minutes before serving.

Country Chicken Casserole

Succulent chicken joints in a vegetable sauce are
excellent served with brown rice or pasta.

NUTRITIONAL NOTES
PER PORTION:

CALORIES 377
FAT 11.7 g **SATURATED FAT** 2.9 g
CHOLESTEROL 76.1 mg

Serves 4

INGREDIENTS
2 chicken breasts, skinned
2 chicken legs, skinned
2 tablespoons whole wheat flour
1 tablespoon sunflower oil
1¼ cups chicken broth
1¼ cups white wine
2 tablespoons crushed tomatoes
1 tablespoon tomato paste
4 strips lean bacon
1 large onion, sliced
1 garlic clove, crushed
1 green bell pepper, seeded
 and sliced
3 cups button mushrooms
8 ounces carrots, sliced
1 bouquet garni
8 ounces frozen Brussels sprouts
1½ cups frozen peas
salt and ground black pepper
chopped fresh parsley, to garnish

1 Preheat the oven to 350°F.
Coat the chicken pieces with
seasoned flour.

2 Heat the oil in a large flameproof
casserole, add the chicken and cook
until browned all over. Remove the
chicken using a slotted spoon and
keep warm.

3 Add any remaining flour to the pan
and cook for 1 minute. Gradually stir
in the broth and wine, then add the
crushed tomatoes and tomato paste.

*chicken breasts
and legs*

 *whole wheat
flour*

 *sunflower
oil*

 *chicken
broth*

*dry
white
wine*

 *crushed
tomatoes*

*tomato
paste*

 bacon

onion

garlic

*green
pepper*

 *button
mushrooms*

carrots

 *bouquet
garni*

 *Brussels
sprouts*

 peas

4 Bring to the boil, stirring continuously, then add the chicken, bacon, onion,
garlic, pepper, mushrooms, carrots and bouquet garni and stir. Cover and bake for
1½ hours, stirring once or twice.

COOK'S TIP
Use fresh Brussels sprouts and peas if available, and use red wine in place of white for a change.

5 Stir in the Brussels sprouts and peas, re-cover and bake for 30 more minutes.

6 Remove and discard the bouquet garni. Add seasoning to the casserole, garnish with chopped fresh parsley and serve immediately.

Tagine of Chicken

Based on a traditional Moroccan dish. The chicken and couscous can be cooked the day before and reheated for serving.

Serves 8

INGREDIENTS
8 chicken legs (thighs and
    drumsticks)
2 tbsp olive oil
1 medium onion, finely chopped
2 garlic cloves, crushed
1 tsp ground turmeric
½ tsp ground ginger
½ tsp ground cinnamon
scant 2 cups fresh or canned chicken
    stock
1¼ cups pitted green olives
1 lemon, sliced
salt and freshly ground black pepper
fresh cilantro sprigs, to garnish

FOR THE VEGETABLE COUSCOUS
2½ cups chicken stock
1 lb couscous
4 zucchini, thickly sliced
2 carrots, thickly sliced
2 small turnips, peeled and cubed
¼ cup chopped fresh cilantro
3 tbspolive oil
15-oz can chick peas, drained

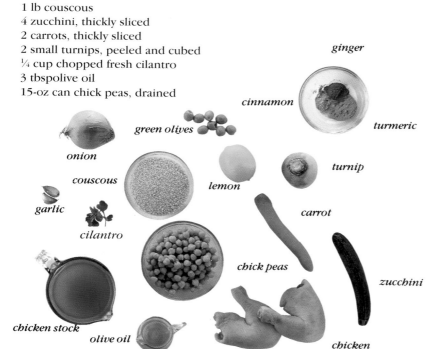

ginger
cinnamon
turmeric
green olives
onion
couscous
lemon
turnip
garlic
cilantro
carrot
chick peas
zucchini
chicken stock
olive oil
chicken

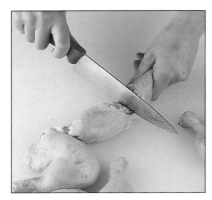

1 Preheat the oven to 350°F. Cut the chicken legs into two through the joint.

2 Heat the oil in a large flameproof casserole and working in batches, brown the chicken on both sides. Remove and keep warm.

3 Add the onion and crushed garlic to the flameproof casserole and cook gently until tender. Add the spices and cook for 1 minute. Pour over the stock, bring to the boil, and return the chicken. Cover and bake for 45 minutes until tender.

4 Transfer the chicken to a bowl, cover and keep warm. Remove any fat from the cooking liquid and boil to reduce by one-third. Meanwhile, blanch the olives and lemon slices in a pan of boiling water for 2 minutes until the lemon skin is tender. Drain and add to the cooking liquid, adjusting the seasoning to taste.

5 To cook the couscous, bring the stock to the boil in a large pan and sprinkle in the couscous slowly, stirring all the time. Remove from the heat, cover and leave to stand for 5 minutes.

COOK'S TIP

The couscous can be reheated with
2 tbsp olive oil in a steamer over a pan
of boiling water, stirring occasionally.
If you cook the chicken in advance,
undercook it by 15 minutes and
reheat in the oven for 20–30 minutes.

NUTRITIONAL NOTES

PER PORTION:

CALORIES 350
FAT 10.8 g **SATURATED FAT** 2.3 g
CHOLESTEROL 65.7 mg

6 Meanwhile, cook the vegetables,
drain and put them into a large bowl.
Add the couscous and oil and season.
Stir the grains to fluff them up, add the
chickpeas and finally the chopped
cilantro. Spoon onto a large serving plate,
cover with the chicken pieces, and spoon
over the liquid. Garnish with fresh
cilantro sprigs.

Oat-crusted Chicken with Sage

Oats make a good coating for savory foods, and sealing in the natural juices means that you do not need to add extra fat.

Serves 4

INGREDIENTS
3 tablespoons skim milk
2 teaspoons mustard powder
½ cup rolled oats
3 tablespoons chopped sage leaves
8 skinned chicken thighs or
    drumsticks
½ cup low fat sour cream
1 teaspoon wholegrain mustard
salt and ground black pepper
fresh sage leaves, to garnish

skim milk

mustard powder

rolled oats

sage leaves

chicken thighs

low fat sour cream

wholegrain mustard

1 Preheat the oven to 400°F. Mix the milk and mustard powder in a cup. Mix the oats with 2 tablespoons of the sage in a shallow dish. Add salt and pepper to taste. Brush the chicken with the mustard and milk mixture and press into the oats to coat evenly.

2 Place the chicken on a baking sheet and bake for about 40 minutes, or until the juices run clear, not pink, when pierced through the thickest part.

3 Meanwhile, mix the low fat sour cream, mustard and remaining sage. Season to taste. Garnish with fresh sage and serve hot or cold, with the sauce.

COOK'S TIP
If fresh sage is not available, choose another fresh herb such as thyme or parsley, instead of using a dried alternative.

NUTRITIONAL NOTES
PER PORTION:

CALORIES 214
FAT 6.6 g **SATURATED FAT** 1.8 g
CHOLESTEROL 64.6 mg

Tuscan Chicken

This simple peasant casserole has all the flavors of traditional Italian ingredients.

Serves 4

INGREDIENTS
1 teaspoon olive oil
8 skinned chicken thighs
1 onion, thinly sliced
2 red bell peppers, seeded
  and sliced
1 garlic clove, crushed
1¼ cups crushed tomatoes
⅔ cup dry white wine
1 large fresh oregano sprig, or
  1 teaspoon dried oregano
14-ounce can cannellini
  beans, drained
3 tablespoons white bread crumbs
salt and ground black pepper

chicken thighs

olive oil

red pepper

oregano sprig

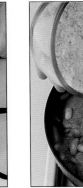

cannellini beans

onion

fresh bread crumbs

dry white wine

garlic

1 Heat the oil in a non-stick frying pan and fry the chicken until golden brown. Remove with a slotted spoon and keep hot. Add the onion and peppers to the pan and sauté gently until softened, but not brown. Stir in the garlic.

2 Add the chicken, crushed tomatoes, wine and oregano. Season well, then bring to a boil with the lid on.

NUTRITIONAL NOTES

PER PORTION:

CALORIES 248
FAT 7.5 g **SATURATED FAT** 2.1 g
CHOLESTEROL 73 mg

3 Lower the heat and simmer gently, without a lid, for 30–35 minutes or until the chicken is tender and cooked through. Stir occasionally.

4 Stir in the cannellini beans and simmer for 5 minutes more to heat through. Sprinkle evenly with the bread crumbs and put under the broiler until golden brown.

Piquant Chicken with Spaghetti

Serves 4

INGREDIENTS

1 onion, finely chopped
1 carrot, diced
1 garlic clove, crushed
1¼ cups vegetable stock or water
4 small chicken breasts, boned and skinned
bouquet garni (bay leaf, parsley and thyme)
4 ounces button mushrooms, sliced thinly
1 teaspoon wine vinegar or lemon juice
12 ounces spaghetti
½ cucumber, peeled and sliced lengthwise
2 firm ripe tomatoes, peeled, seeded and chopped
2 tablespoons low-fat sour cream
1 tablespoon chopped fresh parsley
1 tablespoon snipped chives
salt and ground black pepper

carrot

chicken breasts

tomatoes

cucumber

chives

spaghetti

thyme

parsley

button mushrooms

vegetable stock

onion

bay leaf

1 Put the onion, carrot, garlic, stock or water into a saucepan with the chicken breasts and bouquet garni. Bring to the boil, cover and simmer gently for 15–20 minutes or until tender. Transfer the chicken to a plate and cover with foil.

2 Remove the chicken and strain the liquid. Discard the vegetables and return the liquid to the pan. Add the sliced mushrooms, wine vinegar or lemon juice and simmer for 2–3 minutes until tender.

3 Cook the spaghetti in a large pan of boiling, salted water until *al dente*. Drain thoroughly.

4 Blanch the cucumber in boiling water for 10 seconds. Drain and rinse under cold water.

5 Cut the chicken breasts into bite-size pieces. Boil the stock to reduce by half, then add the chicken, tomatoes, sour cream, cucumber and herbs. Season with salt and pepper to taste.

6 Transfer the spaghetti to a warmed serving dish and spoon over the piquant chicken. Serve at once.

NUTRITIONAL NOTES

PER PORTION:

ENERGY 472 calories **FAT** 7.6g
SATURATED FAT 2.5g **CHOLESTEROL** 65mg
CARBOHYDRATE 72g **FIBER** 4.8g

Tortellini

Serves 6–8 as a starter or 4–6 as a main course

INGREDIENTS
4 ounces smoked lean ham
4 ounces chicken breast, boned and
    skinned
3¾ cups chicken or vegetable stock
cilantro stalks
2 tablespoons grated Parmesan
    cheese, plus extra for serving
1 egg, beaten, plus egg white
    for brushing
2 tablespoons chopped
    fresh cilantro
1 recipe basic pasta dough
flour, for dusting
salt and ground black pepper
cilantro leaves, to garnish

basic pasta dough

smoked ham

chicken breast

grated Parmesan cheese

stock

egg

cilantro

1 Cut the ham and chicken into large chunks and put them into a saucepan with ⅔ cup of the chicken or vegetable stock and some cilantro stalks. Bring to a boil, cover and simmer for 20 minutes until tender. Cool the stock slightly.

2 Drain the ham and chicken and mince finely (reserve the stock). Put into a bowl with the Parmesan cheese, beaten egg, chopped coriander and season with salt and pepper.

3 Roll the pasta into thin sheets, cut into 1½-inch squares. Put ½ teaspoon of filling on each. Brush edges with egg white and fold each square into a triangle; press out any air and seal firmly.

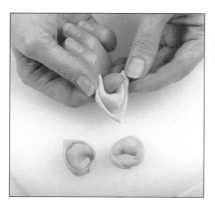

4 Curl each triangle around the tip of a forefinger and press the two ends together firmly.

5 Lay on a lightly floured tea towel to rest for 30 minutes before cooking.

NUTRITIONAL NOTES

PER PORTION:

ENERGY 335 calories **FAT** 9.7g
SATURATED FAT 3.6g **CHOLESTEROL** 193mg
CARBOHYDRATE 39g **FIBER** 1.6g

6 Strain the reserved stock and add to the remainder. Put into a pan and bring to a boil. Lower the heat to a gentle boil and add the tortellini. Cook for 5 minutes. Then turn off the heat, cover the pan and let stand for 20–30 minutes. Serve in soup plates with some of the stock and garnish with cilantro leaves. Serve grated Parmesan separately.

Stir-fried Duck with Blueberries

Serve this conveniently quick dinner party dish with sprigs of fresh mint, which will give a wonderful fresh aroma as you bring the meal to the table.

Serves 6

INGREDIENTS
2 duck breasts, about 6 oz each
2 tbsp sunflower oil
1 tbsp red wine vinegar
1 tsp sugar
1 tsp red wine
1 tsp *crème de cassis* (black currant liqueur)
4 oz fresh blueberries
1 tbsp fresh mint, chopped
salt and freshly ground black pepper
fresh mint sprigs, to garnish
mixed green vegetables, steamed, to serve

duck

red wine vinegar

blueberries

red wine

mint

1 Cut the duck breasts into neat slices. Season well with salt and pepper.

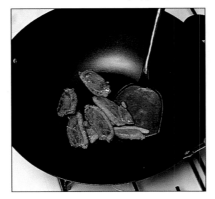

2 Heat the wok, then add the oil. When the oil is hot, stir-fry the duck for 3 minutes.

NUTRITIONAL NOTES
PER PORTION:

ENERGY 186 Kcals FAT 11.2 g
SATURATED FAT 2.4 g

3 Add the red wine vinegar, sugar, red wine and *crème de cassis*. Bubble for 3 minutes, to reduce to a thick syrup.

4 Stir in the blueberries, sprinkle over the mint and serve garnished with sprigs of fresh mint.

Duck and Ginger Chop Suey

Chicken can also be used in this recipe, but duck gives a richer contrast of flavors.

Serves 4

INGREDIENTS
2 duck breasts, about 6 oz each
3 tbsp sunflower oil
1 medium egg, lightly beaten
1 clove garlic
2 cups bean sprouts
2 slices ginger, cut into
    matchsticks
2 tsp oyster sauce
2 scallions, cut into matchsticks
salt and freshly ground pepper

FOR THE MARINADE
1 tbsp honey
2 tsp rice wine
2 tsp light soy sauce
2 tsp dark soy sauce

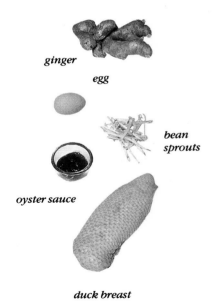

ginger

egg

bean sprouts

oyster sauce

duck breast

NUTRITIONAL NOTES
PER PORTION:

ENERGY 186 Kcals **FAT** 7.5 g
SATURATED FAT 0.2 g

1 Remove the fat from the duck, cut the breasts into thin strips and place in a bowl. Mix the marinade ingredients together, pour over the duck, cover, chill and marinate overnight.

2 Next day, make the egg omelette. Heat a small frying pan and add 1 tbsp of the oil. When the oil is hot, pour in the egg and swirl around to make an omelet. Once cooked, leave it to cool and cut into strips. Drain the duck and discard the marinade.

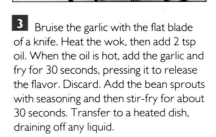

3 Bruise the garlic with the flat blade of a knife. Heat the wok, then add 2 tsp oil. When the oil is hot, add the garlic and fry for 30 seconds, pressing it to release the flavor. Discard. Add the bean sprouts with seasoning and then stir-fry for about 30 seconds. Transfer to a heated dish, draining off any liquid.

4 Heat the wok and add the remaining oil. When the oil is hot, stir-fry the duck for 3 minutes until cooked. Add the ginger and oyster sauce and stir-fry for a further 2 minutes. Add the bean sprouts, egg strips and scallions, stir-fry briefly and serve immediately.

Duck Breast Salad

Serves 6

INGREDIENTS

2 duck breasts, boned
1 teaspoon coriander seeds, crushed
12 ounces rigatoni
²/₃ cup fresh orange juice
1 tablespoon lemon juice
2 teaspoons honey
1 shallot, finely chopped
1 garlic clove, crushed
1 stalk celery, chopped
3 ounces dried cherries
3 tablespoons port
1 tablespoon chopped fresh mint,
    plus extra for garnish
2 tablespoons chopped fresh
    cilantro, plus extra for garnish
1 apple, diced
2 oranges, segmented
salt and ground black pepper

rigatoni *port* *cilantro* *coriander seeds*
duck breasts
orange
apple *mint*
shallot *dried cherries*
garlic
celery

1 Remove the skin and fat from the duck breasts and season with salt and pepper. Rub with crushed coriander seeds. Cook under a preheated broiler for 7–10 minutes depending on size. Wrap in foil and leave for 20 minutes.

2 Cook the pasta in a large pan of boiling, salted water until *al dente*. Drain thoroughly and rinse under cold running water. Leave to cool.

3 To make the dressing, put the orange juice, lemon juice, honey, shallot, garlic, celery, cherries, port, mint and fresh cilantro into a bowl, whisk together and leave to marinate for 30 minutes.

4 Slice the duck very thinly. (It should be pink in the center.)

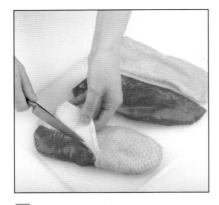

5 Put the pasta into a bowl, add the dressing, diced apple and segments of orange. Toss well to coat the pasta. Transfer the salad to a serving plate with the duck slices and garnish with the extra coriander and mint.

NUTRITIONAL NOTES

PER PORTION:

ENERGY 348 calories **FAT** 3.8g
SATURATED FAT 0.9g **CHOLESTEROL** 55mg
CARBOHYDRATE 64g **FIBER** 1.3g

Turkey and Tomato Hot-pot

Turkey is not just for festive occasions. Here, it's turned into tasty meatballs and simmered with rice in a tomato sauce.

Serves 4

INGREDIENTS
1 oz white bread, crusts removed
2 tbsp skim milk
1 garlic clove, crushed
½ tsp caraway seeds
8 oz ground turkey
1 egg white
1½ cups fresh or canned low salt
    chicken stock
14 oz can plum tomatoes
1 tbsp tomato paste
½ cup rice
salt and freshly ground black pepper
1 tbsp chopped fresh basil, to garnish
carrot and zucchini ribbons, to serve

COOK'S TIP
To make carrot and zucchini ribbons, cut the vegetables lengthwise into thin strips using a vegetable peeler, and blanch or steam until cooked through.

NUTRITIONAL NOTES
PER SERVING:

CALORIES 190 **PROTEIN** 18.04 g
FAT 1.88 g **SATURATED FAT** 0.24 g
CARBOHYDRATE 26.96 g **FIBER** 1.04 g
ADDED SUGAR 0 **SODIUM** 0.32 g

1 Cut the bread into small cubes and put into a mixing bowl. Sprinkle over the milk and leave to soak for 5 minutes.

2 Add the garlic clove, caraway seeds, turkey, salt and freshly ground black pepper to the bread. Mix together well.

3 Whisk the egg white until stiff, then fold, half at a time, into the turkey mixture. Chill for 10 minutes in the refrigerator.

basil

ground turkey

rice

bread

tomato paste

plum tomatoes

caraway seeds

garlic

4 Put the stock, tomatoes and tomato paste into a large, heavy-based saucepan and bring to a boil.

5 Add the rice, stir and cook briskly for about 5 minutes. Turn the heat down to a gentle simmer.

6 Meanwhile, shape the turkey mixture into 16 small balls. Carefully drop them into the tomato stock and simmer for a further 8-10 minutes, or until the turkey balls and rice are cooked. Garnish with chopped basil, and serve with carrot and zucchini ribbons.

Turkey Tonnato

This low fat version of the Italian dish "vitello tonnato" is garnished with fine strips of red bell pepper instead of the traditional anchovy fillets.

NUTRITIONAL NOTES

PER SERVING:

CALORIES 235 **PROTEIN** 35.47 g
FAT 7.09 g **SATURATED FAT** 1.33 g
CARBOHYDRATE 7.80 g **FIBER** 1.37 g
ADDED SUGAR 1.04 g **SODIUM** 0.87 g

Serves 4

INGREDIENTS
1 lb turkey fillets
1 small onion, sliced
1 bay leaf
4 black peppercorns
1½ cups fresh chicken stock
7 oz can tuna in water, drained
5 tbsp reduced calorie mayonnaise
2 tbsp lemon juice
2 red bell peppers, seeded and
   thinly sliced
about 25 capers, drained
pinch of salt
mixed salad and tomatoes, to serve

tuna

lemon

bay leaf

onion

capers

mayonnaise

pepper

turkey fillet

stock

1 Put the turkey fillets in a single layer in a large, heavy-based saucepan. Add the onion, bay leaf, peppercorns and stock. Bring to the boil and reduce the heat. Cover and simmer for 12 minutes, or until tender.

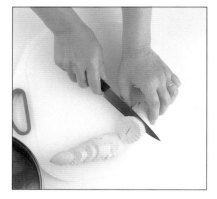

2 Turn off the heat and leave the turkey to cool in the stock, then remove with a slotted spoon. Slice thickly and arrange on a serving plate.

3 Boil the stock until reduced to about 5 tbsp. Strain and leave to cool.

4 Put the tuna, mayonnaise, lemon juice, 3 tbsp of the reduced stock and salt into a blender or food processor and purée until smooth.

5 Stir in enough of the remaining stock to reduce the sauce to the thickness of double cream. Spoon over the turkey.

6 Arrange the strips of red pepper in a lattice pattern over the turkey. Put a caper in the centre of each square. Chill in the refrigerator for 1 hour and serve with a fresh mixed salad and tomatoes.

Penne with Spinach

Serves 4

INGREDIENTS

8 ounces fresh spinach
1 garlic clove, crushed
1 shallot or small onion,
    finely chopped
1/2 small red bell pepper, seeded and
    finely chopped
1 small red chili, seeded
    and chopped
2/3 cup stock
12 ounces penne
5 ounces smoked turkey bacon
3 tablespoons low-fat sour cream
2 tablespoons grated
    Parmesan cheese
shavings of Parmesan cheese,
    to garnish

 red pepper

 grated Parmesan cheese

 red chili

 shallot

 *smoked turkey bacon*

 penne

 stock

 *low-fat sour cream*

garlic

spinach

2 Put the garlic, shallot or small onion, pepper and chili into a large frying pan. Add the stock, cover and cook for about 5 minutes until tender. Add the prepared spinach and cook quickly for another 2–3 minutes until it has wilted.

1 Wash the spinach and remove the hard central stalks. Shred finely.

3 Cook the pasta in a large pan of boiling, salted water until *al dente*. Drain thoroughly.

4 Grill the smoked turkey rashers, cool a little, and chop finely.

5 Stir the sour cream and grated Parmesan into the pasta with the spinach, and toss carefully together.

6 Transfer to serving plates and sprinkle with chopped turkey and shavings of Parmesan cheese.

NUTRITIONAL NOTES
PER PORTION:

ENERGY 422 calories **FAT** 6.8g
SATURATED FAT 3.2g **CHOLESTEROL** 38mg
CARBOHYDRATE 71g **FIBER** 4.4g

Turkey and Pasta Casserole

Serves 4

INGREDIENTS
10 ounces ground turkey
5 ounces smoked turkey
    bacon, chopped
1–2 garlic cloves, crushed
1 onion, finely chopped
2 carrots, diced
2 tablespoons concentrated
    tomato paste
1¼ cups chicken stock
8 ounces rigatoni
2 tablespoons grated
    Parmesan cheese
salt and ground black pepper

turkey bacon   *carrots*   *onion*

rigatoni

garlic

tomato purée

Parmesan cheese

ground turkey   *stock*

1 Brown the ground turkey in a non-stick saucepan, breaking up any large pieces with a wooden spoon, until well browned all over.

2 Add the chopped turkey bacon, garlic, onion, carrots, paste, stock and seasoning. Bring to a boil, cover and simmer for 1 hour until tender.

3 Preheat the oven to 350°F. Cook the pasta in a large pan of boiling, salted water until *al dente*. Drain thoroughly and mix with the turkey sauce.

4 Transfer to a shallow ovenproof dish and sprinkle with grated Parmesan cheese. Bake in the preheated oven for 20–30 minutes until lightly browned.

NUTRITIONAL NOTES
PER PORTION:

ENERGY 391 calories **FAT** 4.9g
SATURATED FAT 2.2g **CHOLESTEROL** 60mg
CARBOHYDRATE 55g **FIBER** 3.5g

Macaroni and Cheese

Serves 4

INGREDIENTS

1 medium onion, chopped
²/₃ cup vegetable or chicken stock
1 ounce low-fat margarine
1½ ounces flour
¼ cup skim milk
2 ounces reduced-fat Cheddar
    cheese, grated
1 teaspoon mustard
8 ounces macaroni
4 slices turkey bacon, cut in half
2–3 firm tomatoes, sliced
a few fresh basil leaves
1 tablespoon grated Parmesan
    cheese
salt and ground black pepper

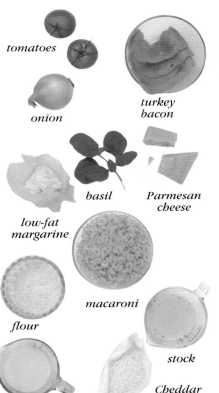

tomatoes

turkey bacon

onion

basil   *Parmesan cheese*

low-fat margarine

macaroni

flour

stock

skim milk   *Cheddar cheese*

1 Put the onion and stock into a non-stick frying pan. Bring to the boil, stirring occasionally and cook for 5–6 minutes or until the stock has reduced entirely and the onions are transparent.

2 Put the margarine, flour, milk, and seasoning into a saucepan and whisk together over the heat until thickened and smooth. Draw aside and add the cheese, mustard and onions.

NUTRITIONAL NOTES

PER PORTION:

ENERGY 152 calories **FAT** 2.8g
SATURATED FAT 0.7g **CHOLESTEROL** 12mg
CARBOHYDRATE 23g **FIBER** 1.1g

3 Cook the macaroni in a large pan of boiling, salted water for 6 minutes or according to the instructions on the packet. Drain thoroughly and stir into the sauce. Transfer the macaroni to a shallow ovenproof dish.

4 Layer the turkey bacon and tomatoes on top of the macaroni and cheese, sprinkling the basil leaves over the tomatoes. Lightly sprinkle with Parmesan cheese and broil to lightly brown the top.

Rolled Stuffed Cannelloni

Serves 4

INGREDIENTS
12 sheets lasagne
fresh basil leaves, to garnish

FOR THE FILLING
2–3 garlic cloves, crushed
1 small onion, finely chopped
²/₃ cup white wine
1 pound ground turkey
1 tablespoon dried basil
1 tablespoon dried thyme
1½ ounces fresh white bread
    crumbs

FOR THE SAUCE
1 ounce low-fat margarine
1 ounce flour
1¼ cups skim milk
4 sun-dried tomatoes, chopped
1 tablespoon chopped fresh herbs
    (basil, parsley, marjoram)
2 tablespoons grated
    Parmesan cheese
salt and ground black pepper

skim milk

*sliced
white bread*

lasagne

*sun-dried
tomatoes*

*ground
turkey*

garlic

parsley

*grated
Parmesan
cheese*

*white
wine*

onion

flour

*low-fat
margarine*

basil

1 Put the garlic, onion and half the wine into a pan. Cover and cook for about 5 minutes until tender. Increase the heat, add the turkey and break up with a wooden spoon. Cook quickly until all the liquid has evaporated and the turkey begins to brown slightly.

2 Lower the heat, add the remaining wine, seasoning and dried herbs. Cover and cook for 20 minutes. Draw off the heat and stir in the breadcrumbs. Leave to cool.

3 Cook the lasagne sheets in a large pan of boiling, salted water until *al dente*. Cook in batches to prevent them sticking together. Drain thoroughly and rinse in cold water. Pat dry on a clean dish towel.

4 Lay the lasagne on a chopping board. Spoon the turkey mixture along one short edge and roll it up to encase the filling. Cut the tubes in half.

5 Preheat the oven to 400°F. Put the margarine, flour and skim milk into a pan, heat and whisk until smooth. Add the chopped tomatoes, fresh herbs and seasoning.

6 Spoon a thin layer of the sauce into a shallow ovenproof dish and arrange a layer of cannelloni on top. Spoon over a layer of sauce and cover with more cannelloni and sauce. Sprinkle with grated Parmesan and bake for 10–15 minutes until lightly browned. Serve at once, garnished with fresh basil leaves.

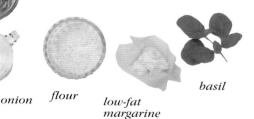

NUTRITIONAL NOTES
PER PORTION:

ENERGY 336 calories **FAT** 7.4g
SATURATED FAT 2.7g **CHOLESTEROL** 65mg
CARBOHYDRATE 26g **FIBER** 1.4g

Fish & Shellfish Dishes

Herbed Fishcakes with Lemon and Chive Sauce

The wonderful flavors of fresh herbs make these fishcakes the catch of the day.

Serves 4

INGREDIENTS
12 oz potatoes, peeled
5 tbsp skim milk
12 oz haddock fillets, skinned
1 tbsp lemon juice
1 tbsp grated horseradish
2 tbsp chopped fresh parsley
flour, for dusting
2 cups fresh whole-wheat bread
   crumbs
salt and freshly ground black pepper
sprig of flat-leaf parsley, to garnish
snow peas and a sliced tomato and
   onion salad, to serve

FOR THE LEMON AND CHIVE SAUCE
thinly pared zest and juice of ½
   small lemon
½ cup dry white wine
2 thin slices of fresh ginger
2 tsp cornstarch
2 tbsp snipped fresh chives

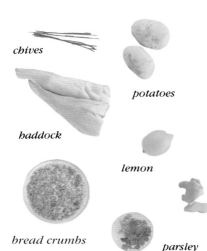

chives

potatoes

haddock

lemon

ginger

bread crumbs   *parsley*

1 Cook the potatoes in a large saucepan of boiling water for 15-20 minutes. Drain and mash with the milk and season to taste.

2 Purée the fish together with the lemon juice and horseradish sauce in a blender or food processor. Mix together with the potatoes and parsley.

3 With floured hands, shape the mixture into eight fishcakes and coat with the breadcrumbs. Chill in the refrigerator for 30 minutes.

4 Cook the fishcakes under a preheated medium broiler for 5 minutes on each side, until browned.

5 To make the sauce, cut the lemon zest into julienne strips and put in a large saucepan with the lemon juice, wine and ginger, and season to taste.

6 Simmer uncovered for 6 minutes. Blend the cornstarch with 1 tbsp of cold water. Add to the saucepan and simmer until clear. Stir in the chives just before serving. Serve the sauce hot with the fishcakes, garnished with sprigs of flat-leaf parsley an accompanied by snow peas and a sliced tomato and onion salad.

Salmon and Broccoli Pilaff

This quick and easy pilaff is an ideal choice for a tasty suppertime meal.

Serves 4

INGREDIENTS
1 red onion, chopped
1 garlic clove, crushed
4 stalks celery, chopped
1 yellow bell pepper, diced
1 cup brown basmati rice
2½ cups fish stock
1¼ cups dry white wine
1 can (14 ounces) pink salmon, drained and flaked
1 can (14 ounces) red kidney beans, rinsed and drained
12 ounces small broccoli florets
3 tablespoons chopped fresh parsley
1–2 tablespoons light soy sauce
salt and ground black pepper
1 ounce toasted flaked almonds, to garnish

red onion

garlic

celery

yellow pepper

brown basmati rice

fish stock

dry white wine

pink salmon

red kidney beans

broccoli

fresh parsley

1 Put the onion, garlic, celery, pepper, rice, stock and wine in a saucepan and bring to the boil, stirring. Simmer uncovered for 25–30 minutes, until almost all the liquid has been absorbed, stirring occasionally.

2 Stir the salmon and kidney beans into the rice mixture. Cook gently for a further 5–10 minutes until the pilaff is piping hot.

NUTRITIONAL NOTES
PER PORTION:

CALORIES 550 PROTEIN 33.38g
FAT 11.98g SATURATED FAT 2.00g
CARBOHYDRATE 69.55g FIBER 9.51g
ADDED SUGAR 0.71g SODIUM 1.39g

3 Meanwhile, cook the broccoli florets in boiling water for about 5 minutes, until tender. Drain thoroughly and keep warm.

4 Fold the broccoli into the pilaff, then stir in the parsley and soy sauce, and season to taste. Garnish with flaked almonds and serve immediately.

Sole Provençal

Re-create the taste of the Mediterranean with this easy-to-make fish casserole.

Serves 4

INGREDIENTS
4 large sole fillets
2 small red onions
½ cup vegetable stock
4 tbsp dry red wine
1 garlic clove crushed
2 zucchini sliced
1 yellow bell pepper, seeded and
   sliced
14-oz can chopped tomatoes
1 tbsp chopped fresh thyme
salt and freshly ground black pepper
potato gratin, to serve

plaice

thyme   *sole*

zucchini

red onion   *bell pepper*

NUTRITIONAL NOTES
Per portion:

ENERGY 167 Kcals PROTEIN 27.5 g
FAT 2.55 g SATURATED FAT 0.39 g
CARBOHYDRATE 6.60 g
FIBER 1.6 g SUGAR 6.3 g
SODIUM 222 mg

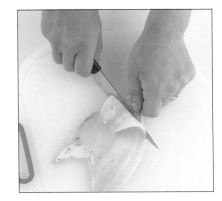

1 Preheat the oven to 350°F. Skin the sole with a sharp knife by laying it skin-side down. Holding the tail end, push the knife between the skin and flesh in a sawing movement. Hold the knife at a slight angle with the blade toward the skin.

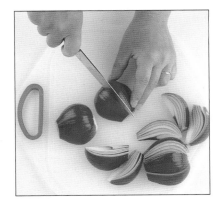

2 Cut each onion into eight wedges. Put into a heavy-based saucepan with the stock. Cover and simmer for 5 minutes. Uncover and continue to cook, stirring occasionally, until the stock has reduced entirely. Add the wine and garlic clove to the pan and continue to cook until the onions are soft.

3 Add the zucchini, yellow bell pepper, tomatoes and thyme and season to taste. Simmer for 3 minutes. Spoon the sauce into a large casserole.

4 Fold each fillet in half and place on top of the sauce. Cover and cook in the pre-heated oven for 15-20 minutes until the fish is opaque and cooked. Serve with potato gratin.

Spicy Seafood and Okra Stew

This spicy combination of seafood and vegetables is good served with herbed brown rice.

Serves 4–6

INGREDIENTS
2 teaspoons olive oil
1 onion, chopped
1 garlic clove, crushed
2 stalks celery, chopped
1 red bell pepper, seeded and diced
1 teaspoon each ground coriander,
  ground cumin and ground ginger
½ teaspoon chili powder
½ teaspoon garam masala
2 tablespoons whole-wheat flour
1¼ cups each fish stock and dry
  white wine
1 can (8 ounces) chopped tomatoes
1 can (8 ounces) okra, trimmed
  and sliced
3 cups mushrooms, sliced
1 pound frozen, cooked, shelled
  seafood, defrosted
1 can (6 ounces) corn kernels
8 ounces long grain brown rice
2–3 tablespoons chopped fresh
  mixed herbs
salt and ground black pepper
fresh parsley sprigs, to garnish

1 Heat the oil in a large saucepan. Add the onion, garlic, celery and pepper and cook for 5 minutes, stirring occasionally.

2 Add the spices and cook for 1 minute, stirring, then add the flour and cook for a further 1 minute, stirring.

3 Gradually stir in the stock and wine and add the tomatoes, okra and mushrooms. Bring to the boil, stirring continuously, then cover and simmer for 20 minutes, stirring occasionally.

4 Stir in the seafood and corn and cook for another 10–15 minutes, until piping hot.

olive oil

onion

garlic

celery

red pepper

ground coriander

ground cumin

ground ginger

chili powder

garam masala

whole-wheat flour

fish stock

dry white wine

chopped tomatoes

okra

mushrooms

seafood

corn

long grain brown rice

fresh mixed herbs

NUTRITIONAL NOTES
PER PORTION:

CALORIES 541 PROTEIN 34.96g
FAT 7.18g SATURATED FAT 1.42g
CARBOHYDRATE 76.05g FIBER 7.25g
ADDED SUGAR 0.01g SODIUM 1.35g

COOK'S TIP
Use fresh cooked seafood in place of the frozen if it is available.

5 Meanwhile, cook the rice in a large saucepan of lightly salted, boiling water for about 35 minutes, until tender.

6 Rinse the rice in fresh boiling water and drain thoroughly, then toss together with the mixed herbs. Season the stew and serve on a bed of herby rice. Garnish with fresh parsley sprigs.

Steamed Chile Mussels

Make sure all the mussels open when the dish is cooked, and discard any that remain closed. Add more red chiles if you really enjoy spicy food.

Serves 6

INGREDIENTS
2 fresh red chiles
6 ripe tomatoes
2 tbsp peanut oil
2 garlic cloves, crushed
2 shallots, finely chopped
2½ lb fresh mussels
2 tbsp white wine
2 tbsp chopped fresh parsley, to garnish
French bread, to serve

mussels

red chile

tomato

shallot

parsley

garlic

1 Roughly chop and deseed the chiles. Roughly chop the tomatoes.

2 Heat the oil in a large, heavy saucepan and gently sauté the garlic and shallots until soft.

NUTRITIONAL NOTES
PER PORTION:

ENERGY 106 Kcals **FAT** 5.2 g
SATURATED FAT 0.8 g

3 Stir in the tomatoes and chile and simmer for 10 minutes.

4 Clean the mussels. Add the mussels and white wine to the pan, cover and cook until all the mussel shells are open – this should take about 5 minutes. Scatter over the chopped parsley. Serve in a large bowl with chunks of fresh French bread.

Fishballs with Quick Tomato Sauce

This quick sauce is ideal to serve with fishballs and makes a good choice for children. If you like, add a dash of chili sauce.

Serves 4

INGREDIENTS
1 pound white fish fillets, skinned
4 tablespoons fresh whole-wheat
    bread crumbs
2 tablespoons snipped chives
    or scallions
14-ounce can chopped tomatoes
¾ cup button mushrooms, sliced
salt and pepper

white fish fillets

scallions

fresh whole-wheat bread crumbs

chopped tomatoes

button mushrooms

1 Cut the fish fillets into large chunks and place in a food processor. Add the whole-wheat bread crumbs and chives or scallions. Season to taste with salt and pepper and process until the fish is finely chopped but still has some texture left.

2 Divide the fish mixture into about 16 even-size pieces, then mold them into balls with your hands.

3 Place the tomatoes and mushrooms in a wide saucepan and cook over a medium heat until boiling. Add the fish balls, cover and simmer for about 10 minutes, until cooked. Serve hot.

COOK'S TIP
Cod is a good choice for this dish but if it's not available, use flounder or sole instead.

NUTRITIONAL NOTES
PER PORTION:

CALORIES 137 **FAT** 1.4 g
SATURATED FAT 0.2 g **PROTEIN** 22.3 g
CARBOHYDRATE 9.4 g **FIBER** 1.8 g

Salmon, Zucchini and Corn Frittata

A delicious change from an omelet, serve this filling frittata with a mixed tomato and pepper salad and warm whole-wheat rolls.

NUTRITIONAL NOTES

PER PORTION:

ENERGY 336Kcals/1415KJ PROTEIN 25.85g
FAT 12.20g SATURATED FAT 3.57g
CARBOHYDRATE 32.83g FIBRE 4.34g
ADDED SUGAR 0.00g SODIUM 0.49g

COOK'S TIP
Use canned tuna or crab in place of the salmon and mushrooms instead of the courgettes.

Serves 4–6

INGREDIENTS
2 teaspoons olive oil
1 onion, chopped
6 ounces zucchini, thinly sliced
8 ounces boiled potatoes (with skins left on), diced
3 eggs, plus 2 egg whites
2 tablespoons skim milk
1 can (7 ounces) pink salmon in water, drained and flaked
1 can (7 ounces) corn kernels, drained
2 teaspoons dried mixed herbs
salt and ground black pepper
½ cup reduced-fat, aged Cheddar cheese, finely grated
chopped fresh mixed herbs and basil leaves, to garnish

olive oil
onion
zucchini
potatoes
eggs
skim milk
pink salmon
corn
dried mixed herbs
Cheddar cheese
salt
black pepper

1 Heat the oil in a large nonstick frying pan. Add the onion and zucchini and cook for 5 minutes, stirring occasionally.

2 Add the potatoes and cook for 5 minutes, stirring occasionally.

3 Beat the eggs, egg whites and milk together, add the salmon, corn, herbs and seasoning and pour the mixture evenly over the vegetables.

4 Cook over a medium heat until the eggs are beginning to set and the frittata is golden brown underneath.

5 Preheat the broiler. Sprinkle the cheese over the frittata and place it under medium heat until the cheese has melted and the top is golden brown.

6 Sprinkle with chopped fresh herbs, garnish with basil leaves and serve immediately cut into wedges.

Red Snapper in Banana Leaves

Watch out for the bones in the snapper as there tend to be a lot of them. Fresh red snapper is worth looking for, as the flavor is exceptional.

Serves 4

INGREDIENTS
8 small red snapper or kingfish about
    6 oz each
4 sprigs fresh rosemary
banana leaves or wax paper
2 tbsp olive oil
salt and freshly ground black pepper

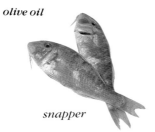

rosemary

banana leaves

olive oil

snapper

1 Preheat the oven to 425°F. Wash, scale and gut the fish.

2 Lay the fresh rosemary inside the cavity of each fish.

3 Cut a piece of banana leaf or wax paper large enough to wrap up each fish.

4 Drizzle each one with a little olive oil.

5 Season each fish well.

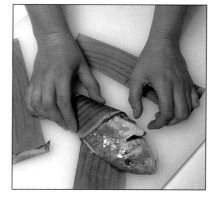

6 Wrap each fish tightly with the seam of the parcel on the underside. Bake for about 12 minutes in the pre-heated oven and unwrap to serve.

NUTRITIONAL NOTES
PER PORTION:

ENERGY 338 Kcals **FAT** 15.6 g
SATURATED FAT 3.6 g

Salmon Steaks with Sorrel Sauce

The sharp flavor of the sorrel sauce balances the richness of the fish. If sorrel is not available, use finely chopped watercress instead.

Serves 2

INGREDIENTS

2 salmon steaks (about
  9 ounces each)
1 teaspoon olive oil
1 tablespoon butter
2 shallots, finely chopped
3 tablespoons low fat crème fraîche
3½ ounces fresh sorrel leaves,
  washed and patted dry
salt and pepper
fresh sage, to garnish

salmon

olive oil

shallots

butter

*low fat crème
fraîche*

*sorrel
leaves*

sage

1 Season the salmon steaks with salt and pepper. Brush a non-stick frying pan with the oil.

2 In a small saucepan, melt the butter over a medium heat. Add the shallots and fry for 2–3 minutes, stirring frequently, until just softened.

3 Add the crème fraîche and the sorrel to the shallots and cook until the sorrel is completely wilted, stirring constantly.

4 Meanwhile, place the frying pan over a medium heat until hot.

COOK'S TIP

If preferred, cook the salmon steaks in a microwave oven for about 4–5 minutes, tightly covered, or according to the manufacturer's guidelines.

5 Add the salmon steaks and cook for about 5 minutes, turning once, until the flesh is opaque next to the bone. If you're not sure, pierce with the tip of a sharp knife; the juices should run clear.

6 Arrange the salmon steaks on two warmed plates, garnish with sage and serve with the sorrel sauce.

NUTRITIONAL NOTES

PER PORTION:

CALORIES 86 **FAT** 6.8 g
SATURATED FAT 3.9 g **PROTEIN** 3.7 g
CARBOHYDRATE 2.8 g **FIBER** 1.0 g

Fillets of Striped Bass Baked with Thyme and Garlic

Quick cooking is the essence of this dish. Use the freshest garlic available and half the amount of dried thyme if fresh is not available.

Serves 4

INGREDIENTS

4 × 4 oz striped bass fillets
1 shallot, finely chopped
2 garlic cloves, thinly sliced
4 sprigs fresh thyme, plus extra to
    garnish
grated zest and juice of 1 lemon, plus
    extra juice for drizzling
2 tbsp extra virgin olive oil
salt and freshly ground black pepper

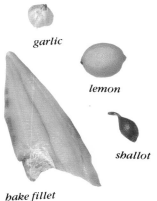

garlic

lemon

shallot

bake fillet

thyme

1 Preheat the oven to 350°F. Lay the bass fillets into the base of a large roasting pan. Scatter the shallot, garlic cloves and thyme on top.

2 Season well with salt and pepper.

3 Drizzle over the lemon juice and oil. Bake for about 15 minutes in the preheated oven. Serve scattered with finely grated lemon zest and garnished with thyme sprigs.

VARIATION

If striped bass is not available you can use cod or haddock fillets for this recipe. You can also use a mixture of fresh herbs rather than just thyme.

NUTRITIONAL NOTES

PER PORTION:

ENERGY 169 Kcals **FAT** 8.3 g
SATURATED FAT 1.2 g

Cod and Spinach Parcels

The best way to serve this dish is to slice each parcel into about four and reveal the meaty large flakes of white fish. Drizzle the sauce over the slices.

Serves 4

INGREDIENTS
4 pieces of thick cod fillet, skinned
    about 6 oz each
8 oz large spinach leaves
½ tsp freshly ground nutmeg
3 tbsp white wine
salt and freshly ground black pepper

white wine

spinach

cod fillet

1 Preheat the oven to 350°F. Season the fish well with salt and freshly ground black pepper.

2 Blanch the spinach leaves in boiling water for a minute and refresh under cold water.

NUTRITIONAL NOTES

PER PORTION:

ENERGY 162 Kcals **FAT** 1.7 g
SATURATED FAT 0.2 g

3 Pat the spinach leaves dry on absorbent paper towels.

4 Wrap the spinach around each fish fillet. Sprinkle with nutmeg. Place in a roasting tin, pour over the wine and poach for 15 minutes. Slice and serve hot.

Thick Cod Fillet with Fresh Mixed-herb Crust

Mixed fresh herbs make this a delicious crust. Season well and serve with large lemon wedges.

Serves 4

INGREDIENTS
2 tbsp butter
1 tbsp fresh chervil
1 tbsp fresh parsley
1 tbsp fresh chives
3 cups wholewheat bread
   crumbs
4 × 8 oz thickly cut cod fillets,
   skinned
1 tbsp olive oil
lemon wedges, to garnish
salt and freshly ground black pepper

butter

breadcrumbs

parsley

cod fillets

chervil

lemon

NUTRITIONAL NOTES
PER PORTION:

ENERGY 348 Kcals FAT 10.6 g
SATURATED FAT 2 g

I Preheat the oven to 400°F. Melt the butter and chop the fresh herbs finely.

2 Mix the butter with the breadcrumbs, herbs and seasoning.

3 Press a quarter of the mixture on top of each fillet. Place on a baking sheet and drizzle over the olive oil. Bake in the pre-heated oven for 15 minutes until the fish flesh is firm and the top turns golden. Serve garnished with lemon wedges.

Grilled Salmon with Spicy Sauce

A spicy, tomato and mustard sauce makes grilled salmon fillets delicious—cook them on a grill or under a hot broiler.

NUTRITIONAL NOTES
Per portion:
Calories 125 **Fat** 3.5 g
Saturated Fat 1.4 g **Protein** 2.8 g
Carbohydrate 21.9 g **Fiber** 1.6 g

Serves 4

INGREDIENTS
1 small red onion
1 garlic clove
6 plum tomatoes
1 tsp butter
3 tbsp ketchup
2 tbsp Dijon mustard
2 tbsp dark brown sugar
1 tbsp honey
1 tsp ground cayenne pepper
1 tbsp ancho chili powder
1 tbsp ground paprika
1 tbsp Worcestershire sauce
4 × 5 oz salmon fillets

cayenne pepper

Dijon mustard

dark brown sugar

plum tomatoes

red onion

salmon fillet

tomato ketchup

1 Finely chop the red onion and finely dice the garlic.

2 Dice the tomatoes.

3 Melt the butter in a large, heavy-based saucepan and gently cook the onion and garlic until translucent.

4 Add the tomatoes and simmer for 15 minutes.

5 Add the remaining ingredients except the salmon and simmer for a further 20 minutes. Process the mixture in a food processor fitted with a metal blade and leave to cool.

6 Brush the salmon with the sauce and chill for at least 2 hours. Barbecue or broil for about 2–3 minutes either side, brushing on the sauce when necessary.

Millionaire's Lobster Salad

When money is no object and you're in a decadent mood, this salad will satisfy your every whim. It is ideally served with a cool Chardonnay, Chablis or Pouilly-Fuissé wine.

Serves 4

INGREDIENTS
1 medium lobster, live or cooked
1 bay leaf
1 sprig thyme
1½ lb new potatoes, scraped
2 ripe tomatoes
4 plump, juicy oranges
½ frisée lettuce
6 oz lamb's lettuce
7 oz can artichoke hearts in brine, quartered
2 tbsp extra-virgin olive oil
salt
1 small bunch tarragon, chervil or flat-leaf parsley, to garnish

DRESSING
2 tbsp frozen concentrated orange juice, thawed
3 oz low fat spread, diced
salt and cayenne pepper

COOK'S TIP
This rich delicate flavor of this salad depends on using the freshest lobsters. If North America lobsters (pictured here) are not available, use spiny rock lobsters or crawfish.

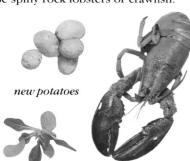
new potatoes

lamb's lettuce

lobster

orange

frisée lettuce

tarragon

tomato

1 If the lobster needs cooking, add to a large pan of salted water with the bay leaf and thyme. Bring to the boil and simmer for 15 minutes. Cool under running water. Twist off the legs and claws, and separate the tail piece from the body section. Break the claws open with a hammer and remove the meat intact. Cut the tail piece open from the underside with a pair of kitchen shears. Slice the meat and set aside.

2 Bring the potatoes to the boil in salted water and simmer for 20 minutes. Drain, cover and keep warm. Cover the tomatoes with boiling water and leave for 20 seconds to loosen their skins. Cool under running water and slip off the skins. Halve the tomatoes, discard the seeds, then cut the flesh into large dice.

3 To segment the oranges, remove the peel from the top, bottom and sides with a serrated knife. With a small paring knife, loosen the orange segments by cutting between the flesh and the membranes, holding the fruit over a small bowl.

4 To make the dressing, measure the thawed orange juice into a glass bowl and set it over a saucepan containing 1 in of simmering water. Heat the juice for 1 minute, remove from heat, then whisk in the low fat spread a little at a time until the dressing reaches a coating consistency. Season to taste with salt and a pinch of cayenne pepper. Cover and keep warm.

5 Wash the salad leaves and spin dry. Dress with olive oil, then divide between 4 large serving plates. Moisten the potatoes, artichokes and orange segments with olive oil and distribute among the leaves. Lay the sliced lobster over the salad, spoon on the warm butter dressing, add the diced tomato and decorate with fresh herbs. Serve at room temperature.

NUTRITIONAL NOTES
PER PORTION:

ENERGY 371 Kcals **FAT** 14.2 g
SATURATED FAT 3.3 g

Grilled Salmon and Spring Vegetable Salad

Spring is the time to enjoy sweet young vegetables. Cook them briefly, cool to room temperature, dress and serve with a piece of lightly grilled salmon topped with sorrel and quail's eggs.

Serves 4

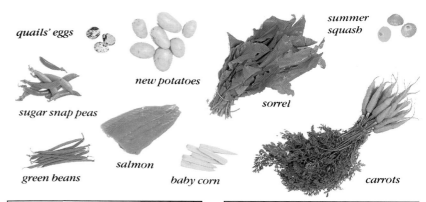

quails' eggs

new potatoes

summer squash

sorrel

sugar snap peas

salmon

green beans

baby corn

carrots

INGREDIENTS

12 oz small new potatoes, scrubbed or scraped
salt and pepper
4 quails' eggs
¼ lb young carrots, peeled
¼ lb baby corn
¼ lb sugar snap peas, trimmed and stringed
¼ lb fine green beans, trimmed and stringed
¼ lb young zucchini
¼ lb summer squash (optional)

½ cup French Dressing
4 salmon fillets, each weighing 5 oz, skinned
¼ lb sorrel or young spinach, stems removed

NUTRITIONAL NOTES
PER PORTION:

ENERGY 335 Kcals **FAT** 14 g
SATURATED FAT 2.6 g

1 Bring the potatoes to the boil in salted water and cook for 15–20 minutes. Drain, cover and keep warm.

2 Cover the quails' eggs with boiling water and cook for 8 minutes. Refresh under cold water, shell and cut in half.

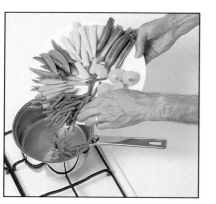

3 Bring a saucepan of salted water to the boil, add all the vegetables and cook for 2–3 minutes. Drain well. Place the hot vegetables and potatoes in a salad bowl, moisten with French Dressing and allow to cool.

4 Brush the salmon fillets with French Dressing and broil for about 6 minutes, turning once.

5 Place the sorrel in a stainless steel or enamel saucepan with 2 tbsp French Dressing, cover, and soften over a gentle heat for 2 minutes. Strain, then allow to cool to room temperature. Toss the vegetables in the remaining French Dressing.

6 Divide the potatoes and vegetables between 4 large plates, then position a piece of salmon to one side of each plate. Finally place a spoonful of sorrel on each piece of salmon and top with a halved quail's egg. Season and serve at room temperature.

Vietnamese Stuffed Squid

The smaller the squid the sweeter the dish will taste.
Be very careful not to overcook the flesh as it becomes
tough very quickly.

NUTRITIONAL NOTES
Per portion:

ENERGY 339 Kcals **FAT** 11.4 g
SATURATED FAT 3 g

Serves 4

INGREDIENTS
1½ lb (appx. 8 small) squid, cleaned
2 oz cellophane noodles
2 tbsp safflower oil
2 scallions, finely chopped
8 shiitake mushrooms, halved if large
9 oz ground pork
1 garlic clove, chopped
2 tbsp Thai fish sauce
1 tsp sugar
1 tbsp finely chopped cilantro
1 tsp lemon juice
salt and freshly ground pepper

noodles

garlic

cilantro

ground pork

squid

scallions

shitake mushrooms

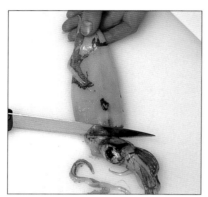

1 Preheat the oven to 400°F. Clean the squid and remove any excess membrane and tentacles.

2 Put the noodles into a saucepan of boiling water. Remove the pan from the heat and soak the noodles for 20 minutes.

3 Heat 1 tbsp of the oil in a wok and stir-fry the scallions, mushrooms, pork and garlic for 4 minutes until the meat is golden.

4 Add the noodles, fish sauce, sugar, seasoning, cilantro and lemon juice.

5 Stuff the squid two-thirds full with the mixture and secure with toothsticks or satay sticks. Drizzle over the remaining oil, prick the squid twice and bake in the preheated oven for 10 minutes. Serve hot.

Roast Monkfish with Garlic and Fennel

Monkfish was sometimes used as a substitute for lobster meat because it is very similar in texture. It is now appreciated in its own right and is delicious quickly roasted.

NUTRITIONAL NOTES
PER PORTION:

ENERGY 117 Kcals **FAT** 3.3 g
SATURATED FAT 0.5 g

Serves 4

INGREDIENTS
1¼ lb monkfish tail
8 garlic cloves
1 tbsp olive oil
2 bulbs fennel, sliced
juice of 1 lemon
1 bay leaf
salt and freshly ground black pepper

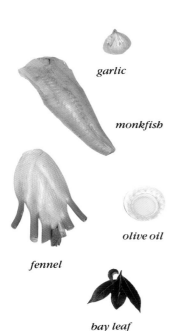

garlic

monkfish

olive oil

fennel

bay leaf

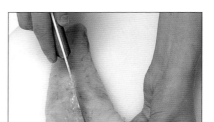

1 Preheat the oven to 425°F. With a filleting knife, cut away the thin membrane covering the outside of the fish.

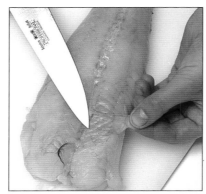

2 Cut along one side of the central bone to remove the fillet. Repeat on the other side.

3 Tie the fillets together with string.

4 Peel and slice the garlic cloves and cut incisions into the fish flesh. Place the garlic slices into the incisions.

5 Heat the oil in a large, heavy-based saucepan and seal the fish on all sides.

6 Place the fish in a roasting dish together with the fennel, lemon juice, seasoning and bay leaf. Roast in the preheated oven for about 20 minutes and serve immediately.

Sea Bass en Papillote

A dramatic presentation to delight your guests. Bring the unopened parcels to the table and let them unfold their own fish to release the delicious aroma.

Serves 4

INGREDIENTS
4 small sea bass, gutted
1 tbsp butter
1 lb spinach, washed well
3 shallots, finely chopped
4 tbsp white wine
4 bay leaves
salt and freshly ground black pepper

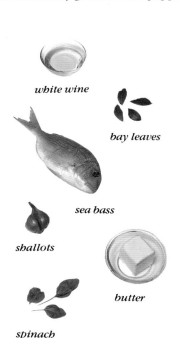

white wine

bay leaves

sea bass

shallots

butter

spinach

NUTRITIONAL NOTES
Per portion:

ENERGY 264 Kcals **FAT** 10.4 g
SATURATED FAT 4.2 g

1 Preheat the oven to 350°F. Season both the inside and outside of the fish. Melt 4 tbsp of the butter in a large, heavy-based saucepan and add the spinach. Cook gently until the spinach has broken down into a smooth purée. Set aside to cool.

2 Melt another 4 tbsp of the butter in a clean pan and add the shallots. Gently sauté for 5 minutes until soft. Add to the spinach and leave to cool.

3 Stuff the insides of the fish with the spinach filling.

4 For each fish, fold a large sheet of wax paper in half and cut around the fish laid on one half, to make a heart shape when unfolded. It should be at least 2 in larger than the fish. Melt the remaining butter and brush a little onto the paper. Set the fish on one side of the paper.

5 Add a little wine and a bay leaf to each package.

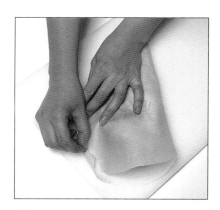

6 Fold the other side of the paper over the fish and make small pleats to seal the two edges, starting at the curve of the heart. Brush the outsides with butter. Transfer the packages to a baking sheet and bake for 20–25 minutes until the packages are brown. Serve with new potatoes and glazed carrots.

Penne with Salmon and Dill

Serves 6

INGREDIENTS
12 ounces fresh salmon
  fillet, skinned
4 ounces sliced smoked salmon
1–2 shallots, finely chopped
4 ounces button mushrooms,
  quartered
²/₃ cup light red or rosé wine
²/₃ cup fish stock
²/₃ cup low-fat sour cream
2 tablespoons chopped fresh dill
12 ounces penne
salt and ground black pepper
sprigs of dill, to garnish

1 Cut the fresh salmon into 1-inch cubes. Cut the smoked salmon into ¹/₂-inch strips.

2 Put the shallots and mushrooms into a non-stick pan with the red or rosé wine. Bring to the boil and cook for about 5 minutes or until the wine has reduced almost completely.

3 Add the fish stock and sour cream and stir until smooth. Then add the fresh salmon, cover the pan and cook gently for 2–3 minutes.

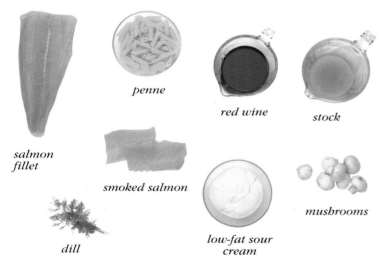

penne

red wine

stock

salmon
fillet

smoked salmon

low-fat sour
cream

mushrooms

dill

4 Remove from the heat and stir in the chopped dill and seasoning.

5 Meanwhile cook the pasta in a large pan of boiling, salted water according to the instructions on the packet. Drain thoroughly and transfer to a warm serving dish. Add the smoked salmon to the sauce and pour over the pasta. Toss lightly to mix. Serve at once, garnished with sprigs of dill.

NUTRITIONAL NOTES
PER PORTION:

ENERGY 394 calories **FAT** 12.8g
SATURATED FAT 4.6g **CHOLESTEROL** 64mg
CARBOHYDRATE 45g **FIBER** 2g

Shellfish Pasta Shells with Spinach Sauce

You'll need very large pasta shells, measuring about 1½ in long for this dish; don't try stuffing smaller shells—it would take much too long!

NUTRITIONAL NOTES

PER PORTION:

ENERGY 363 Kcals **PROTEIN** 34.94 g
FAT 6.08 g **SATURATED FAT** 2.09 g
CARBOHYDRATE 45 g
FIBER 3.98 g **SUGAR** 9.16 g
SODIUM 622 mg

Serves 4

INGREDIENTS
1 tbsp low fat margarine
8 scallions, finely sliced
6 tomatoes
32 large dried pasta shells
1 cup low fat cream cheese
6 tbsp skim milk
pinch of freshly grated nutmeg
8 oz shrimp
6-oz can white crabmeat, drained
    and flaked
4 oz frozen chopped spinach,
    thawed and drained
salt and freshly ground black pepper

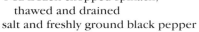
scallions

shrimp

pasta shells

crabmeat

spinach

tomatoes

1 Preheat the oven to 300°F. Melt the low fat margarine in a small saucepan and gently cook the scallions for 3–4 minutes or until softened.

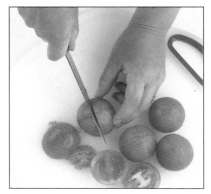
2 Plunge the tomatoes into a saucepan of boiling water for 1 minute, then into a saucepan of cold water. Slip off the skins. Halve the tomatoes, remove the seeds and cores and roughly chop the flesh.

3 Cook the pasta shells in lightly salted boiling water for about 10 minutes, or until *al dente*. Drain well.

4 Put the low fat cream cheese and skim milk into a saucepan and heat gently, stirring until blended. Season with salt, freshly ground black pepper and a pinch of nutmeg. Measure 2 tbsp of the sauce into a bowl.

5 Add the scallions, tomatoes, shrimp and crabmeat to the bowl. Mix well. Spoon the filling into the shells and place in a single layer in a shallow ovenproof dish. Cover with foil and cook for 10 minutes.

6 Stir the spinach into the remaining sauce. Bring to a boil and simmer gently for 1 minutes, stirring constantly. Drizzle on the pasta shells and serve hot.

Smoked Haddock in Parsley Sauce

Serves 4

INGREDIENTS

1 pound smoked haddock fillet
1 small leek or onion, sliced thickly
1¼ cups skim milk
a bouquet garni (bay leaf, thyme
   and parsley)
1 ounce low-fat margarine
1 ounce flour
2 tablespoons chopped fresh parsley
8 ounces pasta shells
salt and ground black pepper
½ ounce toasted slivered almonds,
   to serve

leek

haddock fillet

salt

parsley

bay leaves

pepper

pasta shells

skim milk

flour

low-fat margarine

1 Remove all the skin and any bones from the haddock. Put into a pan with the leek or onion, milk and bouquet garni. Bring to the boil, cover and simmer gently for about 8–10 minutes until the fish flakes easily.

2 Strain, reserving the milk for making the sauce, and discard the bouquet garni.

NUTRITIONAL NOTES

PER PORTION:

ENERGY 405 calories **FAT** 6.9g
SATURATED FAT 1.0g **CHOLESTEROL** 42mg
CARBOHYDRATE 58g **FIBER** 3.7g

3 Put the margarine, flour and reserved milk into a pan. Bring to the boil and whisk until smooth. Season and add the fish and leek or onion.

4 Cook the pasta in a large pan of boiling water until *al dente*. Drain thoroughly and stir into the sauce with the chopped parsley. Serve immediately, scattered with almonds.

Fusilli with Smoked Trout

Serves 4–6

INGREDIENTS

2 carrots, cut in julienne sticks
1 leek, cut in julienne sticks
2 sticks celery, cut in julienne sticks
²/₃ cup vegetable stock
8 ounces fresh trout fillets, skinned
  and cut into strips
7 ounces low-fat cream cheese
²/₃ cup white wine or fish stock
1 tablespoon chopped fresh dill
  or fennel
8 ounces fusilli
salt and ground black pepper
dill sprigs, to garnish

leek
carrots
low-fat cream cheese
celery
dill
white wine
trout fillets
stock
fusilli

1 Put the carrots, leek and celery into a pan with the vegetable stock. Bring to the boil and cook quickly for 4–5 minutes until tender and most of the stock has evaporated. Remove from the heat and add the smoked trout.

2 To make the sauce, put the cream cheese and wine or fish stock into a saucepan, heat and whisk until smooth. Season with salt and pepper. Add the chopped dill or fennel.

3 Cook the fusilli in a large pan of boiling, salted water until *al dente*. Drain thoroughly.

4 Return the fusilli to the pan with the sauce, toss lightly and transfer to a serving bowl. Top with the cooked vegetables and trout. Serve immediately, garnished with dill sprigs.

NUTRITIONAL NOTES

PER PORTION:

ENERGY 339 calories **FAT** 4.7g
SATURATED FAT 0.8g **CHOLESTEROL** 57mg
CARBOHYDRATE 49g **FIBER** 4.1g

Saffron Pappardelle

Serves 4

INGREDIENTS
large pinch of saffron strands
4 sun-dried tomatoes, chopped
1 teaspoon fresh thyme
12 large shrimp in their shells
8 ounces baby squid
8 ounces monkfish fillet
2–3 garlic cloves, crushed
2 small onions, quartered
1 small bulb fennel, trimmed
    and sliced
²/₃ cup white wine
8 ounces pappardelle
salt and ground black pepper
2 tablespoons chopped fresh
    parsley, to garnish

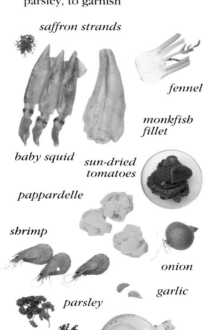

saffron strands

fennel

monkfish fillet

baby squid   *sun-dried tomatoes*

pappardelle

shrimp

onion

garlic

parsley

thyme   *white wine*

1 Put the saffron, sun-dried tomatoes and thyme into a bowl with 4 tablespoons hot water. Let soak for 30 minutes.

2 Wash the shrimp and carefully remove the shells, leaving the heads and tails intact. Pull the head from the body of each squid and remove the quill. Cut the tentacles from the head and rinse under cold water. Pull off the outer skin and cut into ¼-inch rings. Cut the monkfish into 1-inch cubes.

3 Put the garlic, onions and fennel into a pan with the wine. Cover and simmer for 5 minutes until tender.

4 Add the monkfish, saffron, tomatoes and thyme in their liquid. Cover and cook for 3 minutes. Then add the shrimp and squid. Cover and cook gently for 1–2 minutes. (Do not overcook or the squid will become tough.)

5 Meanwhile cook the pasta in a large pan of boiling, salted water until *al dente*. Drain thoroughly.

6 Divide the pasta among four serving dishes and top with the fish and shellfish sauce. Sprinkle with parsley and serve at once.

NUTRITIONAL NOTES
PER PORTION:

ENERGY 381 calories **FAT** 3.5g
SATURATED FAT 0.6g **CHOLESTEROL** 34mg
CARBOHYDRATE 52g **FIBER** 3.2g

Sweet and Sour Shrimp with Chinese Egg Noodles

Serves 4–6

INGREDIENTS

½ ounce dried porcini mushrooms
1¼ cups hot water
bunch of scallions, cut into thick
    diagonal slices
1-inch piece of fresh ginger, peeled
    and grated
1 red bell pepper, seeded and diced
8 ounce can water chestnuts, sliced
3 tablespoons light soy sauce
2 tablespoons sherry
12 ounces large peeled shrimp
8 ounces Chinese egg noodles

*fresh
ginger*

red pepper

shrimp

scallions

*water
chestnuts*

egg noodles

*soy
sauce*

*porcini
mushrooms*

1 Put the dried porcini mushrooms into a bowl with the hot water and soak for 15 minutes.

2 Put the scallions, ginger and diced red pepper into a pan with the mushrooms and their liquid. Bring to a boil, cover and cook for about 5 minutes until tender

NUTRITIONAL NOTES

PER PORTION:

ENERGY 391 calories **FAT** 7.1g
SATURATED FAT 0.3g **CHOLESTEROL** 88mg
CARBOHYDRATE 54g **FIBER** 2.8g

3 Add the water chestnuts, soy sauce, sherry and shrimp. Cover and cook gently for 2 minutes.

4 Cook the egg noodles according to the instructions on the package. Drain thoroughly and transfer to a warmed serving dish. Spoon the hot shrimp on top. Serve at once.

Pasta with Scallops in Warm Green Tartar Sauce

Serves 4

INGREDIENTS

½ cup low fat sour cream
2 teaspoons coarse-grained mustard
2 garlic cloves, crushed
2–3 tablespoons fresh lime juice
4 tablespoons chopped fresh parsley
2 tablespoons snipped chives
12 ounces black tagliatelle
12 large scallops
4 tablespoons white wine
⅔ cup fish stock
salt and ground black pepper
lime wedges and parsley sprigs,
    to garnish

lime

chives

parsley

*black
tagliatelle*

scallops

white wine

*low fat sour
cream*

fish stock

garlic

1 To make the tartar sauce, mix the sour cream, mustard, garlic, lime juice, herbs and seasoning together in a bowl.

2 Cook the pasta in a large pan of boiling, salted water until *al dente*. Drain thoroughly.

NUTRITIONAL NOTES

PER PORTION:

ENERGY 433 calories **FAT** 3.4g
SATURATED FAT 0.6g **CHOLESTEROL** 45mg
CARBOHYDRATE 68g **FIBER** 3.4g

3 Slice the scallops in half, horizontally. Keep any coral whole. Put the white wine and fish stock into a saucepan. Heat to simmering point. Add the scallops and cook very gently for 3–4 minutes (no longer or they will become tough).

4 Remove the scallops. Boil the wine and stock to reduce by half and add the green sauce to the pan. Heat gently to warm, replace the scallops and cook for 1 minute. Spoon over the pasta and garnish with lime wedges and parsley.

Cod with a Spicy Mushroom Sauce

The cod is grilled before it is added to the sauce to prevent it from breaking up during cooking.

Serves 4

INGREDIENTS
4 cod fillets
1 tbsp lemon juice
1 tbsp olive oil
1 medium onion, chopped
1 bay leaf
4 black peppercorns, crushed
4 oz mushrooms
⅔ cup low fat plain yogurt
1 tsp minced garlic
1 tsp minced ginger
½ tsp garam marsala
½ tsp chili powder
1 tsp salt
1 tbsp fresh cilantro leaves,
   to garnish
lightly cooked green beans, to serve

minced ginger   *onion*

lemon juice   *cod fillets*
   mushrooms

chili powder   *bay leaf*

garam masala   *minced garlic*   *fresh cilantro*   *yogurt*

NUTRITIONAL NOTES
PER PORTION:

ENERGY 170 Kcals PROTEIN 25.80 g
FAT 4.32 g SATURATED FAT 0.79 g
CARBOHYDRATE 7.67 g FIBER 1.00 g
ADDED SUGAR 0 SALT 0.61 g

1 Remove the skin and any bones from the cod fillets. Sprinkle with lemon juice, then cook under a preheated broiler about 5 minutes on each side. Remove from heat and set aside.

2 Heat the oil in a non-stick wok or frying pan and fry the onion with the bay leaf and peppercorns for 2–3 minutes. Lower the heat, then add the mushrooms and stir-fry for 4–5 minutes.

3 In a bowl, combine the yogurt, ginger and garlic, garam masala, chili powder and salt. Pour this over the onions and stir-fry for about 3 minutes.

4 Add the cod to the sauce and cool for another 2 minutes. Serve garnished with the cilantro and accompanied by lightly cooked green beans.

Stir-fried Vegetables with Monkfish

Monkfish is a rather expensive fish, but ideal to use in stir-fry recipes as it is quite tough and does not break easily.

Serves 4

INGREDIENTS
2 tablespoons corn oil
2 medium onions, sliced
1 teaspoon garlic pulp
1 teaspoon ground cumin
1 teaspoon ground coriander
1 teaspoon chili powder
6 ounces monkfish, cut into cubes
2 tablespoons fresh fenugreek
   leaves
2 tomatoes, seeded and sliced
1 zucchini, sliced
1 tablespoon lime juice
salt

onions   *zucchini*   *monkfish*

tomatoes   *fenugreek*   *lime juice*

chili powder   *ground cumin*
ground coriander   *garlic pulp*

NUTRITIONAL NOTES
Per portion:
ENERGY 86 K Cals   **PROTEIN** 9.18g
FAT 2.38g   **SATURATED FAT** 0.35g
CARBOHYDRATE 8.30g   **FIBER** 1.87g
ADDED SUGAR 0.02g
SALT 0.27g

1 Heat the oil in a nonstick wok or frying pan and fry the onions over a low heat until soft.

2 Meanwhile mix together the garlic, cumin, coriander and chili powder. Add this spice mixture to the onions and stir for about 1 minute.

COOK'S TIP
Try to use monkfish for this recipe, but if it is not available, either cod or shrimp make a suitable substitute.

3 Add the fish and continue to stir-fry for 3–5 minutes until the fish is well cooked through.

4 Add the fenugreek, tomatoes and zucchini, followed by salt to taste, and stir-fry for a further 2 minutes. Sprinkle with lime juice before serving.

Shrimp and Vegetable Balti

This makes a simple and delicious accompaniment to many other Balti dishes.

Serves 4

INGREDIENTS

6 ounces frozen cooked, peeled
   shrimp
2 tablespoons corn oil
¼ teaspoon onion seeds
4–6 curry leaves
4 ounces frozen peas
4 ounces frozen corn
1 large zucchini, sliced
1 medium red bell pepper, seeded
   and roughly diced
1 teaspoon crushed coriander seeds
1 teaspoon crushed dried red chilies
1 tablespoon lemon juice
salt
1 tablespoon fresh cilantro leaves,
   to garnish

shrimp   *peas*   *corn*

red bell *curry leaves*
pepper
            zucchini

fresh cilantro

onion *dried red* *coriander*
seeds *chilies* *seeds*

lemon juice

NUTRITIONAL NOTES
Per portion:

ENERGY 134 K Cals **PROTEIN** 13.94g
FAT 3.04g **SATURATED FAT** 0.51g
CARBOHYDRATE 14.03g **FIBER** 2.96g
ADDED SUGAR 0g
SALT 1.03g

 Thaw the shrimp and drain them of any excess liquid.

 Next add the peas, corn, zucchini and red bell pepper. Continue to stir for 3–5 minutes.

2 Heat the oil with the onion seeds and curry leaves in a nonstick wok or frying pan.

5 Finally, add the coriander seeds, chilies, salt to taste and lemon juice.

COOK'S TIP
The best way to crush whole seeds is to use an electric spice grinder or a small marble pestle and mortar.

3 Add the shrimp to the wok and stir-fry until the liquid has evaporated.

6 Serve immediately, garnished with fresh cilantro leaves.

Vegetarian
Dishes

Sweet Potato Roulade

Sweet potato works particularly well as the base for this roulade. Serve in thin slices for a truly impressive dinner party dish.

Serves 6

INGREDIENTS

1 cup low-fat ricotta cheese
5 tbsp low-fat yogurt
6–8 scallions, finely sliced
2 tbsp chopped brazil nuts, roasted
1 lb sweet potatoes, peeled and
    coarsely cubed
12 allspice berries, crushed
4 eggs, separated
¼ cup Edam or Gouda cheese, finely
    grated
salt and freshly ground black pepper
1 tbsp sesame seeds

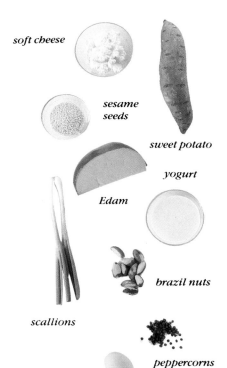

soft cheese

sesame seeds

sweet potato

yogurt

Edam

brazil nuts

scallions

peppercorns

egg

1 Preheat the oven to 400°F. Grease and line a 13 × 10 in jelly roll pan with parchment paper, snipping the corners with scissors to fit neatly into the pan.

2 In a small bowl, mix together the ricotta, yogurt, scallions and brazil nuts. Set aside.

3 Boil or steam the sweet potato until tender. Drain well. Place in a food processor with the allspice and blend until smooth. Spoon into a bowl and stir in the egg yolks and Edam. Season to taste.

4 Whisk the egg whites until stiff but not dry. Fold ⅓ of the egg whites into the sweet potatoes to lighten the mixture before gently folding in the rest.

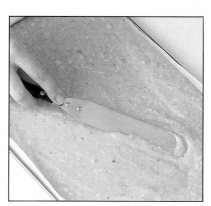

5 Pour into the prepared pan, tipping it to get the mixture right into the corners. Smooth gently with a spatula and cook in the oven for 10–15 minutes.

COOK'S TIP
Choose the orange-fleshed variety of sweet potato for the most striking color.

NUTRITIONAL NOTES
PER PORTION:

ENERGY 240 Kcals **FAT** 11.8 g
SATURATED FAT 3.8 g

6 Meanwhile, lay a large sheet of waxed paper on a clean dish-towel and sprinkle with the sesame seeds. When the roulade is cooked, tip it onto the paper, trim the edges and roll it up. Leave to cool. When cool carefully unroll, spread with the filling and roll up again. Cut into slices to serve.

221

Pumpkin and Pistachio Risotto

This elegant combination of creamy golden rice and orange pumpkin can be as pale or bright as you like by adding different quantities of saffron.

Serves 4

INGREDIENTS

5 cups fresh vegetable stock or water
generous pinch of saffron threads
2 tbsp olive oil
1 medium onion, chopped
2 garlic cloves, crushed
1 lb arborio rice
2 lb pumpkin, peeled, seeded and cut into ¾ in cubes
¾ cup dry white wine
½ oz Parmesan cheese, finely grated
½ cup pistachios
3 tbsp chopped fresh marjoram or oregano, plus extra leaves, to garnish
salt, freshly grated nutmeg and ground black pepper

saffron

pumpkin

white wine

onion

garlic

marjoram

Parmesan

arborio rice

pistachios

1 Bring the stock or water to the boil and reduce to a low simmer. Ladle a little stock into a small bowl. Add the saffron threads and leave to infuse.

4 Gradually add the stock or water, a ladleful at a time, allowing the rice to absorb the liquid before adding more and stirring all the time. After 20–30 minutes the rice should be golden yellow and creamy, and *al dente* when tested.

2 Heat the oil in a large saucepan. Add the onion and garlic and cook gently for about 5 minutes until softened. Add the rice and pumpkin and cook for a few more minutes until the rice looks transparent.

3 Pour in the wine and allow it to bubble hard. When it is absorbed add ¼ of the stock and the infused saffron and liquid. Stir constantly until all the liquid is absorbed.

NUTRITIONAL NOTES
PER PORTION:

ENERGY 427 Kcals **FAT** 11.7 g
SATURATED FAT 2.4 g

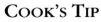 Stir in the Parmesan cheese, cover the pan and leave to stand for 5 minutes.

6 To finish, stir in the pistachios and marjoram or oregano. Season to taste with a little salt, nutmeg and pepper, and scatter over a few extra marjoram or oregano leaves.

COOK'S TIP
Italian arborio rice must be used to make an authentic risotto. Choose unpolished white arborio as it contains more starch.

Wild Rice Rösti with Carrot and Orange Purée

Rösti is a traditional dish from Switzerland. This variation has the extra nuttiness of wild rice and a bright simple sauce as a fresh accompaniment.

Serves 6

INGREDIENTS
½ cup wild rice
2 lb large potatoes
3 tbsp walnut oil
1 tsp yellow mustard seeds
1 onion, coarsely grated and drained
  in a sieve
2 tbsp fresh thyme leaves
salt and freshly ground black pepper

FOR THE PURÉE
12 oz carrots, peeled and roughly
  chopped
rind and juice of 1 large orange

onion

thyme

carrot

wild rice

potatoes

yellow mustard seeds

orange

COOK'S TIP
Make individual rösti and serve topped with a mixed julienne of vegetables for an unusual starter.

NUTRITIONAL NOTES
PER PORTION:

ENERGY 221 Kcals **FAT** 6.5 g
SATURATED FAT 0.7 g

1 For the purée, place the carrots in a pan, cover with cold water and add 2 pieces of orange rind. Bring to the boil and cook for 10 minutes or until tender. Drain well and discard the rind.

2 Purée the mixture in a blender with 4 tbsp of the orange juice. Return to the pan to reheat.

3 Place the wild rice in a clean pan and cover with water. Bring to the boil and cook for 30–40 minutes, until the rice is just starting to split, but still crunchy. Drain the rice.

4 Scrub the potatoes, place in a large pan and cover with cold water. Bring to the boil and cook for 10–15 minutes until just tender. Drain well and leave to cool slightly. When the potatoes are cool, peel and coarsely grate them into a large bowl. Add the cooked rice.

5 Heat 2 tbsp of the walnut oil in a non-stick frying pan and add the mustard seeds. When they start to pop, add the onion and cook gently for 5 minutes until softened. Add to the bowl of potato and rice, together with the thyme, and mix thoroughly. Season to taste with salt and pepper.

6 Heat the remaining oil in the frying pan and add the potato mixture. Press down well and cook for 10 minutes or until golden brown. Cover the pan with a plate and flip over, then slide the rösti back into the pan for another 10 minutes to cook the other side. Serve with the reheated carrot and orange purée.

Sweet Vegetable Couscous

A wonderful combination of sweet vegetables and spices, this makes a substantial winter dish.

Serves 4–6

INGREDIENTS

1 generous pinch of saffron threads
3 tbsp boiling water
1 tbsp olive oil
1 red onion, sliced
2 garlic cloves
1–2 fresh red chiles, seeded and finely chopped
½ tsp ground ginger
½ tsp ground cinnamon
14-oz can chopped tomatoes
1¼ cups fresh vegetable stock or water
4 medium carrots, peeled and cut into ¼-in slices
2 medium turnips, peeled and cut into ¾-in cubes
1 lb sweet potatoes, peeled and cut into ¾-in cubes
⅓ cup raisins
2 medium zucchini, cut into ¼-in slices
14-oz can chickpeas, drained and rinsed
3 tbsp chopped fresh parsley
3 tbsp chopped fresh cilantro
1 lb couscous

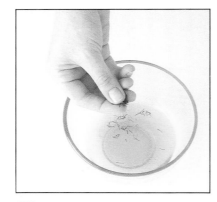

1 Leave the saffron to infuse in the boiling water.

2 Heat the oil in a large saucepan. Add the onion, garlic and chiles and cook gently for 5 minutes.

3 Add the ground ginger and cinnamon and cook for a further 1–2 minutes.

4 Add the tomatoes, stock or water, infused saffron and liquid, carrots, turnips, sweet potatoes and raisins, cover and simmer for 25 minutes.

red onion

zucchini

chickpeas

carrot

red chile

garlic

couscous

turnip

chopped tomatoes

raisins

sweet potato

5 Add the zucchini, chickpeas, parsley and cilantro and cook for another 10 minutes.

6 Meanwhile prepare the couscous following the packet instructions and serve with the vegetables.

NUTRITIONAL NOTES
Per portion:

ENERGY 402 Kcals **FAT** 5.2 g
SATURATED FAT 1.2 g

Vegetarian Cassoulet

Every town in south-west France has its own version of this popular classic. Warm French bread is all that is needed to complete this hearty vegetable version.

Serves 4–6

INGREDIENTS
2 cups dried white beans
1 bay leaf
2 onions
3 whole cloves
3 garlic cloves, crushed
1 tsp olive oil
2 leeks, thickly sliced
12 baby carrots
4 oz button mushrooms
14-oz can chopped tomatoes
1 tbsp tomato paste
1 tsp paprika
1 tbsp chopped fresh thyme
2 tbsp chopped fresh parsley
2 cups fresh white bread crumbs
salt and freshly ground black pepper

COOK'S TIP
If you're short on time use canned white beans—you'll need two 14-oz cans. Drain, reserving the bean liquid, and make up to 1⅔ cups with vegetable stock.

1 Soak the beans overnight in plenty of cold water. Drain and rinse under cold running water. Put them in a saucepan with 7½ cups of cold water and the bay leaf. Bring to a boil and cook rapidly for 10 minutes.

2 Peel one of the onions and spike with cloves. Add to the beans, and reduce the heat. Cover and simmer gently for 1 hour, until the beans are almost tender. Drain, reserving the stock but discarding the bay leaf and onion.

3 Chop the remaining onion and put it into a large flameproof casserole with the garlic cloves and olive oil. Cook gently for 5 minutes or until softened.

chopped tomatoes   *bay leaf*

bread crumbs   *leek*

carrots   *mushrooms*

4 Preheat the oven to 325°F. Add the leeks, carrots, mushrooms, chopped tomatoes, tomato paste, paprika, thyme and 1⅔ cups of the reserved stock to the casserole.

5 Bring to the boil, cover and simmer gently for 10 minutes. Stir in the cooked beans and parsley. Season to taste.

NUTRITIONAL NOTES

Per portion:

ENERGY 305.5 Kcals **PROTEIN** 18.8 g
FAT 3.33 g **SATURATED FAT** 0.58 g
CARBOHYDRATE 53.3 g
FIBER 16.33 g **SUGAR** 12.16 g
SODIUM 208.66 mg

6 Sprinkle with the breadcrumbs and bake uncovered in the pre-heated oven for 35 minutes, or until the topping is golden brown and crisp.

Chili Casserole

The contrasting textures of beans, vegetables and cornbread topping make this a memorable meal.

Serves 4

INGREDIENTS
1⅓ cups red kidney beans
1 bay leaf
1 large onion, finely chopped
1 garlic clove, crushed
2 celery stalks, sliced
1 tsp ground cumin
1 tsp chili powder
14-oz can chopped tomatoes
1 tbsp tomato paste
1 tsp dried mixed herbs
1 tbsp lemon juice
1 yellow bell pepper, seeded and sliced
salt and freshly ground black pepper
mixed salad, to serve

FOR THE CORNBREAD TOPPING
1½ cups corn meal
1 tbsp whole-wheat flour
1 tsp baking powder
1 egg, beaten
¾ cup skim milk

kidney beans

celery

tomato purée

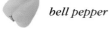
bell pepper

NUTRITIONAL NOTES
PER PORTION:

ENERGY 396.75 Kcals **PROTEIN** 22.73 g
FAT 4.67 g **SATURATED FAT** 0.65 g
CARBOHYDRATE 68.75
FIBER 11.9 g **SUGAR** 9.89 g
SODIUM 272 mg

1 Soak the beans overnight in cold water. Drain and rinse well. Pour 4 cups of water into a large heavy saucepan with the beans and bay leaf and boil rapidly for 10 minutes. Lower the heat, cover and simmer for 30–35 minutes or until the beans are tender.

2 Add the onions, garlic clove, celery, cumin, chili powder, chopped tomatoes, tomato paste and dried mixed herbs. Half-cover the pan with a lid, and simmer for another 10 minutes.

3 Stir in the lemon juice, yellow pepper and seasoning. Simmer for a further 8-10 minutes, stirring occasionally, until the vegetables are just tender. Discard the bay leaf and spoon the mixture into a large casserole.

4 Preheat the oven to 425°F. For the topping, put the corn meal, flour, baking powder a pinch of salt into a bowl and combine. Make a well in the center and add the egg and milk. Mix and pour over the bean mixture. Bake for 20 minutes or until brown.

Cheese and Onion Slice

This inexpensive supper dish is made substantial with the addition of porridge oats.

Serves 4

INGREDIENTS
2 large onions, thinly sliced
1 garlic clove, crushed
⅔ cup vegetable stock
3 cups rolled oats
1 cup grated Edam cheese
2 tbsp chopped fresh parsley
2 eggs, lightly beaten
1 medium potato, peeled
salt and freshly ground black pepper
coleslaw and tomatoes, halved,
    to serve

rolled oats

Edam cheese

eggs   *parsley*

onion

potato

NUTRITIONAL NOTES
PER SERVING:

CALORIES 436 **PROTEIN** 20.68 g
FAT 15.81 g **SATURATED FAT** 6.50 g
CARBOHYDRATE 56.38 g **FIBER** 6.18 g
ADDED SUGAR 0 **SODIUM** 1.05 g

1 Preheat the oven to 350°F. Line the base of a 8 in sandwich pie pan with non-stick baking paper. Put the onions, garlic clove and stock into a heavy-based saucepan and simmer until the stock has reduced entirely.

2 Spread the oats on a baking sheet and toast in the oven for 10 minutes. Mix with the onions, cheese, parsley, eggs, salt and freshly ground black pepper.

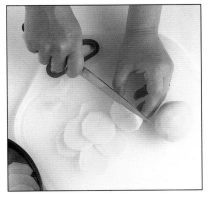

3 Thinly slice the potato and use it to line the base of the pan. Spoon in the oat mixture. Cover with a piece of foil.

4 Bake in the preheated oven for 35 minutes. Turn out onto a baking sheet and remove the lining paper. Put under a preheated hot broiler to brown the potatoes. Cut into wedges and serve hot with coleslaw and halved tomatoes.

Carrot Mousse with Mushroom Sauce

The combination of fresh vegetables in this impressive yet easy-to-make mousse makes healthy eating a pleasure.

NUTRITIONAL NOTES

PER PORTION:

ENERGY 179.75 Kcals **PROTEIN** 13.43 g
FAT 6.53 g **SATURATED FAT** 1.85 g
CARBOHYDRATE 17.77 g
FIBER 2.81 g **SUGAR** 11.29 g
SODIUM 170.73 mg

Serves 4

INGREDIENTS
12 oz carrots, roughly chopped
1 small red bell pepper, seeded and
    roughly chopped
3 tbsp vegetable stock or water
2 eggs
1 egg white
½ cup low fat cream cheese
1 tbsp chopped fresh tarragon
salt and freshly ground black pepper
sprig of fresh tarragon, to garnish
boiled rice and leeks, to serve

FOR THE MUSHROOM SAUCE
2 tbsp low fat margarine
6 oz mushrooms, sliced
2 tbsp flour
1 cup skim milk

carrots

egg white

bell pepper

eggs

mushrooms

flour

cream cheese

low fat margarine

1 Preheat the oven to 375°F. Line the bases of four ⅔-cup ramekins with non-stick baking paper. Put the carrots and pepper in a small saucepan with the vegetable stock or water. Cover and cook for 5 minutes or until tender. Drain well.

2 Lightly beat the eggs and egg white. Mix with the low fat cream cheese. Season to taste. Puree the cooked vegetables in a food processor or blender. Add the cheese mixture and process for a few more seconds until smooth. Stir in the chopped tarragon.

3 Divide the carrot mixture between the prepared ramekins and cover with foil. Place the dishes in a roasting pan filled with hot water. Bake in the pre-heated oven for 35 minutes or until set.

4 For the mushroom sauce, melt 1 tbsp of the low fat margarine in a frying pan. Add the mushrooms and gently saute for 5 minutes, until soft.

5 Put the remaining low fat margarine in a small saucepan together with the flour and milk. Cook over medium heat stirring constantly until the sauce thickens. Stir in the mushrooms and season to taste.

6 Transfer each mousse to a serving plate. Spoon on a little a sauce and serve the remainder separately. Garnish with a sprig of fresh tarragon and serve with boiled rice and leeks.

Ratatouille Crepes

These crepes are made slightly thicker than usual to hold the juicy vegetable filling.

Serves 4

INGREDIENTS
¾ cup flour
¼ cup oatmeal
1 egg
1¼ cups skim milk
mixed salad, to serve

FOR THE FILLING
1 large eggplant, cut into 1 in
    cubes
1 garlic clove, crushed
2 medium zucchini, sliced
1 green bell pepper, seeded and sliced
1 red bell pepper, seeded and sliced
5 tbsp vegetable stock
7 oz can chopped tomatoes
1 tsp cornstarch
salt and freshly ground black pepper

1 Sift the flour and a pinch of salt into a bowl. Stir in the oatmeal. Make a well in the center, add the egg and half the milk and mix to a smooth batter. Gradually beat in the remaining milk. Cover the bowl and leave to stand for 30 minutes.

2 Spray a 7 in crepe pan or heavy-based frying pan with non-stick cooking spray. Heat the pan, then pour in just enough batter to cover the base of the pan thinly. Cook for 2-3 minutes, until the underside is golden brown. Flip over and cook for a further 1-2 minutes.

zucchini

oatmeal

pepper

cornstarch

chopped tomatoes

eggplant

flour

egg

3 Slide the crepe out onto a plate lined with non-stick baking paper. Stack the other crepes on top as they are made, interleaving each with non-stick baking paper. Keep warm.

4 For the filling, put the eggplant in a colander and sprinkle well with salt. Leave to stand on a plate for 30 minutes. Rinse thoroughly and drain well.

5 Put the garlic clove, zucchini, peppers, stock and tomatoes into a large saucepan. Simmer uncovered and stir occasionally for 10 minutes. Add the eggplant and cook for a further 15 minutes. Blend the cornstarch with 2 tsp water and add to the saucepan. Simmer for 2 minutes. Season to taste.

NUTRITIONAL NOTES

Per serving:

CALORIES 182 **PROTEIN** 9.36 g
FAT 3.07 g **SATURATED FAT** 0.62 g
CARBOHYDRATE 31.40 g **FIBER** 4.73 g
ADDED SUGAR 0 **SODIUM** 0.22 g

6 Spoon the ratatouille mixture into the middle of each crepe. Fold each one in half, then in half again to make a cone shape. Serve hot with a mixed salad.

Vegetable Biryani

This exotic dish made from everyday ingredients will be appreciated by vegetarians and meat eaters alike.

Serves 4–6

NUTRITIONAL NOTES
PER PORTION:

ENERGY 152 Kcals **PROTEIN** 4.5 g
FAT 1.18 g **SATURATED FAT** 0.1 g
CARBOHYDRATE 34.16 g
FIBER 1.86 g **SUGAR** 3.22 g
SODIUM 0.05 mg

INGREDIENTS
1 cup long-grain rice
2 whole cloves
seeds of 2 cardamom pods
scant 2 cups vegetable stock
2 garlic cloves
1 small onion, roughly chopped
1 tsp cumin seeds
1 tsp ground coriander
½ tsp ground tumeric
½ tsp chili powder
1 large potato, peeled and cut into
　1-in cubes
2 carrots, sliced
½ cauliflower broken into florets
2 oz green beans, cut into 1-in
　lengths
2 tbsp chopped fresh cilantro
2 tbsp lime juice
salt and freshly ground black pepper
sprig of fresh cilantro to garnish

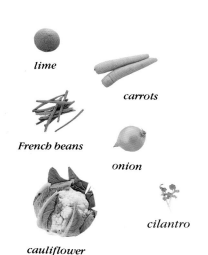

lime

carrots

French beans

onion

cilantro

cauliflower

1 Put the rice, cloves and cardamom seeds into a large, heavy saucepan. Pour on the stock and bring to a boil.

2 Reduce the heat, cover and simmer for 20 minutes, or until all the stock has been absorbed.

3 Meanwhile, put the garlic cloves, 1 onion, cumin seeds, coriander, tumeric, chili powder and seasoning into a blender or coffee grinder with 2 tbsp water. Blend to a paste.

4 Preheat the oven to 350°F. Spoon the spicy paste into a flameproof casserole and cook over low heat for 2 minutes, stirring occasionally.

5 Add the potato, carrots, cauliflower, beans and 6 tbsp of water. Cover and cook over low heat for another 12 minutes, stirring occasionally. Add the chopped cilantro.

6 Spoon the rice over the vegetables. Sprinkle on the lime juice. Cover and cook for 25 minutes or until the vegetables are tender. Fluff up the rice with a fork before serving, and garnish with a fresh sprig of cilantro.

Mixed Mushroom Ragout

These mushrooms are delicious served hot or cold and can be made up to two days in advance.

Serves 4

NUTRITIONAL NOTES
PER PORTION:

ENERGY 36 Kcals **PROTEIN** 2.25 g
FAT 0.63 g **SATURATED FAT** 0.07g
CARBOHYDRATE 4.92 g
FIBER 0.94 g **SUGAR** 4.04 g
SODIUM 32.75 mg

INGREDIENTS
1 small onion, finely chopped
1 garlic clove, crushed
1 tsp coriander seeds, crushed
2 tbsp red wine vinegar
1 tbsp soy sauce
1 tbsp dry sherry
2 tsp tomato paste
2 tsp light brown sugar
⅔ cup vegetable stock
4 oz button mushrooms
4 oz chestnut mushrooms, quartered
4 oz oyster mushrooms, sliced
salt and freshly ground black pepper
sprig of fresh cilantro, to garnish

oyster mushrooms

sherry

chestnut mushrooms

soy sauce

vinegar

coriander seeds

tomato paste   *garlic*

cilantro

button mushrooms

onion

1 Put the first nine ingredients into a large saucepan. Bring to the boil and reduce the heat. Cover and simmer for 5 minutes.

2 Uncover the saucepan and simmer for 5 more minutes, or until the liquid has reduced by half.

3 Add the baby button and chestnut mushrooms and simmer for 3 minutes. Stir in the oyster mushrooms and cook for a further 2 minutes.

4 Remove the mushrooms with a slotted spoon and transfer them to a serving dish.

5 Boil the juices for another 5 minutes or until reduced to about 5 tbsp. Season to taste.

6 Let cool for 2–3 minutes, then pour over the mushrooms. Serve hot or well chilled, garnished with a sprig of fresh cilantro.

Spicy Bean and Lentil Loaf

An appetizing, meat-free and high-fiber savory loaf, ideal for picnics or a packed lunch.

Serves 12

INGREDIENTS
2 teaspoons olive oil
1 onion, finely chopped
1 garlic clove, crushed
2 stalks celery, finely chopped
1 can (14 ounces) red kidney
  beans, rinsed and drained
1 can (14 ounces) lentils, rinsed
  and drained
1 egg
1 carrot, coarsely grated
½ cup hazelnuts, finely chopped
½ cup reduced-fat aged Cheddar
  cheese, finely grated,
1 cup fresh whole-wheat
  bread crumbs
1 tablespoon tomato paste
1 tablespoon ketchup
1 teaspoon each ground cumin,
  ground coriander and
  chili powder
salt and ground black pepper

olive oil   *onion*   *garlic*

celery

egg

red kidney beans   *lentils*

carrot   *hazelnuts*   *reduced-fat aged Cheddar cheese*

fresh whole-wheat bread crumbs   *tomato paste*

ketchup   *ground coriander*   *ground cumin*   *chili powder*

1 Preheat the oven to 350°F. Lightly grease a 2-pound loaf pan. Heat the oil in a saucepan, add the onion, garlic and celery and cook gently for 5 minutes, stirring occasionally. Remove the pan from the heat and cool slightly.

2 Rinse and drain the beans and lentils. Put in a blender or food processor with the onion mixture and egg and process until smooth.

3 Transfer the mixture to a bowl, add all the remaining ingredients and mix well. Season to taste.

4 Spoon the mixture into the prepared pan and level the surface. Bake for about 1 hour, then remove from the pan and serve hot or cold in slices.

NUTRITIONAL NOTES
PER PORTION:

CALORIES 119 PROTEIN 7.22g
FAT 4.85g SATURATED FAT 0.88g
CARBOHYDRATE 12.57g FIBER 3.31g
ADDED SUGAR 0.19g SODIUM 0.17g

Leek and Caraway Gratin with a Carrot Crust

Tender leeks are mixed with a creamy caraway sauce and a crunchy carrot topping.

Serves 4–6

INGREDIENTS
1½ lb leeks, cut into 2 in pieces
⅔ cup fresh vegetable stock or water
3 tbsp dry white wine
1 tsp caraway seeds
pinch of salt
1¼ cups skim milk, or as required
2 tbsp butter
¼ cup plain flour

FOR THE TOPPING
2 cups fresh wholewheat
  breadcrumbs
2 cups grated carrot
2 tbsp chopped fresh parsley
3 oz Jarlsberg cheese, coarsely grated
2 tbsp slivered almonds

parsley

vegetable stock

Jarlsberg

breadcrumbs

leek

butter

1 Place the leeks in a large pan. Add the stock or water, wine, caraway seeds and salt. Bring to a simmer, cover and cook for 5–7 minutes until the leeks are just tender.

2 With a slotted spoon, transfer the leeks to an ovenproof dish. Reduce the remaining liquid to half then make the amount up to 1½ cups with skim milk.

3 Preheat the oven to 350°F. Melt the butter in a saucepan, stir in the flour and cook without allowing it to color for 1–2 minutes. Gradually add the stock and milk, stirring well after each addition, until you have a smooth sauce. Simmer for 5–6 minutes then pour over the leeks in the dish.

4 Mix all the topping ingredients together in a bowl and sprinkle over the leeks. Bake for 20–25 minutes until golden.

NUTRITIONAL NOTES
PER PORTION:

ENERGY 194 Kcals **FAT** 8.52 g
SATURATED FAT 2.04 g

Vegetable and Macaroni Casserole

A tasty change from macaroni cheese, this recipe is delicious served with steamed fresh vegetables.

COOK'S TIP
Use another reduced-fat hard cheese such as Red Leicester or Double Gloucester in place of the Cheddar cheese.

Serves 6

INGREDIENTS
2¼ cups whole-wheat macaroni
2 cups sliced leeks
3 tablespoons vegetable stock
8 ounces broccoli florets
4 tablespoons reduced-fat spread
½ cup all-purpose whole-wheat
 flour
3¾ cups skim milk
1¼ cups grated reduced-fat
 aged Cheddar cheese
1 teaspoon prepared
 English mustard
1 can (11 ounces) corn kernels
salt and ground black pepper
½ cup fresh whole-wheat
 bread crumbs
2 tablespoons chopped fresh
 parsley
2 tomatoes, cut into eighths

wholewheat macaroni

leeks

vegetable stock

broccoli

reduced-fat spread

all-purpose whole-wheat flour

skim milk

reduced-fat aged Cheddar cheese

English mustard

fresh whole-wheat bread crumbs

corn

fresh parsley

tomatoes

1 Preheat the oven to 400°F. Cook the macaroni in lightly salted boiling water for about 10 minutes, until just tender, then drain and keep warm.

2 Cook the leeks in the stock for about 10 minutes, until tender, then strain and set aside. Blanch the broccoli for 2 minutes, drain and set aside.

3 Put the reduced-fat spread, flour and milk in a saucepan. Heat gently, whisking constantly, until the sauce comes to a boil and thickens. Simmer gently for 3 minutes, stirring.

4 Remove the pan from the heat, add 1 cup cheese and stir until melted and well blended.

5 Add the macaroni, leeks, broccoli, mustard, corn and seasoning and mix well. Transfer the mixture to an oven-proof dish.

6 Mix the remaining cheese, bread-crumbs and parsley together and sprinkle over the top. Arrange the tomatoes on top and then bake for 30–40 minutes, until golden brown and bubbling.

NUTRITIONAL NOTES
PER PORTION:

CALORIES 376 PROTEIN 23.30g
FAT 9.68g SATURATED FAT 3.82g
CARBOHYDRATE 52.34g FIBER 7.12g
ADDED SUGAR 0.01g SODIUM 0.53g

Zucchini, Corn and Plum Tomato Whole-wheat Pizza

This tasty whole-wheat pizza can be served hot or cold with a mixed bean salad and fresh crusty bread or baked potatoes. It is also ideal as a snack for the road.

NUTRITIONAL NOTES
PER PORTION:
CALORIES 291 PROTEIN 12.56g
FAT 12.35g SATURATED FAT 3.69g
CARBOHYDRATE 34.54g FIBER 4.93g
ADDED SUGAR 0.00g SODIUM 0.25g

Serves 6

INGREDIENTS
2 cups whole-wheat flour
pinch of salt
2 teaspoons baking powder
¼ cup polyunsaturated margarine
¾ cup skim milk
2 tablespoons tomato paste
2 teaspoons dried *herbes de Provence*
2 teaspoons olive oil
1 onion, sliced
1 garlic clove, crushed
2 small zucchini, sliced
1½ cups mushrooms, sliced
¾ cup frozen corn kernels
2 plum tomatoes, sliced
½ cup reduced-fat Cheddar cheese, finely grated
½ cup mozzarella cheese, finely grated
salt and ground black pepper
basil sprigs, to garnish

1 Preheat the oven to 425°F. Line a baking sheet with nonstick baking paper. Put the flour, salt and baking powder in a bowl and rub the margarine lightly into the flour until the mixture resembles bread crumbs.

2 Add enough milk to form a soft dough and knead lightly. On a lightly floured surface, roll the dough out to a circle about 10 inches in diameter.

3 Place the dough on the prepared baking sheet and pinch the edges until they are slightly thicker than the center. Spread the tomato paste over the base and sprinkle the herbs on top.

4 Heat the oil in a frying pan, add the onion, garlic, zucchini and mushrooms and cook gently, stirring occasionally, for 10 minutes.

5 Spread the vegetable mixture over the pizza crust and sprinkle with the corn and seasoning. Arrange the tomato slices on top.

polyunsaturated margarine *skim milk* *tomato paste*

dried herbes de Provence *olive oil* *onion*

 garlic

whole-wheat flour *salt* *baking powder*

mushrooms *plum tomatoes* *reduced-fat Cheddar cheese* *mozzarella cheese*

zucchini *corn*

6 Mix together the cheeses and sprinkle over the pizza. Bake for 25–30 minutes, until cooked and golden brown. Serve the pizza hot or cold in slices, garnished with basil sprigs.

COOK'S TIP
This pizza is ideal for freezing in portions or slices. Freeze for up to 3 months.

Vegetable Paella

A delicious change from the more traditional seafood-based paella, this recipe is full of flavor and nutrients, including fiber.

Serves 6

INGREDIENTS
1 onion, chopped
2 garlic cloves, crushed
8 ounces leeks (trimmed weight), washed and sliced
3 stalks celery, chopped
1 red bell pepper, seeded and sliced
2 zucchini, sliced
6 ounces crimini mushrooms, sliced
1½ cups frozen peas
2 cups long grain brown rice
1 can (14 ounces) cannellini beans, rinsed and drained
3¾ cups vegetable stock
4 tablespoons dry white wine
few saffron strands
2 cups cherry tomatoes, halved
3–4 tablespoons chopped fresh mixed herbs
salt and ground black pepper
lemon wedges and celery leaves, to garnish

onion garlic leeks
celery
red pepper
zucchini
cannellini beans vegetable stock dry white wine
crimini mushrooms frozen peas brown rice
saffron strands cherry tomatoes
fresh mixed herbs salt black pepper

1 Put the onion, garlic, leeks, celery, pepper, zucchini and mushrooms in a large saucepan and mix together.

2 Add the peas, rice, cannellini beans, stock, wine and saffron.

3 Bring to the boil, stirring, then simmer uncovered for about 35 minutes, until almost all the liquid has been absorbed and the rice is tender, stirring occasionally.

4 Stir in the tomatoes, chopped herbs and seasoning. Serve garnished with lemon wedges and celery leaves.

NUTRITIONAL NOTES

PER PORTION:

CALORIES 416 PROTEIN 13.69g
FAT 3.95g SATURATED FAT 0.86g
CARBOHYDRATE 84.87g FIBER 8.85g
ADDED SUGAR 0.03g SODIUM 0.54g

Vegetable Chili

This alternative to traditional chili con carne is delicious served with brown rice.

Serves 4

INGREDIENTS
2 onions, chopped
1 garlic clove, crushed
3 stalks celery, chopped
1 green bell pepper, seeded and
  diced
8 ounces mushrooms, sliced
2 zucchini, diced
1 can (14 ounces) red kidney
  beans, rinsed and drained
1 can (14 ounces) chopped
  tomatoes
⅔ cup strained tomatoes
2 tablespoons tomato paste
1 tablespoon ketchup
1 teaspoon chili powder, ground
  cumin and ground coriander
salt and ground black pepper
cilantro sprigs, to garnish
plain yogurt and cayenne pepper,
  to serve

onions *garlic*

*green
pepper* *mushrooms* *celery*

zucchini

*red kidney
beans* *chopped
tomatoes*

*strained
tomatoes*

ketchup

*chili
powder*

*tomato
paste*

*ground
cumin* *ground
coriander*

1 Put the onions, garlic, celery, pepper, mushrooms and zucchini in a large saucepan and mix together.

2 Add the kidney beans, chopped and strained tomatoes, tomato paste and ketchup.

3 Add the spices and seasoning and mix well.

4 Cover, bring to a boil and simmer, stirring occasionally, for 20–30 minutes, until the vegetables are tender. Garnish with cilantro sprigs. Serve with plain yogurt, sprinkled with cayenne pepper.

NUTRITIONAL NOTES

PER PORTION:

CALORIES 158 PROTEIN 9.96g
FAT 1.59g SATURATED FAT 0.27g
CARBOHYDRATE 27.55g FIBER 8.58g
ADDED SUGAR 0.57g SODIUM 0.39g

Sweet and Sour Mixed Bean Hot-pot

An appetizing mixture of beans and vegetables in a tasty sweet and sour sauce, topped with potato.

Serves 6

INGREDIENTS
1 pound unpeeled potatoes
1 tablespoon olive oil
3 tablespoons reduced-fat spread
¼ cup whole-wheat flour
1¼ cups strained tomatoes
⅔ cup unsweetened apple juice
4 tablespoons each light brown
  sugar, ketchup, dry sherry,
  cider vinegar and light soy sauce
1 can (14 ounces) lima beans
1 can (14 ounces) red kidney beans
1 can (14 ounces) cannellini beans
1 can (14 ounces) chickpeas
6 ounces green beans, chopped
  and blanched
8 ounces shallots, sliced and
  blanched
3 cups mushrooms, sliced
1 tablespoon each chopped fresh
  thyme and marjoram
salt and ground black pepper
fresh herb sprigs, to garnish

1 Preheat the oven to 400°F. Thinly slice the potatoes and parboil them for 4 minutes. Drain thoroughly, toss them in the oil so they are lightly coated all over and set aside.

2 Place the reduced-fat spread, flour, strained tomatoes, apple juice, sugar, ketchup, sherry, vinegar and soy sauce in a saucepan. Heat gently, whisking constantly, until the sauce comes to a boil and thickens. Simmer gently, stirring, for 3 minutes.

3 Rinse and drain the beans and chick-peas and add to the sauce with all the remaining ingredients, except the herb garnish. Mix well.

potatoes

olive oil

reduced-fat spread

all-purpose whole-wheat flour

strained tomatoes

unsweetened apple juice

light brown sugar

ketchup

dry sherry

cider vinegar

light soy sauce

lima beans

red kidney beans

cannellini beans

chick-peas

green beans

shallots

mushrooms

fresh thyme

fresh marjoram

4 Spoon the bean mixture into a casserole.

5 Arrange the potato slices over the top, completely covering the bean mixture.

6 Cover the dish with foil and bake for about 1 hour, until the potatoes are cooked and tender. Remove the foil for the last 20 minutes of the cooking time, to lightly brown the potatoes. Serve garnished with fresh herb sprigs.

NUTRITIONAL NOTES
PER PORTION:

CALORIES 410 PROTEIN 17.36g
FAT 7.43g SATURATED FAT 1.42g
CARBOHYDRATE 70.40g FIBER 12.52g
ADDED SUGAR 15.86g SODIUM 1.54g

NUTRITIONAL NOTES
PER PORTION:

ENERGY 484 Kcals **FAT** 10.9 g
SATURATED FAT 1.5 g

Pasta Shells with Tomatoes and Arugula

This pretty-colored pasta dish relies for its success on a salad green called arugula. Available in large supermarkets, it is a leaf easily grown in the garden or a window box and tastes slightly peppery.

Serves 4

INGREDIENTS
1 lb shell pasta
salt and pepper
1 lb very ripe cherry tomatoes
3 tbsp olive oil
3 oz fresh arugula
Parmesan cheese

olive oil

pasta shells

cherry tomatoes

Parmesan cheese

arugula

1 Cook the pasta in plenty of boiling salted water according to the manufacturer's instructions. Drain well.

2 Halve the tomatoes. Trim, wash, and dry the arugula.

3 Heat the oil in a large saucepan, add the tomatoes and cook for barely 1 minute. The tomatoes should only just heat through and not disintegrate.

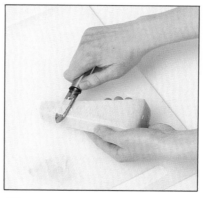

4 Shave the Parmesan cheese using a rotary vegetable peeler.

5 Add the pasta, then the arugula. Carefully stir to mix and heat through. Season well with salt and freshly ground black pepper. Serve immediately with plenty of shaved Parmesan cheese.

Pasta, Asparagus and Fava Beans with Creamy Pea Sauce

A creamy pea sauce makes a wonderful combination with crunchy young vegetables.

Serves 4

INGREDIENTS
1 tbsp olive oil
1 garlic clove, crushed
6 scallions, sliced
1 cup fresh or frozen baby peas, defrosted
12 oz fresh young asparagus
2 tbsp chopped fresh sage, plus extra leaves, to garnish
finely grated zest of 2 lemons
1¾ cups fresh vegetable stock or water
8 oz fresh or frozen fava beans, defrosted
1 lb tagliatelle
4 tbsp low fat yogurt

lemon

garlic

asparagus

fava beans

peas

yogurt

tagliatelle

sage

scallions

1 Heat the oil in a pan. Add the garlic and scallions and cook gently for 2–3 minutes until softened.

2 Add the peas and ⅓ of the asparagus, together with the sage, lemon zest and stock or water. Bring to a boil, reduce the heat and simmer for 10 minutes, until tender. Purée in a blender until smooth.

3 Meanwhile remove the outer skins from the fava beans and discard.

4 Cut the remaining asparagus into 2-in lengths, trimming off any tough fibrous stems, and blanch in boiling water for 2 minutes.

5 Cook the tagliatelle following the instructions on the side of the packet until *al dente*. Drain well.

NUTRITIONAL NOTES

PER PORTION:

CALORIES 522 **FAT** 6.9 g
SATURATED FAT 0.9 g **PROTEIN** 23.8 g
CARBOHYDRATE 97.1 g **FIBER** 11.2 g

COOK'S TIP

Frozen peas and beans have been used here to cut down the preparation time, but the dish tastes even better if you use fresh young vegetables when in season.

6 Add the cooked asparagus and shelled beans to the sauce and reheat. Stir in the yogurt and toss into the tagliatelle. Garnish with a few extra sage leaves and serve.

Pasta Primavera

Serves 4

INGREDIENTS
8 ounces thin asparagus spears, cut in half
4 ounces snow peas, trimmed
4 ounces whole baby corn
8 ounces whole baby carrots, trimmed
1 small red bell pepper, seeded and chopped
8 scallions, sliced
8 ounces torchietti or rotini
$2/3$ cup low-fat cottage cheese
$2/3$ cup low-fat yogurt
1 tablespoon lemon juice
1 tablespoon chopped parsley
1 tablespoon snipped chives
skim milk (optional)
salt and ground black pepper
sun-dried tomato bread, to serve

scallions

red pepper

baby corn

parsley

baby carrots

lemon

chives

torchietti

snow peas

asparagus spears

low-fat yogurt

low-fat cottage cheese

1 Cook the asparagus spears in a pan of boiling, salted water for 3–4 minutes. Add the snow peas halfway through the cooking time. Drain and rinse both under cold water.

2 Cook the baby corn, carrots, red pepper and spring onions in the same way until tender. Drain and rinse.

3 Cook the pasta in a large pan of boiling, salted water until *al dente*. Drain thoroughly.

NUTRITIONAL NOTES
PER PORTION:

ENERGY 320 calories **FAT** 3.1g
SATURATED FAT 0.4g **CHOLESTEROL** 3mg
CARBOHYDRATE 58g **FIBER** 6.2g

4 Put the cottage cheese, yogurt, lemon juice, parsley, chives and seasoning into a food processor or blender and process until smooth. Thin the sauce with skim milk, if necessary. Put into a large pan with the pasta and vegetables, heat gently and toss carefully. Transfer to a serving plate and serve with sun-dried tomato bread.

Tagliatelle with Mushrooms

Serves 4

INGREDIENTS

1 small onion, finely chopped
2 garlic cloves, crushed
²/₃ cup vegetable stock
8 ounces mixed fresh mushrooms, such as button, oyster, or chanterelles
4 tablespoons white or red wine
2 teaspoons tomato paste
1 tablespoon soy sauce
1 teaspoon chopped fresh thyme
2 tablespoons chopped fresh parsley
8 ounces fresh sun-dried tomato and herb tagliatelle
salt and ground black pepper
shavings of Parmesan cheese, to serve (optional)

tomato paste *Parmesan cheese* *onion*

mixed mushrooms

thyme *parsley*

vegetable stock

garlic

white wine *tagliatelle*

soy sauce

1 Put the onion and garlic into a pan with the stock. Then cover and cook for 5 minutes or until tender.

2 Add the mushrooms (quartered or sliced if large or left whole if small), wine, tomato paste and soy sauce. Cover and cook for 5 minutes.

3 Remove the lid from the pan and boil until the liquid has reduced by half. Stir in the chopped fresh herbs and season to taste.

4 Cook the pasta in a large pan of boiling, salted water until *al dente*. Drain thoroughly and toss lightly with the mushrooms. Serve at once with shavings of Parmesan cheese, if using.

NUTRITIONAL NOTES

PER PORTION:

ENERGY 241 calories **FAT** 2.4g
SATURATED FAT 0.7g **CHOLESTEROL** 3mg
CARBOHYDRATE 45g **FIBER** 3g

Vegetarian Lasagne

Serves 6–8

INGREDIENTS

1 small eggplant
1 large onion, finely chopped
2 garlic cloves, crushed
$^2/_3$ cup vegetable stock
8 ounces mushrooms, sliced
14 ounce can chopped tomatoes
2 tablespoons tomato paste
$^2/_3$ cup red wine
$^1/_4$ teaspoon ground ginger
1 teaspoon mixed dried herbs
10–12 sheets lasagne
1 ounce low-fat margarine
1 ounce flour
$1^1/_4$ cups skim milk
large pinch of grated nutmeg
7 ounces low-fat cottage cheese
1 egg, beaten
$^1/_2$ ounce grated Parmesan cheese
1 ounce reduced-fat Cheddar
    cheese, grated
salt and ground black pepper

1 Wash the eggplant and cut it into 1-inch cubes. Put the onion and garlic into a saucepan with the stock, cover and cook for about 5 minutes or until tender.

2 Add the diced eggplant, sliced mushrooms, tomatoes, tomato paste, wine, ginger, seasoning and herbs. Bring to a boil, cover and cook for 15–20 minutes. Remove the lid and cook rapidly to reduce the liquid by half.

3 To make the sauce, put the margarine, flour, skim milk and nutmeg into a pan. Whisk together over the heat until thickened and smooth. Season to taste.

egg
garlic
eggplant
mushrooms
tomato paste
vegetable stock
lasagne
Parmesan cheese
red wine
onion
low-fat cottage cheese
chopped tomatoes
nutmeg
reduced-fat Cheddar cheese
skim milk
flour
low-fat margarine

NUTRITIONAL NOTES

PER PORTION:

ENERGY 428 calories **FAT** 7.2g
SATURATED FAT 1.4g **CHOLESTEROL** 50mg
CARBOHYDRATE 69g **FIBER** 4.7g

4 Preheat the oven to 400°F. Spoon about a quarter of the vegetable mixture into the base of a 12 x 8 x 2 inch ovenproof dish. Cover with a layer of lasagne noodles and a quarter of the sauce.

5 Repeat with two more layers, then cover with the cottage cheese. Beat the egg into the remaining sauce and pour over the top. Sprinkle with the two grated cheeses.

6 Bake for 25–30 minutes or until the top is golden brown.

Crescent Spinach Ravioli

Serves 4–6

INGREDIENTS
1 bunch of scallions, finely chopped
1 carrot, coarsely grated
2 garlic cloves, crushed
7 ounces low-fat cottage cheese
1 tablespoon chopped dill
4 halves sun-dried tomatoes,
    finely chopped
1 ounce grated Parmesan cheese
1 recipe basic pasta dough, with
    4 ounces frozen spinach, thawed
    and chopped added
egg white, beaten, for brushing
flour, for dusting
salt and ground black pepper
2 halves sun-dried tomatoes, finely
    chopped, and fresh dill,
    to garnish

carrot

*sun-dried
tomatoes*

dill

garlic

scallions

*Parmesan
cheese*

spinach

*low-fat
cottage cheese*

1 Put the scallions, carrot, garlic and cottage cheese into a bowl. Add the chopped dill, tomatoes, seasoning and Parmesan cheese.

2 Roll the spinach pasta into thin sheets, cut into 3-inch rounds with a fluted pastry cutter.

3 Place a small spoonful of filling in the center of each circle. Brush the edges with egg white.

4 Fold each in half to make crescents. Press the edges together to seal. Transfer to a floured dish towel to rest for 1 hour before cooking. Makes about 80 crescents.

5 Cook the pasta in a large pan of boiling, salted water for 5 minutes (cook in batches to stop them sticking together). Drain well.

6 Put the crescents on to warmed serving plates and garnish with sun-dried tomatoes and dill.

NUTRITIONAL NOTES
PER PORTION:

ENERGY 312 calories **FAT** 7.3g
SATURATED FAT 2.4g **CHOLESTEROL** 119mg
CARBOHYDRATE 43g **FIBER** 3.4g

Vegetarian Cannelloni

Serves 4–6

INGREDIENTS
1 onion, finely chopped
2 garlic cloves, crushed
2 carrots, coarsely grated
2 stalks celery, finely chopped
²⁄₃ cup vegetable stock
4 ounces red or green lentils
14-ounce can chopped tomatoes
2 tablespoons tomato paste
½ teaspoon ground ginger
1 teaspoon fresh thyme
1 teaspoon chopped fresh rosemary
1½ ounces low fat margarine
1½ ounces flour
2½ cups skim milk
1 bay leaf
large pinch grated nutmeg
16–18 cannelloni tubes
1 ounce reduced-fat Cheddar
    cheese, grated
1 ounce grated Parmesan cheese
1 ounce fresh white bread crumbs
salt and ground black pepper
flat-leaf parsley, to garnish

1 To make the filling put the onion, garlic, carrots and celery into a large saucepan, add half the stock, cover and cook for 5 minutes or until tender.

2 Add the lentils, chopped tomatoes, tomato paste, ginger, thyme, rosemary and seasoning. Bring to a boil, cover and cook for 20 minutes. Remove the lid and cook for about 10 minutes until thick and soft. Let cook.

3 To make the sauce, put the margarine, flour, skim milk and bay leaf into a pan and whisk over the heat until thick and smooth. Season with salt, pepper and nutmeg. Discard the bay leaf.

flour

low fat margarine

reduced-fat Cheddar cheese

onion   *garlic*   *celery*
              rosemary

white bread crumbs

bay leaf   *thyme*

carrots

nutmeg

red lentils

Parmesan cheese

skim milk

cannelloni tubes

chopped tomatoes   *vegetable stock*   *tomato paste*

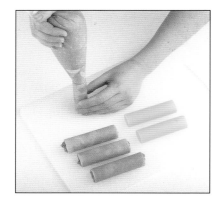

4 Fill the uncooked cannelloni by piping the filling into each tube. (It is easiest to hold them upright with one end flat on a board, while piping into the other end.)

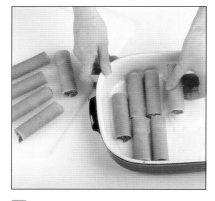

5 Preheat the oven to 350°F. Spoon half the sauce into the bottom of an 8-inch square ovenproof dish. Lay two rows of filled cannelloni on top and spoon over the remaining sauce.

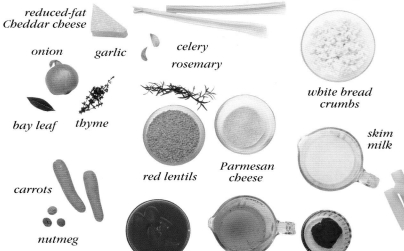

6 Top with the cheeses and bread crumbs. Bake in the preheated oven for 30–40 minutes. Place under broiler to brown the top, if necessary. Garnish with flat-leaf parsley.

NUTRITIONAL NOTES

PER PORTION:

ENERGY 579 calories **FAT** 9.8g
SATURATED FAT 2.7g **CHOLESTEROL** 13mg
CARBOHYDRATE 100g **FIBER** 5.7g

Tofu Stir-fry with Egg Noodles

Serves 4

INGREDIENTS

8 ounces firm tofu
3 tablespoons dark soy sauce
2 tablespoons sherry or vermouth
3 leeks, sliced thinly
1-inch piece fresh ginger, peeled and finely grated
1–2 red chilies, seeded and sliced in rings
1 small red bell pepper, seeded and sliced thinly
2/3 cup vegetable stock
2 teaspoons honey
2 teaspoons cornstarch
8 ounces medium egg noodles
salt and ground black pepper

leeks

egg noodles   *fresh ginger*   *tofu*

red chilies   *red bell pepper*

soy sauce   *vegetable stock*   *vermouth*

1 Cut the tofu into ¾-inch cubes. Put it into a bowl with the soy sauce and the sherry or vermouth. Toss to coat each piece and marinate for about 30 minutes.

2 Put the leeks, ginger, chili, pepper and stock into a frying pan. Bring to a boil and cook quickly for 2–3 minutes until just soft.

3 Strain the tofu, reserving the marinade. Mix the honey and cornstarch into the marinade.

4 Put the egg noodles into a large pan of boiling water and leave to stand for about 6 minutes until cooked (or follow the instructions on the packet).

5 Heat a non-stick frying pan and quickly fry the tofu until lightly golden brown on all sides.

6 In a saucepan, add the vegetable mixture to the tofu with the marinade, and stir well until the liquid is thick and glossy. Spoon on to the egg noodles and serve at once.

NUTRITIONAL NOTES

PER PORTION:

ENERGY 345 calories **FAT** 8.2g
SATURATED FAT 0.7g **CHOLESTEROL** 0mg
CARBOHYDRATE 55g **FIBER** 2.5g

Ratatouille Penne Bake

Serves 6

INGREDIENTS

1 small eggplant
2 zucchini, thickly sliced
7 ounces firm tofu, cubed
3 tablespoons dark soy sauce
1 garlic clove, crushed
2 teaspoons sesame seeds
1 small red bell pepper, seeded
    and sliced
1 onion, finely chopped
1–2 garlic cloves, crushed
²/₃ cup vegetable stock
3 firm ripe tomatoes, peeled, seeded
    and quartered
1 tablespoon chopped mixed herbs
8 ounces penne
salt and ground black pepper
crusty bread, to serve

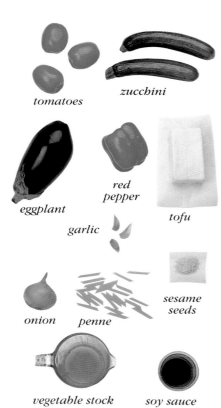

tomatoes   zucchini

eggplant   red pepper   tofu

garlic

onion   penne   sesame seeds

vegetable stock   soy sauce

1 Wash and cut the eggplant into 1-inch cubes. Put into a colander with the zucchini, sprinkle with salt and leave to drain for 30 minutes.

2 Mix the tofu with the soy sauce, garlic and sesame seeds. Cover and marinate for 30 minutes.

NUTRITIONAL NOTES

PER PORTION:

ENERGY 208 calories **FAT** 3.7g
SATURATED FAT 0.5g **CHOLESTEROL** 0mg
CARBOHYDRATE 36g **FIBER** 3.9g

3 Put the pepper, onion and garlic into a saucepan, with the stock. Bring to the boil, cover and cook for 5 minutes until tender. Remove the lid and boil until all the stock has evaporated. Add the tomatoes and herbs and cook for a further 3 minutes. Season to taste.

4 Meanwhile cook the pasta in a large pan of boiling, salted water until *al dente*. Drain thoroughly. Toss the pasta with the vegetables and tofu. Transfer to a shallow 10-inch square ovenproof dish and grill until lightly browned. Transfer to a serving dish and serve with fresh crusty bread.

Fettuccine with Broccoli and Garlic

Serves 4

INGREDIENTS

3–4 garlic cloves, crushed
12 ounces broccoli florets
$2/3$ cup chicken stock
4 tablespoons white wine
2 tablespoons chopped fresh basil
4 tablespoons grated
   Parmesan cheese
12 ounces fettuccine or tagliatelle
salt and pepper
fresh basil leaves, to garnish

garlic

broccoli

basil

white wine

fettuccine

chicken stock

grated Parmesan cheese

1 Put the garlic, broccoli and stock into a saucepan. Bring to the boil and cook for 5 minutes until tender, stirring from time to time.

2 Mash with a fork or potato masher, until roughly chopped. Return to the pan with the white wine, basil and Parmesan cheese. Season to taste.

NUTRITIONAL NOTES

PER PORTION:

ENERGY 477 calories **FAT** 8.3g
SATURATED FAT 3.4g **CHOLESTEROL** 15mg
CARBOHYDRATE 71g **FIBER** 5g

3 Cook the fettuccine in a large pan of boiling, salted water until *al dente*. Drain thoroughly.

4 Return to the pan with half the broccoli sauce, toss to coat the pasta and transfer to serving plates. Top with the remaining broccoli sauce and garnish with basil leaves.

Salsas, Salads & Side Dishes

Tomato Salsas

Salsa is Spanish for sauce, but elsewhere it has come to mean a side dish of finely chopped vegetables or fruits, which really enhances the meals it accompanies.

Serves 6

INGREDIENTS

6 medium tomatoes
1 green chile
2 scallions, chopped
4 in length cucumber, peeled and
  diced
2 tbsp lemon juice
2 tbsp fresh cilantro, chopped
1 tbsp fresh parsley, chopped
salt and pepper

tomatoes

basil

orange bell pepper

parsley

lemon

scallions

cilantro   *garlic*

cucumber

capers

green chile

1 Cut a small cross in the stalk end of each tomato. Place in a bowl and cover with boiling water.

2 After 30 seconds or as soon as the skins split, drain and plunge into cold water. Gently slide off the skins. Quarter the tomatoes, remove the seeds and dice the flesh.

3 Halve the chile, remove the stalk, seeds and membrane, and chop finely.

4 Combine all the ingredients and transfer to a serving bowl Chill for 1–2 hours before serving.

NUTRITIONAL NOTES
PER PORTION:

CALORIES 14 **FAT** 0.3 g
SATURATED FAT 0 **PROTEIN** 0.8 g
CARBOHYDRATE 2.4 g **FIBER** 0.9 g

VARIATIONS

Tomato and Caper Salsa:
Prepare the tomatoes and stir in
the onion and lemon juice. Add
six torn sprigs of basil and 1 tbsp
coarsely chopped capers. Season
to taste.

Tomato and Roast Pepper Salsa:
Prepare 4 tomatoes and stir in
the chile, onion and herbs. Add
a roasted, peeled and a crushed
garlic clove. Season to taste.

Roasted Bell Pepper and Ginger Salsa

Broiling to remove the skins will take away any bitterness from the peppers.

Serves 6

NUTRITIONAL NOTES
PER PORTION:

CALORIES 33 **FAT** 0.6 g
SATURATED FAT 0 **PROTEIN** 1.4 g
CARBOHYDRATE 5.9 g **FIBER** 1.6 g

INGREDIENTS
1 large red bell pepper
1 large yellow bell pepper
1 large orange bell pepper
1 in piece fresh ginger
1/2 tsp coriander seeds
1 tsp cumin seeds
1 small garlic clove
2 tbsp lime or lemon juice
1 small red onion, finely chopped
2 tbsp chopped fresh cilantro
1 tsp chopped fresh thyme
salt and pepper

red pepper

thyme

yellow pepper

coriander and cumin seeds

garlic

orange pepper

lime

ginger

cilantro

1 Quarter the peppers and remove the stalk, seeds and membranes.

2 Grill the quarters, skin side up, until charred and blistered. Rub away the skins and slice very finely.

3 Peel or scrape the root ginger and chop roughly.

4 Over a moderate heat, gently dry-fry the spices for 30 seconds to 1 minute, making sure they don't scorch.

5 Crush the spices in a pestle and mortar. Add the ginger and garlic and continue to work to a pulp. Work in the lime or lemon juice.

6 Mix together the peppers, spice mixture, onion and herbs. Season to taste and spoon into a serving bowl. Chill for 1–2 hours before serving as an accompaniment to barbecued meats or kebabs.

Mango and Red Onion Salsa

A very simple salsa, which is livened up by the addition of passion-fruit pulp.

NUTRITIONAL NOTES

PER PORTION:

CALORIES 61 **FAT** 0.3 g
SATURATED FAT 0 **PROTEIN** 1.1 g
CARBOHYDRATE 14.5 g **FIBER** 2.9 g

Serves 4

INGREDIENTS
1 large ripe mango
1 red onion
2 passion fruit
6 large fresh basil leaves
juice of 1 lime, to taste
sea salt

mango   *red onion*

passion fruit   *basil*

lime juice

1 Holding the mango upright on a chopping board, use a large knife to slice the flesh away from either side of the large flat stone in two portions.

2 Using a smaller knife, trim away any flesh still clinging to the top and bottom of the stone.

3 Score the flesh of the mango halves deeply, taking care to avoid cutting through the skin. Make parallel incisions about ½ in apart; turn and cut lines in the opposite direction. Carefully turn the skin inside out so the flesh stands out like porcupine spikes. Slice the dice away from the skin.

4 Finely chop the red onion and place it in a bowl with the mango.

5 Halve the passion fruit, scoop out the seeds and pulp, and add to the mango mixture.

6 Tear the basil leaves coarsely and stir them into the salsa with lime juice and a little sea salt to taste. Serve immediately.

VARIATION
Corn kernels are a delicious addition to this salsa.

Tuna, Chickpea and Cherry Tomato Salad

A quick and easy salad that makes a satisfying light meal when served with thick slices of whole-wheat bread.

NUTRITIONAL NOTES
PER PORTION:

CALORIES 198 PROTEIN 20.98g
FAT 4.30g SATURATED FAT 0.62g
CARBOHYDRATE 20.70g FIBER 5.88g
ADDED SUGAR 0.00g SODIUM 0.45g

Serves 6

INGREDIENTS
1 teaspoon olive oil
1 garlic clove, crushed
1 teaspoon ground coriander
1 teaspoon garam masala
1 teaspoon chili powder
½ cup tomato juice
2 tablespoons balsamic vinegar
dash of Tabasco sauce
1½ pounds cherry tomatoes, halved
½ cucumber, sliced
1 bunch radishes, sliced
1 bunch scallions, chopped
2 ounces watercress, chopped
2 cans (14 ounces) chickpeas,
  rinsed and drained
2 cans (14 ounces) tuna in water,
  drained and flaked
1 tablespoon chopped fresh parsley
1 tablespoon chopped fresh chives
salt and ground black pepper

1 Heat the oil in a small saucepan. Add the garlic and spices and cook gently for 1 minute, stirring.

2 Stir in the tomato juice, vinegar and Tabasco sauce, and heat gently until the mixture is boiling. Remove the pan from the heat and set aside to cool slightly.

3 Put the tomatoes and cucumber in a serving bowl.

olive oil   garlic   ground coriander   garam masala   chili powder   tomato juice

balsamic vinegar   Tabasco sauce   cherry tomatoes   cucumber   radishes   scallions

watercress   chick-peas   tuna   fresh parsley   fresh chives

4 Add the radishes, scallions and watercress.

5 Stir in the chick-peas, the tuna and the herbs.

6 Pour the tomato dressing over the salad and toss the ingredients together to mix. Season to taste and serve.

Apple Coleslaw

The term coleslaw stems from the Dutch *koolsla*, meaning 'cool cabbage'. There are many variations of this salad; this recipe combines the sweet flavors of apple and carrot with celery salt. Coleslaw is traditionally served with cold ham.

Serves 4

INGREDIENTS
1 lb white cabbage
1 medium onion
2 apples, peeled and cored
6 oz carrots, peeled
⅔ cup mayonnaise
1 tsp celery salt
black pepper

carrots

onion

apple

white cabbage

NUTRITIONAL NOTES
Per portion:
ENERGY 91 Kcals **FAT** 3.9 g
SATURATED FAT 0.09 g

COOK'S TIP

This recipe can be easily adapted to suit different tastes. You could add ½ cup chopped walnuts or raisins for added texture. For a richer coleslaw, add ½ cup grated Cheddar cheese. You may find you will need smaller portions, as the cheese makes a more filling dish.

1 Discard the outside leaves of the cabbage if they are dirty, cut the cabbage into 2 in wedges, then remove the stem section.

2 Feed the cabbage and the onion through a food processor fitted with a slicing blade. Change to a grating blade and grate the apples and carrots. Alternatively use a hand grater and vegetable slicer.

3 Combine the salad ingredients in a large bowl. Fold in the mayonnaise and season with celery salt and freshly ground black pepper.

Carrot, Raisin and Apricot Coleslaw

A tasty, high-fiber coleslaw, combining cabbage, carrots and dried fruit in a light yogurt dressing.

Serves 6

INGREDIENTS
3 cups finely shredded white
  cabbage
1½ cups coarsely grated carrots
1 red onion, sliced
3 celery stalks, sliced
1 cup raisins
3 ounces dried apricots, chopped
8 tablespoons reduced-calorie
  mayonnaise
6 tablespoons low-fat plain yogurt
2 tablespoons chopped fresh
  mixed herbs
salt and ground black pepper

*white
cabbage*

carrots

*red
onion*

celery

raisins

*dried
apricots*

*low-fat plain
yogurt*

*reduced-calorie
mayonnaise*

*fresh mixed
herbs*

salt

black pepper

1 Put the cabbage and carrot in a large bowl.

2 Add the onion, celery, raisins and apricots and mix well.

NUTRITIONAL NOTES
PER PORTION:

CALORIES 204 PROTEIN 3.71g
FAT 6.37g SATURATED FAT 0.93g
CARBOHYDRATE 35.04g FIBER 4.25g
ADDED SUGAR 0.50g SODIUM 0.24g

3 In a small bowl, mix together the mayonnaise, yogurt, herbs and seasoning.

COOK'S TIP
Use other dried fruit such as golden raisins and dried pears or peaches in place of the dark raisins and apricots.

4 Add the mayonnaise dressing to the cabbage mixture and toss the ingredients together to mix. Cover and chill for several hours before serving.

Marinated Cucumber Salad

Sprinkling the cucumber with salt draws out some of
the water and makes them crisper.

Serves 4–6

INGREDIENTS
2 medium cucumbers
1 tbsp salt
¼ cup sugar
¾ cup cider
1 tbsp cider vinegar
3 tbsp chopped fresh dill
pinch of pepper

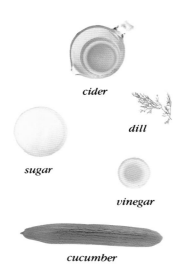

cider

dill

sugar

vinegar

cucumber

NUTRITIONAL NOTES
PER SERVING:

CALORIES 111 **PROTEIN** 0.52 g
FAT 0.14 g **SATURATED FAT** 0.01 g
CARBOHYDRATE 25.59 g **FIBER** 0.62 g
ADDED SUGAR 23.62 g **SODIUM** 0.02 g

1 Slice the cucumbers thinly and place
them in a colander, sprinkling salt
between each layer. Put the colander
over a bowl and leave to drain for 1 hour.

2 Thoroughly rinse the cucumber
under cold running water to remove
excess salt, then pat dry on absorbent
paper towels.

3 Gently heat the sugar, cider and
vinegar in a saucepan, until the sugar has
dissolved. Remove from the heat and
leave to cool. Put the cucumber slices in a
bowl, pour over the cider mixture and
leave to marinate for 2 hours.

4 Drain the cucumber and sprinkle
with the dill and pepper to taste. Mix well
and transfer to a serving dish. Chill in the
refrigerator until ready to serve.

Cachumbar

Cachumbar is a salad relish most commonly served with Indian curries. There are many versions, although this one will leave your mouth feeling cool and fresh after a spicy meal.

Serves 4

INGREDIENTS
3 ripe tomatoes
2 scallions, chopped
¼ tsp superfine sugar
salt
3 tbsp chopped fresh cilantro

tomatoes

cilantro

scallion

COOK'S TIP
Cachumbar also makes a fine accompaniment to fresh crab, lobster and shellfish.

NUTRITIONAL NOTES
PER PORTION:

ENERGY 61 Kcals **FAT** 1.1 g
SATURATED FAT 0.3 g

2 Halve the tomatoes, remove the seeds and dice the flesh.

3 Combine the tomatoes with the scallions, sugar, salt, and chopped cilantro. Serve at room temperature.

1 Remove the tough cores from the tomatoes with a small knife.

Vegetables à la Grecque

This simple side salad is made with winter vegetables, but you can vary it according to the season.

Serves 4

INGREDIENTS
¾ cup white wine
1 tsp olive oil
2 tbsp lemon juice
2 bay leaves
sprig of fresh thyme
4 juniper berries
1 lb leeks, trimmed and cut into 1-in
   lengths
1 small cauliflower, broken into
   florets
4 celery stalks, sliced on the diagonal
2 tbsp chopped fresh parsley
salt and freshly ground black pepper

wine

celery

cauliflower

parsley

olive oil

leeks

1 Put the wine, oil, lemon juice, bay leaves, thyme and juniper berries into a large, heavy saucepan and bring to a boil. Cover and let simmer for 20 minutes.

2 Add the leeks, cauliflower and celery. Simmer very gently for 5–6 minutes or until just tender.

NUTRITIONAL NOTES
PER PORTION:

ENERGY 88.25 Kcals **PROTEIN** 3.61 g
FAT 2.32 g **SATURATED FAT** 0.37 g
CARBOHYDRATE 5.32 g
FIBER 3.86 g **SUGAR** 4.23 g
SODIUM 28 mg

COOK'S TIP

Choose a dry or medium-dry white wine for this dish.

3 Remove the vegetables with a slotted spoon and transfer them to a serving dish. Briskly boil the cooking liquid for 15–20 minutes or until reduced by half. Strain.

4 Stir the parsley into the liquid and season to taste. Pour over the vegetables and let cool. Chill for at least 1 hour before serving.

Green Bean Salad with Egg Topping

When green beans are fresh and plentiful, serve them lightly cooked as a salad starter topped with butter-fried breadcrumbs, egg and parsley.

Serves 6

INGREDIENTS
1½ lb green beans, trimmed
salt
2 tbsp garlic oil
1 oz polyunsaturated margarine
1 cup fresh white bread crumbs
4 tbsp chopped fresh parsley
1 egg, cooked and shelled

parsley

egg

green beans

2 Heat the margarine in a large skillet, add the bread crumbs and fry until golden. Remove from heat, add the parsley, then add diced cooked egg.

3 Place the beans in a shallow serving dish and spoon on the breadcrumb topping. Serve at room temperature.

1 Bring a large saucepan of salted water to the boil. Add the beans and cook for 6 minutes. Drain well, toss in garlic oil and allow to cool.

NUTRITIONAL NOTES
PER PORTION:

ENERGY 132 Kcals **FAT** 9.5 g
SATURATED FAT 1.8 g

COOK'S TIP
Few cooks need reminding how to boil an egg, but many are faced with the problem of a dark ring around the yolk when cooked. This is caused by boiling for longer than the optimum period of 12 minutes. Allow boiled eggs to cool in water for easy peeling.

Sweet Turnip Salad with Horseradish and Caraway

The robust-flavored turnip goes well with the taste of horseradish and caraway seeds. This salad is delicious with cold roast beef or smoked trout.

Serves 4

INGREDIENTS
12 oz medium turnips
2 scallions, white part only, chopped
1 tbsp sugar
salt
2 tbsp prepared horseradish
2 tsp caraway seeds

turnips

scallions

NUTRITIONAL NOTES
PER PORTION:

ENERGY 48 Kcals **FAT** 0.9 g
SATURATED FAT 0.08 g

COOK'S TIP
If turnips are not available, giant white radish (daikon) can be used as a substitute.

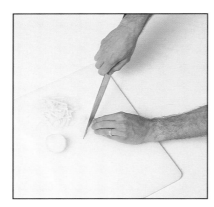

1 Peel, slice, and shred the turnips—or grate them if you wish.

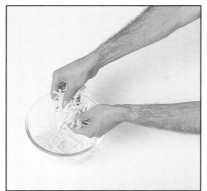

2 Add the scallions, sugar, and salt, then rub together with your hands to soften the turnip.

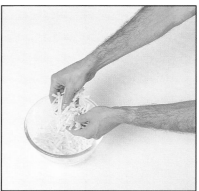

3 Fold in the prepared horseradish and caraway seeds.

Lentil and Cabbage Salad

This warm, crisp salad makes a satisfying meal when served with crusty French bread or whole-wheat rolls.

Serves 4–6

INGREDIENTS
1 cup puy lentils
1 garlic clove
1 bay leaf
1 small onion, peeled and studded
   with 2 cloves
1 tbsp olive oil
1 red onion, finely sliced
2 garlic cloves, crushed
1 tbsp thyme leaves
12 oz cabbage, finely shredded
finely grated zest and juice of
   1 lemon
1 tbsp raspberry vinegar
salt and freshly ground black pepper

NUTRITIONAL NOTES
PER PORTION:

ENERGY 230 Kcals **FAT** 4.1 g
SATURATED FAT 0.5 g

thyme

cabbage

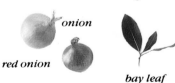
onion

red onion

bay leaf

lemon

garlic

cloves

peppercorns

1 Rinse the lentils in cold water and place in a large pan with 6 cups cold water, peeled garlic clove, bay leaf and clove-studded onion. Bring to a boil and cook for 10 minutes. Reduce the heat, cover and simmer gently for 15–20 minutes. Drain; remove the onion, garlic and bay leaf.

2 Heat the oil in a large pan. Add the red onion, garlic and thyme and cook for 5 minutes until softened.

3 Add the cabbage and cook for 3–5 minutes until just cooked but still crunchy.

4 Stir in the cooked lentils, lemon rind and juice and the raspberry vinegar. Season to taste and serve.

Curried New Potato and Green Bean Salad

Tender new potatoes and green beans tossed together in a subtly flavored light dressing make this salad ideal for serving with grilled vegetables and fresh whole-wheat bread.

Serves 6

INGREDIENTS
1½ cups green beans,
  trimmed and halved
1½ pounds cooked baby new
  potatoes
2 bunches scallions, chopped
⅔ cup golden raisins
3 ounces dried pears, finely chopped
6 tablespoons reduced-calorie
  mayonnaise
4 tablespoons low-fat plain yogurt
2 tablespoons sheep's milk
  yogurt (if available)
1 tablespoon tomato paste
1 tablespoon curry paste
2 tablespoons chopped fresh chives
salt and ground black pepper

green beans   baby new
              potatoes

                          scallions

golden
raisins   dried pears
                          reduced-
                          calorie
              low fat   mayonnaise
              plain
              yogurt   sheep's
                          milk   tomato
                          yogurt   paste

curry paste   chives
              salt   black
                          pepper

1 Cook the beans in boiling water for about 5 minutes, until tender. Rinse under cold running water to cool them quickly, drain and set aside.

2 Put the potatoes, beans, scallions, golden raisins and pears in a bowl and mix together.

3 In a small bowl, mix together the mayonnaise, yogurts, tomato paste, curry paste, chives and seasoning.

4 Add the dressing to the potato mixture and toss the ingredients together to mix. Cover and allow to stand for at least 1 hour before serving.

NUTRITIONAL NOTES
PER PORTION:

CALORIES 235 PROTEIN 5.17g
FAT 6.10 SATURATED FAT 1.06g
CARBOHYDRATE 42.62g FIBER 3.87g
ADDED SUGAR 0.83g SODIUM 0.22g

White Bean and Celery Salad

This simple bean salad is a delicious alternative to the potato salad that seems to appear on every salad menu. If you do not have time to soak and cook dried beans, use canned ones.

Serves 4

INGREDIENTS
1 lb dried white beans (haricot, canellini, navy, or butter beans) or 3 × 14 oz cans white beans
4½ cups vegetable stock, made from a cube
3 stalks celery, cut into ½ in strips
½ cup French Dressing
3 tbsp chopped fresh parsley
salt and pepper

parsley

white beans

celery

1 If using dried beans, cover with plenty of cold water and soak for at least 4 hours. Discard the soaking water, then place the beans in a heavy saucepan. Cover with fresh water, bring to the boil and simmer without a lid for 1½ hours, or until the skins are broken. Cooked beans will squash readily between a thumb and forefinger. Drain the beans. If using canned beans, drain, rinse and use from this stage in the recipe.

NUTRITIONAL NOTES
PER PORTION:

ENERGY 231 Kcals **FAT** 9.05 g
SATURATED FAT 1.9 g

COOK'S TIP

Dried beans that have been kept for longer than 6 months will need soaking overnight to lessen their cooking time. As a rule, the less time beans have been kept in store, the shorter the soaking and cooking time they need. The times given here are suited to freshly purchased beans.

2 Place the cooked beans in a large saucepan. Add the vegetable stock and celery, bring to the boil, cover and simmer for 15 minutes. Drain thoroughly. Moisten the beans with the dressing and leave to cool.

3 Add the chopped parsley and season to taste with salt and pepper.

Roasted Bell Pepper with Wild Mushroom Pasta Salad

A combination of roasted bell peppers and wild mushrooms make this pasta salad colorful as well as nutritious.

Serves 6

INGREDIENTS
1 red bell pepper, halved
1 yellow bell pepper, halved
1 green bell pepper, halved
3 cups whole-wheat
  pasta shells or twists
2 tablespooons olive oil
3 tablespooons balsamic vinegar
5 tablespooons tomato juice
2 tablespooons chopped fresh basil
1 tablespooon chopped fresh thyme
2¼ cups shiitake mushrooms,
  sliced
2¼ cups oyster mushrooms,
  sliced
1 can (14 ounces) black-eyed
  peas, rinsed and drained
⅓ cup golden raisins
2 bunches scallions,
  finely chopped
salt and ground black pepper

red pepper *yellow pepper* *green pepper*

wholewheat pasta shells *olive oil* *balsamic vinegar*

tomato juice *fresh basil* *fresh thyme*

shiitake mushrooms *oyster mushrooms* *black-eyed peas* *golden raisins* *scallions*

1 Preheat the broiler. Put the peppers cut side down on a broiler-pan rack and place under a hot broiler for 10–15 minutes, until the skins are charred. Cover the peppers with a clean, damp dishtowel and set aside to cool.

2 Meanwhile, cook the pasta in lightly salted, boiling water for 10–12 minutes until *al dente*, then drain thoroughly.

3 Mix together the oil, vinegar, tomato juice, basil and thyme, add to the warm pasta and toss together.

NUTRITIONAL NOTES
PER PORTION:

CALORIES 334 PROTEIN 13.58g
FAT 6.02g SATURATED FAT 0.89g
CARBOHYDRATE 60.74g FIBER 9.37g
ADDED SUGAR 0.00g SODIUM 0.11g

4 Remove and discard the skins from the peppers. Seed and slice the peppers and add to the pasta with the mushrooms, black-eyed peas, raisins, scallions and seasoning. Toss the ingredients to mix and serve immediately, or cover and chill in the refrigerator before serving.

Sweet and Sour Peppers with Bows

Serves 4–6

INGREDIENTS

1 red, 1 yellow and 1 orange pepper
1 garlic clove, crushed
2 tablespoons capers
2 tablespoons raisins
1 teaspoon wholegrain mustard
rind and juice of 1 lime
1 teaspoon honey
2 tablespoons chopped
   fresh cilantro
8 ounces pasta bows (farfalle)
salt and ground black pepper
shavings of Parmesan cheese,
   to serve (optional)

raisins

red pepper　*yellow pepper*

cilantro

orange pepper

pasta bows

Parmesan cheese

capers

honey　*garlic*

1 Quarter the peppers, remove the stalk and seeds. Put into boiling water and cook for 10–15 minutes until tender. Drain and rinse under cold water. Peel away the skin and cut the flesh into strips lengthways.

2 Put the garlic, capers, raisins, mustard, lime rind and juice, honey, cilantro and seasoning into a bowl and whisk together.

NUTRITIONAL NOTES
PER PORTION:

ENERGY 268 calories **FAT** 2.0g
SATURATED FAT 0.5g **CHOLESTEROL** 1.3mg
CARBOHYDRATE 57g **FIBER** 4.3g

3 Cook the pasta in a large pan of boiling, salted water for 10–12 minutes until tender. Drain thoroughly.

4 Return the pasta to the pan, add the reserved peppers and dressing. Heat gently and toss to mix. Transfer to a warm serving bowl. Serve with a few shavings of Parmesan cheese, if using.

Fruity Rice Salad

An appetizing and colorful rice salad combining many different flavors, ideal for a packed lunch.

Serves 4–6

INGREDIENTS
1 cup mixed brown and
   wild rice
1 yellow bell pepper,
   seeded and diced
1 bunch scallions, chopped
3 stalks celery, chopped
1 large beefsteak tomato, chopped
2 green apples, chopped
¾ cup dried apricots, chopped
⅔ cup raisins
2 tablespoons unsweetened
   apple juice
2 tablespoons dry sherry
2 tablespoons light soy sauce
dash of Tabasco sauce
2 tablespoons chopped fresh parsley
1 tablespoon chopped fresh
   rosemary
salt and ground black pepper

mixed brown and wild rice

yellow pepper

scallions

celery

beefsteak tomato

apples

dried apricots

raisins

light soy sauce

unsweetened apple juice

dry sherry

Tabasco sauce

fresh parsley

fresh rosemary

1 Cook the rice in a large saucepan of lightly salted, boiling water for about 30 minutes (or according to the instructions on the packet) until tender. Rinse the rice under cold running water to cool quickly and drain thoroughly.

2 Place the pepper, scallions, celery, tomato, apples, apricots, raisins and the cooked rice in a serving bowl and mix well.

3 In a small bowl, mix together the apple juice, sherry, soy sauce, Tabasco sauce, herbs and seasoning.

4 Pour the dressing over the rice mixture and toss the ingredients together to mix. Serve immediately or cover and chill in the fridge before serving.

NUTRITIONAL NOTES

PER PORTION:

CALORIES 428 PROTEIN 8.15g
FAT 2.50g SATURATED FAT 0.52g
CARBOHYDRATE 97.15g FIBER 7.17g
ADDED SUGAR 0.31g SODIUM 0.58g

Bulgur and Fava Bean Salad

This appetizing salad is ideal served with fresh, crusty whole-wheat bread and homemade chutney, and for non-vegetarians it can be served as an accompaniment to grilled lean meat or fish.

Serves 6

INGREDIENTS
2 cups bulgur
8 ounces frozen fava beans
1 cup frozen petit pois
8 ounces cherry tomatoes, halved
1 scallion, chopped
1 red bell pepper, seeded and diced
2 ounces snow peas, chopped
2 ounces watercress
1 tablespoon chopped fresh parsley
1 tablespoon chopped fresh basil
1 tablespoon chopped fresh thyme
salt and ground black pepper
fat-free French dressing

bulgur

frozen fava beans

frozen petit pois

cherry tomatoes

scallion

red pepper

snow peas

watercress

fresh parsley

fresh basil

fresh thyme

fat-free French dressing

salt

black pepper

1 Soak and cook the bulgur according to the packet instructions. Drain thoroughly and put into a serving bowl.

2 Meanwhile, cook the fava beans and petits pois in boiling water for about 3 minutes, until tender. Drain thoroughly and add to the prepared bulgur.

3 Add the cherry tomatoes, scallion, pepper, snow peas and watercress to the bulgur mixture and mix.

NUTRITIONAL NOTES
PER PORTION:

CALORIES 277 PROTEIN 11.13g
FAT 1.81g SATURATED FAT 0.17g
CARBOHYDRATE 55.34g FIBER 4.88g
ADDED SUGAR 0.00g SODIUM 0.02g

4 Add the herbs, seasoning and enough French dressing to taste, tossing the ingredients together. Serve immediately or cover and chill in the fridge before serving.

COOK'S TIP
Use cooked couscous, brown rice or whole-wheat pasta in place of the bulgur.

Thai Fragrant Rice

A lovely, soft, fluffy rice dish, perfumed with fresh lemongrass.

Serves 4

INGREDIENTS
1 piece of lemongrass
2 limes
1 cup brown basmati rice
1 tbsp olive oil
1 onion, chopped
1-in piece of fresh ginger, peeled
   and finely chopped
1½ tsp coriander seeds
1½ tsp cumin seeds
3 cups fresh vegetable stock or water
4 tbsp chopped fresh cilantro
lime wedges, to serve

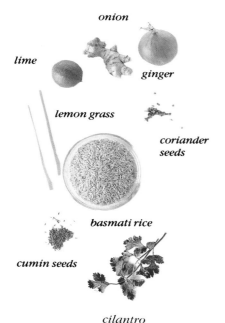

onion
lime
ginger
lemon grass
coriander seeds
basmati rice
cumin seeds
cilantro

1 Finely chop the lemongrass.

2 Remove the zest from the limes using a zester or fine grater.

3 Rinse the rice in plenty of cold water until the water runs clear. Drain through a sieve.

4 Heat the oil in a large pan and add the onion, spices, lemon grass and lime zest and cook gently for 2–3 minutes.

5 Add the rice and cook for another minute, then add the stock and bring to the boil. Reduce the heat to very low and cover the pan. Cook gently for 30 minutes then check the rice. If it is still crunchy, cover the pan again and leave for a further 3–5 minutes. Remove from the heat.

6 Stir in the cilantro, fluff up the grains, cover and let stand for 10 minutes. Serve with lime wedges.

COOK'S TIP

Other varieties of rice, such as white basmati or long grain, can be used for this dish but you will need to adjust the cooking times accordingly.

NUTRITIONAL NOTES
Per portion:

ENERGY 232 Kcals **FAT** 4.4 g
SATURATED FAT 0.8 g

Rice with Mushrooms and Shrimp

Mushrooms and shrimp provide a perfect combination of flavors in this delicious dish.

Serves 4

INGREDIENTS
5 oz basmati rice
1 tbsp corn oil
1 medium onion, chopped
4 black peppercorns
1-in piece cinnamon stick
1 bay leaf
¼ tsp black cumin seeds
2 cardamom pods
1 tsp minced garlic
1 tsp minced ginger
1 tsp garam masala
1 tsp chili powder
1½ tsp salt
4 oz frozen cooked, peeled medium
    shrimp, thawed
4 oz mushrooms, cut into large
    pieces
2 tbsp chopped fresh cilantro
½ cup low fat plain yogurt
1 tbsp lemon juice
2 oz frozen peas
1 cup water
1 red chile, seeded and sliced, to
    garnish

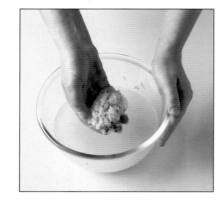

1 Wash the rice well and leave to soak in water.

2 Heat the oil in a non-stick wok or frying pan and add the onion, peppercorns, cinnamon, bay leaf, cumin seeds, cardamoms, minced garlic, minced ginger, garam masala, chili powder and salt. Lower the heat and stir-fry for about 2 minutes.

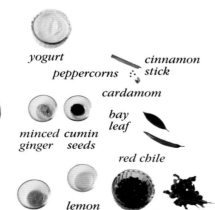

yogurt
peppercorns
cinnamon stick
cardamom
bay leaf
minced ginger
cumin seeds
red chile
basmati rice
mushrooms
shrimp
chili powder
garam masala
onion
salt
minced garlic
lemon juice
peas
fresh cilantro

3 Add the shrimp and cook for 2 minutes, before adding the mushrooms.

4 Add the cilantro and the yogurt, followed by the lemon juice and peas.

NUTRITIONAL NOTES

PER PORTION:

ENERGY 248 Kcals **PROTEIN** 13.12 g
FAT 5.20 g **SATURATED FAT** 0.99 g
CARBOHYDRATE 40.04 g **FIBER** 1.85 g
ADDED SUGAR 0
SALT 1.23 g

5 Drain the rice and add it to the prawn mixture. Pour in the water, cover the pan and cook over a medium heat for about 15 minutes, checking once.

6 Remove from heat and let stand, still covered, for about 5 minutes. Transfer to a serving dish and serve garnished with the sliced red chile.

Vegetable Dishes

Vegetables Provençal

The flavors of the Mediterranean are created in this delicious vegetable dish, ideal for a first course or lunchtime snack, served with fresh, crusty whole-wheat bread.

Serves 6

INGREDIENTS
1 onion, sliced
2 leeks, sliced
2 garlic cloves, crushed
1 each red, green, and yellow bell
  pepper, seeded and sliced
12 ounces zucchini, sliced
3 cups mushrooms, sliced
1 can (14 ounces) chopped
  tomatoes
2 tablespoons ruby port
2 tablespoons tomato paste
1 tablespoon ketchup
1 can (14 ounces) chickpeas
1 cup pitted black olives
3 tablespoons fresh mixed herbs
salt and ground black pepper
chopped fresh mixed herbs,
  to garnish

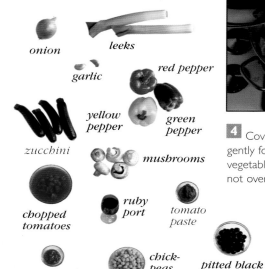

onion   *leeks*

garlic   *red pepper*

yellow pepper   *green pepper*

zucchini   *mushrooms*

chopped tomatoes   *ruby port*   *tomato paste*

tomato ketchup   *chick-peas*   *pitted black olives*   *fresh mixed herbs*

1 Put the onion, leeks, garlic, peppers, zucchini and mushrooms in a large saucepan.

2 Add the tomatoes, port, tomato paste and ketchup and mix well.

3 Rinse and drain the chickpeas and add to the pan.

4 Cover, bring to the boil and simmer gently for 20–30 minutes, until the vegetables are cooked and tender but not overcooked, stirring occasionally.

5 Remove the lid and increase the heat slightly for the last 10 minutes of the cooking time, to thicken the sauce, if liked.

6 Stir in the olives, herbs and seasoning. Serve hot or cold garnished with chopped mixed herbs.

NUTRITIONAL NOTES
PER PORTION:

CALORIES 155 PROTEIN 8.26g
FAT 4.56g SATURATED FAT 0.67g
CARBOHYDRATE 20.19g FIBER 6.98g
ADDED SUGAR 0.52g SODIUM 0.62g

Baked Squash

A creamy, sweet and nutty filling makes the perfect topping for tender buttery squash.

Serves 4

INGREDIENTS
2 butternut or acorn squash, 1 ¼ lb
    each
1 tbsp olive oil
¾ cup canned corn kernels, drained
½ cup unsweetened chestnut purée
5 tbsp low-fat yogurt
salt and freshly ground black pepper
¼ cup fresh goat cheese
snipped chives, to garnish

yogurt

chestnut purée

corn

butternut squash

goat's cheese

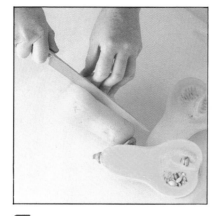

1 Preheat the oven to 350°F. Cut the squash in half lengthwise.

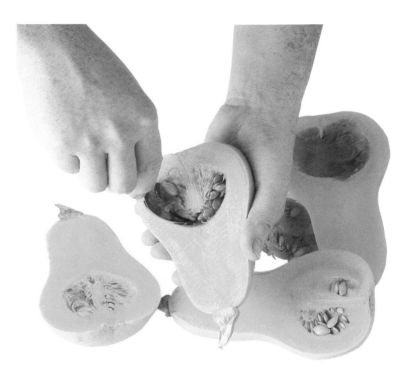

2 Scoop out the seeds with a spoon and discard.

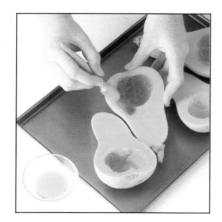

3 Place the squash halves on a cookie sheet and brush the flesh lightly with the oil. Bake in the oven for 30 minutes.

4 Mix together the corn, chestnut purée and yogurt in a bowl. Season to taste.

5 Remove the squash from the oven and divide the chestnut mixture between them, spooning it into the hollows.

COOK'S TIP

Use mozzarella or other mild, soft cheeses in place of goat's cheese. The cheese can be omitted entirely for a lower-fat alternative.

6 Top each half with ¼ of the goat's cheese and return to the oven for a further 10–15 minutes. Garnish with snipped chives.

NUTRITIONAL NOTES
PER PORTION:

ENERGY 212 Kcals **FAT** 5.5 g
SATURATED FAT 1.8 g

Red Cabbage in Port and Red Wine

A sweet and sour, spicy red cabbage dish, with the added crunch of pears and walnuts.

Serves 8

INGREDIENTS
2 tsp walnut oil
1 onion, sliced
2 whole star anise
1 tsp ground cinnamon
pinch of ground cloves
1 lb red cabbage, finely shredded
2 tbsp dark brown sugar
3 tbsp red wine vinegar
1¼ cups red wine
⅔ cup port
2 pears, cut into ½-in cubes
1/2 cup raisins
salt and freshly ground black pepper
¼ cup walnut halves

brown sugar

red cabbage

pears

onion *raisins*

walnut halves

star anise

red wine vinegar

port

red wine

1 Heat the oil in a large pan. Add the onion and cook gently for about 5 minutes until softened.

2 Add the star anise, cinnamon, cloves and cabbage and cook for about 3 minutes more.

NUTRITIONAL NOTES
PER PORTION:

ENERGY 245 Kcals **FAT** 11.5 g
SATURATED FAT 1 g

3 Stir in the sugar, vinegar, red wine and port. Cover the pan and simmer gently for 10 minutes, stirring occasionally.

4 Stir in the cubed pears and raisins and cook for a further 10 minutes or until the cabbage is tender. Season to taste. Mix in the walnut halves and serve.

Herbed Baked Tomatoes

Dress up sliced, sweet tomatoes with fresh herbs and a crisp bread crumb topping.

Serves 4–6

INGREDIENTS

1½ lb (about 8) large red and yellow
    tomatoes
2 tsp red wine vinegar
½ tsp whole grain mustard
1 garlic clove, crushed
2 tsp chopped fresh parsley
2 tsp snipped fresh chives
½ cup fresh fine white bread
    crumbs
salt and freshly ground black pepper
sprigs of Italian parsley, to garnish

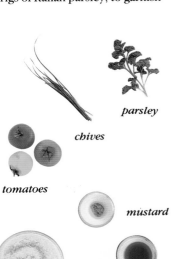

parsley

chives

tomatoes

mustard

vinegar

bread crumbs

NUTRITIONAL NOTES

PER SERVING:

CALORIES 47 **PROTEIN** 1.97 g
FAT 0.73 g **SATURATED FAT** 0.08 g
CARBOHYDRATE 8.63 g **FIBER** 1.98 g
ADDED SUGAR 0 **SODIUM** 0.15 g

1 Preheat the oven to 400°F. Thickly slice the tomatoes and arrange half of them in a 3¾ cup ovenproof dish, overlapping the slices.

2 Mix the vinegar, mustard, garlic clove and seasoning together. Stir in 2 tsp of cold water. Sprinkle the tomatoes with half the parsley and chives, then drizzle over half the dressing.

3 Lay the remaining tomato slices on top, overlapping them slightly. Drizzle with the remaining dressing.

4 Sprinkle over the bread crumbs. Bake in the preheated oven for 25 minutes or until the topping is golden. Sprinkle with the remaining parsley and chives. Serve immediately garnished with sprigs of Italian parsley.

Zucchini and Asparagus en Papillote

An impressive dinner party accompaniment, these puffed paper parcels should be broken open at the table by each guest, so that the wonderful aroma can be fully appreciated.

Serves 4

INGREDIENTS
2 medium zucchini
1 medium leek
8 oz young asparagus, trimmed
4 tarragon sprigs
4 whole garlic cloves, unpeeled
salt and freshly ground black pepper
1 egg, beaten

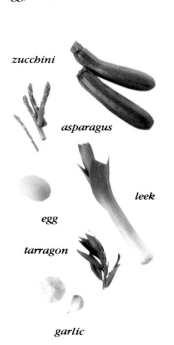

zucchini

asparagus

egg

leek

tarragon

garlic

1 Preheat the oven to 400°F. Using a potato peeler slice the zucchini lengthwise into thin strips.

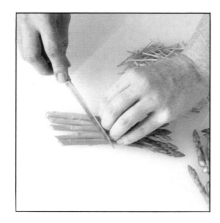

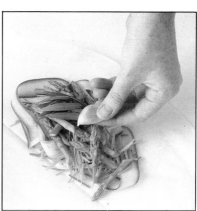

2 Cut the leek into very fine julienne strips and cut the asparagus evenly into 2 in lengths.

3 Cut out 4 sheets of parchment paper 12 × 15 in in size and fold each in half. Draw a large curve to make a heart shape when unfolded. Cut along the inside of the line and open out.

4 Divide the zucchini, asparagus and leek evenly between each paper heart, positioning the filling on one side of the fold line, and topping each with a sprig of tarragon and an unpeeled garlic clove. Season to taste.

NUTRITIONAL NOTES
PER PORTION:

ENERGY 53 Kcals **FAT** 2.3 g
SATURATED FAT 0.5 g

COOK'S TIP

Experiment with other vegetables and herbs such as sugar-snap peas and mint or baby carrots and rosemary. The possibilities are endless.

5 Brush the edges lightly with the beaten egg and fold over.

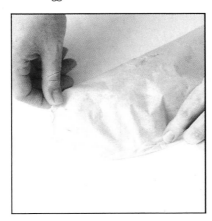

6 Pleat the edges together so that each parcel is completely sealed. Lay the parcels on a baking tray and cook for 10 minutes. Serve immediately.

Bok Choy and Mushroom Stir-fry

Try to buy all the varieties of mushroom for this dish; the wild oyster and shiitake mushrooms have particularly distinctive, delicate flavors.

Serves 4 as an accompaniment

INGREDIENTS
4 dried black Chinese mushrooms
1 lb bok choy
2 oz oyster mushrooms
2 oz shiitake mushrooms
1 tbsp vegetable oil
1 clove garlic, crushed
2 tbsp oyster sauce

Chinese mushrooms

shiitake mushrooms

bok choy

oyster mushrooms

1 Soak the black Chinese mushrooms in ⅔ cup boiling water for 15 minutes to soften them.

2 Tear the bok choy into bite-size pieces with your fingers.

3 Halve any large oyster or shiitake mushrooms, using a sharp knife.

4 Strain the Chinese mushrooms. Heat the wok, then add the oil. When the oil is hot, stir-fry the garlic until softened but not colored.

5 Add the bok choy and stir-fry for 1 minute. Mix in all the mushrooms and stir-fry for 1 minute.

6 Add the oyster sauce, toss well and serve immediately.

NUTRITIONAL NOTES
PER PORTION:

ENERGY 155 Kcals **FAT** 4.2 g
SATURATED FAT 0.5 g

Mixed Roasted Vegetables

Frying Parmesan cheese in this unusual way gives a wonderful crusty coating to the vegetables and creates a truly Mediterranean flavor.

Serves 4 as an accompaniment

INGREDIENTS
1 large eggplant, about 8 oz
salt, for sprinkling
6 oz plum tomatoes
2 red peppers
1 yellow pepper
2 tbsp olive oil
1 oz Parmesan cheese
2 tbsp fresh parsley, chopped
freshly ground black pepper

peppers

plum tomatoes

eggplant

1 Cut the eggplant into segments lengthwise. Place in a colander and sprinkle with salt. Leave for 30 minutes, to allow the salt to draw out the bitter juices.

2 Rinse off the salt under cold water and pat dry on paper towels.

3 Cut the plum tomatoes into segments lengthwise.

4 Cut the red and yellow peppers into quarters lengthwise and deseed.

5 Heat the wok, then add 1 tsp of the olive oil. When the oil is hot, add the Parmesan and stir-fry until golden brown. Remove from the wok, allow to cool and chop into fine flakes.

6 Heat the wok, and then add the remaining oil. When the oil is hot stir-fry the eggplant and peppers for 4–5 minutes. Stir in the tomatoes and stir-fry for a further 1 minute. Toss the vegetables in the Parmesan, parsley and black pepper and serve.

NUTRITIONAL NOTES
PER PORTION:

ENERGY 104 Kcals **FAT** 5.7 g
SATURATED FAT 1.9 g

Spinach with Mushrooms and Red Bell Pepper

A tasty and nutritious vegetable, spinach cooked in this way is wonderful served with chapati.

Serves 4

INGREDIENTS
1 lb fresh and frozen spinach
2 tbsp corn oil
2 medium onions, diced
6–8 curry leaves
¼ tsp onion seeds
1 tsp minced garlic
1 tsp minced ginger
1 tsp chili powder
1 tsp salt
1¼ tsp ground coriander
1 large red bell pepper, seeded and sliced
4 oz mushrooms, roughly chopped
1 cup fromage frais
2 tbsp fresh cilantro leaves

mushrooms

spinach

chili powder

onions

bell pepper

fromage frais

curry leaves

cilantro

onion seeds

minced ginger

minced garlic

NUTRITIONAL NOTES
PER PORTION:

ENERGY 188 Kcals **PROTEIN** 7.28 g
FAT 11.57 g **SATURATED FAT** 5.99 g
CARBOHYDRATE 14.71 g **FIBER** 4.68 g
ADDED SUGAR 0 g **SALT** 0.66 g

1 If using fresh spinach, blanch it briefly in boiling water and drain thoroughly. If using frozen spinach, thaw first, then drain. Set aside.

2 Heat the oil in a non-stick wok or frying pan and fry the onions with the curry leaves and the onion seeds for 1–2 minutes. Add the garlic, ginger, chilli powder, salt and ground coriander. Stir-fry for 2–3 minutes.

3 Add half the red pepper slices and all the mushrooms and continue to stir-fry for 2–3 minutes.

4 Add the spinach and stir-fry for 4–6 minutes. Finally, add the fromage frais and half the fresh cilantro, followed by the remaining red pepper slices. Stir-fry for another 2–3 minutes before serving garnished with the remaining cilantro.

Carrot and Cauliflower Stir-fry

The carrots are thinly sliced, which means that they cook quickly. This dish has a crunchy texture with only a few whole spices.

Serves 4

INGREDIENTS
2 large carrots
1 small cauliflower
1 tbsp olive oil
1 bay leaf
2 cloves
1 small cinnamon stick
2 cardamom pods
3 black peppercorns
1 tsp salt
2 oz frozen peas
2 tsp lemon juice
1 tbsp chopped fresh cilantro
fresh cilantro leaves, to garnish

frozen peas *lemon juice* *salt*
cinnamon *cardamom* *peppercorns*
cloves
bay leaf
cauliflower *carrots*
fresh cilantro

NUTRITIONAL NOTES
PER PORTION:

ENERGY 84 Kcals **PROTEIN** 3.91 g
FAT 3.75 g **SATURATED FAT** 0.6 g
CARBOHYDRATE 9.05 g **FIBER** 3.67 g
ADDED SUGAR 0
SALT 0.5 g

I Cut the carrots into thin batons about 1 in long. Separate the cauliflower into small florets.

2 Heat the oil in a non-stick wok or frying pan and add the bay leaf, cloves, cinnamon, cardamoms and peppercorns. Stir-fry over a medium heat for 30–35 seconds, then add the salt.

3 Next add the carrot and cauliflower and continue to stir-fry for 3–5 minutes.

4 Add the peas, lemon juice and chopped cilantro and cook for another 2–3 minutes. Serve garnished with the whole cilantro leaves.

COOK'S TIP
Stir-fries take only moments to cook so prepare this dish at the last minute.

Spring Vegetable Stir-fry

Beet and Celeriac Gratin

Beautiful ruby-red slices of beets and celeriac make a stunning light accompaniment to any main course dish.

Serves 6

INGREDIENTS
12 oz raw beets
12 oz celeriac
4 thyme sprigs
6 juniper berries, crushed
salt and freshly ground black pepper
½ cup fresh orange juice
½ cup vegetable stock

celeriac

orange juice

juniper berries

beet

thyme

1 Preheat the oven to 375°F. Scrub, peel and slice the beets very finely. Scrub, quarter and peel the celeriac and slice very finely.

2 Fill a 10 in diameter, cast iron, ovenproof or flameproof frying pan with alternate layers of beet and celeriac slices, sprinkling with the thyme, juniper and seasoning between each layer.

3 Mix the orange juice and stock together and pour over the gratin. Place over a medium heat and bring to the boil. Boil for 2 minutes.

4 Cover with foil and place in the oven for 15–20 minutes. Remove the foil and raise the oven temperature to 400°F Cook for a further 10 minutes until tender and bubbling.

NUTRITIONAL NOTES
PER PORTION:

ENERGY 56 Kcals **FAT** 0.4 g
SATURATED FAT 0

Zucchini in Citrus Sauce

If baby zucchini are unavailable, you can use larger ones, but they should be cooked whole so that they don't absorb too much water. Halve them lengthwise and cut into 4 in lengths.

Serves 4

INGREDIENTS
12 oz baby zucchini
4 scallions, finely sliced
1 in fresh ginger root, grated
2 tbsp cider vinegar
1 tbsp light soy sauce
1 tsp soft light brown sugar
3 tbsp vegetable stock
finely grated rind and juice of ½
    lemon and ½ orange
1 tsp cornstarch

orange

lemon

zucchini

ginger

scallions

NUTRITIONAL NOTES

PER SERVING:

CALORIES 33 **PROTEIN** 2.18 g
FAT 0.42 g **SATURATED FAT** 0.09 g
CARBOHYDRATE 5.33 g **FIBER** 0.92 g
ADDED SUGAR 1.31 g **SODIUM** 0.55 g

1 Cook the zucchini in lightly salted boiling water for 3-4 minutes, or until just tender. Drain well.

2 Meanwhile put all the remaining ingredients, except the cornstarch, into a small saucepan and bring to a boil. Simmer for 3 minutes.

3 Blend the cornstarch with 2 tsp of cold water and add to the sauce. Bring to a boil, stirring continuously, until the sauce has thickened.

4 Pour the sauce over the zucchini and gently heat, shaking the pan to coat evenly. Transfer to a warmed serving dish and serve.

Mushrooms in a Creamy Garlic Sauce

This is a simple and delicious recipe, which could be accompanied by a variety of rice dishes.

Serves 4

INGREDIENTS
12 ounces white mushrooms
3 tablespoons olive oil
1 bay leaf
3 garlic cloves, roughly chopped
2 green chilies, seeded and chopped
1 cup low-fat plain yogurt
1 tablespoon chopped fresh mint
1 tablespoon chopped fresh cilantro
1 teaspoon salt
fresh mint and cilantro leaves,
    to garnish

garlic

bay leaf

white mushrooms

mint

cilantro

salt

green chilies

low-fat plain yogurt

NUTRITIONAL NOTES
Per portion:
ENERGY 75 K Cals **PROTEIN** 6.50g
FAT 3.38g **SATURATED FAT** 0.54g
CARBOHYDRATE 4.93g **FIBER** 1.12g
ADDED SUGAR 0.01g
SALT 0.52g

1 Cut the mushrooms in half and set them aside.

2 Heat the oil in a nonstick wok or frying pan, then add the bay leaf, garlic and chilies and cook for about 1 minute.

COOK'S TIP
Cook the mushrooms for longer if you like them well cooked and browned.

3 Add the mushrooms. Stir-fry for about 2 minutes.

4 Remove from the heat and stir in the plain yogurt followed by the mint, cilantro and salt. Stir-fry for about 2 minutes, then transfer to a warmed serving dish and garnish with mint and cilantro leaves.

Potato Gratin

Don't rinse the potato slices before layering because the starch makes a thick sauce during cooking.

Serves 4

INGREDIENTS
1 garlic clove
5 large baking potatoes, unpeeled
3 tbsp freshly grated Parmesan cheese
2½ cups vegetable or low fat chicken stock
pinch of freshly grated nutmeg
salt and freshly ground black pepper

potatoes

Parmesan cheese

stock

NUTRITIONAL NOTES
PER SERVING:

CALORIES 221 **PROTEIN** 7.88 g
FAT 2.71 g **SATURATED FAT** 1.30 g
CARBOHYDRATE 43.77 g **FIBER** 3.30 g
ADDED SUGAR 0 **SODIUM** 0.21 g

1 Preheat the oven to 400°F. Halve the garlic clove and rub over the base and sides of a gratin dish measuring about 8 × 12 in.

2 Slice the potatoes very thinly and arrange a third of them in the dish. Sprinkle with a little grated cheese, salt and freshly ground black pepper. Pour over some of the stock to prevent the potatoes from discoloring.

3 Continue layering the potatoes and cheese as before, then pour over the rest of the stock. Sprinkle with the grated nutmeg.

4 Bake in the oven for 1¼-1½ hours or until the potatoes are tender and the tops well browned.

VARIATION
For a potato and onion gratin, thinly slice one medium onion and layer with the potato.

Breads & Baked Goods

Whole-wheat Herb Triangles

Stuffed with cooked chicken and salad these make a good lunchtime snack and are also an ideal accompaniment to a bowl of steaming soup.

Makes 8

INGREDIENTS
2 cups whole-wheat flour
1 cup flour
1 tsp salt
½ tsp baking soda
1 tsp cream of tartar
½ tsp chili powder
¼ cup soft low fat margarine
4 tbsp chopped mixed fresh herbs
1 cup skim milk
1 tbsp sesame seeds

mixed fresh herbs

chili powder

sesame seeds

whole-wheat flour

baking soda

cream of tartar

soft margarine

skim milk

salt

flour

1 Preheat the oven to 425°F. Lightly flour a baking sheet. Put the whole-wheat flour in a mixing bowl. Sift the remining dry ingredients, including the chili powder, then rub in the soft margarine.

2 Add the herbs and milk, and mix quickly to a soft dough. Transfer to a lightly floured surface. Knead only very briefly or the dough will become tough. Roll out to a 9-in round and place on the prepared baking sheet. Brush lightly with water and sprinkle evenly with the sesame seeds.

3 Carefully cut the dough round into 8 wedges, separate them slightly and bake for 15–20 minutes. Transfer to a wire rack to cool. Serve warm or cold.

NUTRITIONAL NOTES
PER PORTION:

ENERGY 222 Kcals
FAT 7.22 g **SATURATED FAT** 1.25 g
CHOLESTEROL 1.06 g **FIBER** 3.54 g

VARIATION
To make Sun-dried Tomato Triangles, replace the fresh mixed herbs with 2 tbsp drained, chopped sun-dried tomatoes in oil, and add 1 tbsp each mild paprika, chopped fresh parsley and chopped fresh parsley and chopped fresh marjoram.

Caraway Bread Sticks

Ideal to nibble with drinks, these can be made with all sorts of other seeds – try cumin seeds, poppy seeds or celery seeds.

Makes about 20

INGREDIENTS
⅔ cup warm water
½ tsp dried yeast
pinch of sugar
2 cups flour
½ tsp salt
2 tsp caraway seeds

dried yeast

caraway seeds

flour

water

salt

NUTRITIONAL NOTES
PER PORTION:

ENERGY 45 Kcals
FAT 0.24 g **SATURATED FAT** 0.02 g
CHOLESTEROL 0 **FIBER** 0.39 g

VARIATION
To make Coriander and Sesame Sticks, replace the caraway seeds with 1 tbsp crushed coriander seeds. Dampen the bread sticks lightly and sprinkle them with sesame seeds before baking.

1 Grease two baking sheets. Put the warm water in a bowl. Sprinkle the yeast on top. Add the sugar, mix well and let stand for 10 minutes.

2 Sift the flour and salt into a mixing bowl, stir in the caraway seeds and make a well in the centre. Add the yeast mixture and gradually incorporate the flour to make a soft dough, adding a little extra water if necessary.

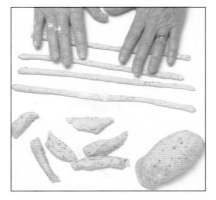

3 Transfer to a lightly floured surface and knead for 5 minutes, until smooth. Divide the mixture into 20 pieces and roll each one into a 12-in stick. Arrange on the baking sheets, leaving room to allow for rising, then let stand for 30 minutes until well risen. Meanwhile preheat the oven to 425°F.

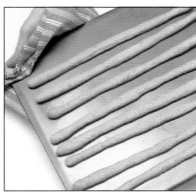

4 Bake the bread sticks for about 10–12 minutes until golden brown. Cool on the baking sheets.

Chive and Potato Scones

These little scones should be fairly thin, soft and crisp on the outside. Serve them for breakfast.

Makes 20

INGREDIENTS
1 lb potatoes
1 cup plain flour, sifted
2 tbsp olive oil
2 tbsp snipped chives
salt and freshly ground black pepper
low fat spread, for topping
   (optional)

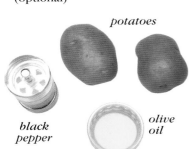

potatoes

black pepper

olive oil

chives

flour

salt

NUTRITIONAL NOTES
PER PORTION:

ENERGY 50 Kcals
FAT 1.24 g **SATURATED FAT** 0.17 g
CHOLESTEROL 0 **FIBER** 0.54 g

1 Cook the potatoes in a saucepan of boiling salted water for 20 minutes or until tender, then drain thoroughly. Return the potatoes to the clean pan and mash them. Preheat a griddle or frying pan.

2 Add the flour, olive oil and snipped chives with a little salt and pepper to the hot mashed potato in the pan. Mix to a soft dough.

COOK'S TIP
Cook the scones over a low heat so that the outsides do not burn before the insides are cooked through.

3 Roll out the dough on a well-floured surface to a thickness of ¼ in and cut out rounds with a 2-in round cookie cutter. Lightly grease the griddle or frying pan.

4 Cook the scones, in batches, on the hot griddle or frying pan for about 10 minutes, turning once, until they are golden brown on both sides. Keep the heat low. Top with a little low fat spread, if you like, and serve immediately.

Ham and Tomato Scones

These make an ideal accompaniment for soup. Choose a strongly flavored ham and chop it fairly finely, so that a little goes a long way.

Makes 12

INGREDIENTS

2 cups self-rising flour
1 tsp dry mustard
1 tsp paprika, plus extra for
  sprinkling
½ tsp salt
2 tbsp soft margarine
1 tbsp snipped fresh basil
⅓ cup drained sun-dried tomatoes in
  oil, chopped
2 oz Black Forest ham, chopped
½–⅔ cup skim milk, plus extra for
  brushing

soft margarine

paprika

salt

skim milk

self-rising flour   *fresh basil*

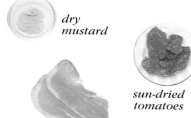
dry mustard

sun-dried tomatoes

Black Forest ham

I Preheat the oven to 400°F. Flour a large baking sheet. Sift the flour, mustard, paprika and salt into a bowl. Rub in the margarine until the mixture resembles bread crumbs.

2 Stir in the basil, sun-dried tomatoes and ham, and mix lightly. Pour in enough milk to mix to a soft dough.

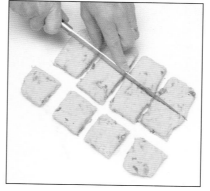

3 Transfer the dough to a lightly floured surface, knead lightly and roll out to a 8 x 6-in rectangle. Cut into 2-in squares and arrange on the baking sheet.

4 Brush lightly with milk, sprinkle with paprika and bake for 12–15 minutes. Transfer to a wire rack to cool.

NUTRITIONAL NOTES

PER PORTION:

ENERGY 113 Kcals
FAT 4.23 g **SATURATED FAT** 0.65 g
CHOLESTEROL 2.98 mg **FIBER** 0.65 g

Banana and Cardamom Bread

The combination of banana and cardamom is delicious in this soft-textured, moist loaf. It is perfect for an afternoon snack, served with low fat spread and jam.

Serves 6

INGREDIENTS
⅔ cup warm water
1 tsp dried yeast
pinch of sugar
10 cardamom pods
3½ cups flour
1 tsp salt
2 tbsp malt extract
2 ripe bananas, mashed
1 tsp sesame seeds

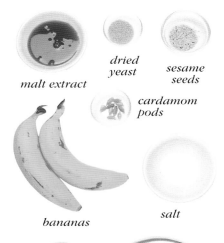

malt extract

dried yeast

sesame seeds

cardamom pods

bananas

salt

water

flour

NUTRITIONAL NOTES
PER PORTION:

ENERGY 299 Kcals
FAT 1.55 g SATURATED FAT 0.23 g
CHOLESTEROL 0 FIBER 2.65 g

COOK'S TIP
Make sure the bananas are really rips, so that they impart maximum flavor to the bread.

If you prefer, place the dough in one piece in a 1 lb loaf pan and bake for an extra 5 minutes.

1 Put the water in a small bowl. Sprinkle the yeast on top, add the sugar and mix well. Leave for 10 minutes.

2 Split the cardamom pods. Remove the seeds and chop them finely.

3 Sift the flour and salt into a mixing bowl and make a well in the centre. Add the yeast mixture with the malt extract, chopped cardamom seeds and bananas.

4 Gradually incorporate the flour and mix to a soft dough, adding a little extra water if necessary. Turn the dough on to a floured surface and knead for about 5 minutes until smooth and elastic. Return to the clean bowl, cover with a damp dish towel and leave to rise for about 2 hours until doubled in bulk.

5 Grease a baking sheet. Transfer the dough to a floured surface, knead briefly, then shape into a braid. Place the braid on the baking sheet and cover loosely with a plastic bag (ballooning it o trap the air). Set aside until well risen. Preheat the oven to 425°F.

6 Brush the braid lightly with water and sprinkle with the sesame seeds. Bake for 10 minutes, then lower the oven temperature to 400°F. Cook for 15 more minutes, or until the loaf sounds hollow when it is tapped underneath. Cool on a wire rack.

Swedish Golden Raisin Bread

A lightly sweetened bread that is delicious served warm. It is also excellent toasted and topped with low fat spread.

NUTRITIONAL NOTES
Per portion:

ENERGY 273 Kcals
FAT 4.86 g **SATURATED FAT** 0.57 g
CHOLESTEROL 0.39 mg **FIBER** 3.83 g

Serves 8–10

INGREDIENTS
⅔ cup warm water
1 tsp dried yeast
1 tbsp honey
2 cups whole-wheat flour
2 cups flour
1 tsp salt
⅔ cup golden raisin
½ cup walnuts, chopped
¾ cup warm skim milk, plus extra for glazing

salt

flour

walnuts

honey

water

skimmed milk

golden raisins

dried yeast

whole-wheat flour

VARIATION

To make Apple and Hazelnut Bread, replace the golden raisins with 2 chopped apples and use chopped toasted hazelnuts instead of the walnuts. Add 1 tsp ground cinnamon with the flour.

1 Put the water in a small bowl. Sprinkle the yeast on top. Add a few drops of the honey to help activate the yeast, mix well and leave for 10 minutes.

2 Put the flours in a bowl with the salt and golden raisins. Set aside 1 tbsp of the walnuts and add the rest to the bowl. Combine lightly and make a well in the center.

3 Add the yeast mixture to the flour mixture with the milk and remaining honey. Gradually incorporate the flour, mixing to a soft dough; add a little extra water if you need to.

4 Turn the dough on to a floured surface and knead for 5 minutes until smooth and elastic. Return to the clean bowl, cover with a damp dish towel and leave in a warm place to rise for about 2 hours until doubled in bulk. Grease a baking sheet.

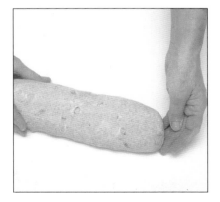

5 Transfer the dough to a floured surface and knead for 2 minutes, then shape into a 11-in long sausage shape. Place the loaf on the prepared baking sheet. Make some diagonal cuts down the whole length of the loaf.

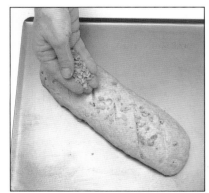

6 Brush the loaf with milk, sprinkle with the reserved walnuts and set aside to rise for about 40 minutes. Preheat the oven to 425°F. Bake the loaf for 10 minutes. Lower the oven temperature to 400°F and bake for about 20 more minutes or until the loaf sounds hollow when it is tapped underneath.

Rye Bread

Rye bread is popular in Northern Europe and makes an excellent base for open-face sandwiches—add a low fat topping of your choice.

Makes 2 loaves, each serving 6

INGREDIENTS
2 cups warm water
2 tsp dried yeast
pinch of sugar
2 cups whole-wheat flour
2 cups rye flour
1 cup flour
1½ tsp salt
2 tbsp caraway seeds
2 tbsp molasses
2 tbsp sunflower oil

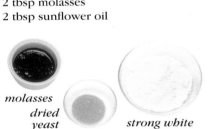

molasses
dried yeast
strong white flour

flour
whole-wheat flour

salt
caraway seeds
sunflower oil
water

1 Put half the water in a bowl. Sprinkle the yeast on top. Add the sugar, mix well and set aside for 10 minutes.

2 Put the flours and salt in a bowl. Set aside 1 tsp of the caraway seeds and add the rest to the bowl.

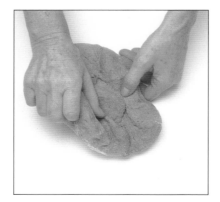

3 Make a well in the flour mixture, then add the yeast mixture with the molasses, oil and the remaining water. Gradually incorporate the flour and mix to a soft dough, adding a little extra water if necessary.

4 Turn the dough on to a floured surface and knead for 5 minutes until smooth and elastic. Return to the clean bowl, cover with a damp dish towel and leave in a warm place to rise for about 2 hours until doubled in bulk. Grease a baking sheet.

5 Transfer the dough to a floured surface and knead for 2 minutes then divide the dough in half, shape into two 9-in long oval loaves. Flatten the loaves slightly and place them on the baking sheet.

6 Brush the loaves with water and sprinkle with the remaining caraway seeds. Cover and set aside in a warm place for about 40 minutes until well risen. Preheat the oven to 400°F. Bake the loaves for 30 minutes or until they sound hollow when they are tapped underneath. Cool on a wire rack. Serve the bread plain, or slice and add a low fat topping.

NUTRITIONAL NOTES
PER PORTION:

ENERGY 224 Kcals
FAT 3.43 g **SATURATED FAT** 0.33 g
CHOLESTEROL 0 **FIBER** 6.04 g

VARIATION
Shape the dough into two loaves and bake in two greased 1-lb loaf pans, if you prefer.

Olive and Oregano Bread

This is an excellent accompaniment to all salads and is particularly good served warm.

NUTRITIONAL NOTES
Per portion:

ENERGY 202 Kcals
FAT 3.28 g **SATURATED FAT** 0.46 g
CHOLESTEROL 0 **FIBER** 22.13 g

Serves 8–10

INGREDIENTS
1¼ cups warm water
1 tsp dried yeast
pinch of sugar
1 tbsp olive oil
1 onion, chopped
4 cups flour
1 tsp salt
¼ tsp freshly ground
    black pepper
⅓ cup pitted black olives,
    roughly chopped
1 tbsp black olive paste
1 tbsp chopped fresh oregano
1 tbsp chopped fresh parsley

fresh oregano *fresh parsley* *black olives*

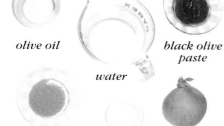

black pepper *flour*

olive oil *black olive paste*

water

dried yeast *salt* *onion*

1 Put half the water in a bowl. Sprinkle the yeast on top. Add the sugar, mix well and set aside for 10 minutes.

2 Heat the olive oil in a frying pan and fry the onion until golden brown.

3 Sift the flour into a mixing bowl with the salt and pepper. Make a well in the centre. Add the yeast mixture, the fried onion (with the oil), the olives, olive paste, herbs and remaining water. Gradually incorporate the flour and mix to a soft dough, adding a little extra water if necessary.

4 Turn the dough on to a floured surface and knead for 5 minutes until smooth and elastic. Place in a mixing bowl, cover with a damp dish towel and leave in a warm place to rise for about 2 hours until doubled in bulk. Lightly grease a baking sheet.

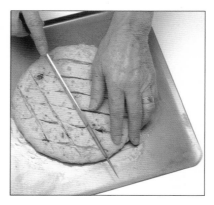

5 Transfer the dough to a floured surface and knead again for a few minutes. Shape into an 8-in round and place on the prepared baking sheet. Using a sharp knife, make criss-cross cuts over the top, cover and set aside in a warm place for 30 minutes, until well risen. Preheat the oven to 425°F.

6 Dust the loaf with a little flour. Bake for 10 minutes, then lower the oven temperature to 400°F. Bake for 20 more minutes or until the loaf sounds hollow when it is tapped underneath. Transfer to a wire rack to cool slightly before serving.

Sun-dried Tomato Braid

This is a delicious Mediterranean-inspired bread to serve at a summer buffet or barbecue.

Serves 8–10

INGREDIENTS
1¼ cups warm water
1 tsp dried yeast
pinch of sugar
2 cups whole-wheat flour
2 cups flour
1 tsp salt
¼ tsp freshly ground
    black pepper
⅔ cup drained sun-dried
    tomatoes in oil, chopped,
    plus 1 tbsp oil from the jar
¼ cup freshly grated Parmesan cheese
2 tbsp red pesto
1 tsp coarse sea salt

Parmesan cheese *red pesto* *black pepper* *whole-wheat flour* *salt* *dried yeast* *sun-dried tomatoes* *water* *flour* *coarse sea salt* *tomato oil*

NUTRITIONAL NOTES
PER PORTION:

ENERGY 294 Kcals
FAT 12.12 g **SATURATED FAT** 2.13 g
CHOLESTEROL 3.40 mg **FIBER** 3.39 g

COOK'S TIP
If you are unable to locate red pesto, use 2 tbsp chopped fresh basil mixed with 1 tbsp sun-dried tomato paste.

1 Put half the water in a bowl. Sprinkle the yeast on top. Add the sugar, mix well and set aside for 10 minutes.

2 Put the whole-wheat flour in a mixing bowl. Sift in the flour, salt and pepper. Make a well in the center and add the yeast mixture, oil, sun-dried tomatoes, Parmesan, pesto and the remaining water. Gradually incorporate the flour and mix to a soft dough, adding a little extra water if necessary.

3 Turn the dough on to a floured surface and knead for 5 minutes until smooth and elastic. Return to the clean bowl, cover with a damp dish towel and leave in a warm place to rise for about 2 hours until doubled in bulk. Lightly grease a baking sheet.

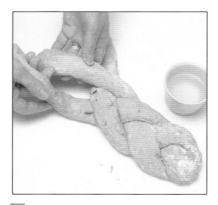

4 Transfer the dough to a lightly floured surface and knead for a few minutes. Divide the dough into three equal pieces and shape each into a 13-in long sausage.

5 Dampen the ends of the three "sausages." Press them together at one end, braid them loosely, them press them together at the other end. Place on the baking sheet, cover and set aside in a warm place for 30 minutes until well risen. Preheat the oven to 425°F.

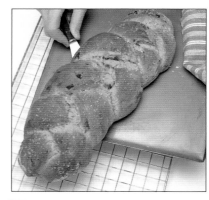

6 Sprinkle the braid with the coarse sea salt. Bake for 10 minutes, then lower the temperature to 400°F and bake for another 15–20 minutes or until the loaf sounds hollow when tapped underneath. Cool on a wire rack.

Focaccia

This flat Italian bread is best served warm. It makes a delicious snack with low fat cheese and chunks of fresh tomato.

Serves 8

INGREDIENTS

1¼ cups warm water
1 tsp dried yeast
pinch of sugar
4 cups flour
1 tsp salt
¼ tsp freshly ground
   black pepper
1 tbsp pesto
⅔ cup pitted black
   olives, chopped
3 tbsp drained sun-dried
   tomatoes in oil, chopped,
   plus 1 tbsp oil from the jar
1 tsp coarse sea salt
1 tsp roughly chopped fresh
   rosemary

1 Put the water in a bowl. Sprinkle the yeast on top. Add the sugar, mix well and set aside for 10 minutes. Lightly grease a 13 x 9-in Swiss roll pan.

2 Sift the flour, salt and pepper into a bowl and make a well in the center.

3 Add the yeast mixture with the pesto, olives and sun-dried tomatoes (reserve the oil). Mix to a soft dough, adding a little extra water if necessary.

black pepper

sun-dried tomatoes

pesto

flour

black olives

coarse sea salt

salt

water

dried yeast

fresh rosemary

tomato oil

4 Turn the dough on to a floured surface and knead for 5 minutes until smooth and elastic. Return to the clean bowl, cover with a damp dish towel and leave in a warm place to rise for about 2 hours until doubled in bulk.

5 Transfer dough to a floured surface, knead briefly, then roll out to a 13 x 9-in rectangle. Lift the dough over the rolling pin and place in the prepared pan. Preheat the oven to 425°F.

NUTRITIONAL NOTES

PER PORTION:

ENERGY 247 Kcals
FAT 6.42 g **SATURATED FAT** 0.93 g
CHOLESTEROL 0.35 mg **FIBER** 2.18 g

6 Using your fingertips, make small indentations all over the dough. Brush with the reserved oil from the sun-dried tomatoes, then sprinkle with the salt and rosemary. Leave to rise for 20 minutes, then bake for 20–25 minutes, or until golden. Transfer to a wire rack, but serve while still warm.

VARIATION

To make Oregano and Onion Focaccia, omit the pesto, olives and sun-dried tomatoes. Add 1 tbsp chopped fresh oregano or 1 tsp dried oregano to the flour. Slice 1 onion very thinly into rounds and scatter over the rolled-out dough. Drizzle with olive oil and sprinkle with sea salt before baking.

Coffee Sandwich Cookies

These are delicious on their own, but taste even better with a filling made by mixing low fat cream cheese with drained and chopped preserved ginger.

Makes 12

INGREDIENTS
½ cup flour
1 tbsp instant coffee powder
2 eggs
6 tbsp sugar

FOR THE FILLING
½ cup low fat cream cheese
¼ cup chopped
    preserved ginger

eggs

*instant coffee
powder*

flour

sugar

ginger

*low fat cream
cheese*

NUTRITIONAL NOTES

PER PORTION:

ENERGY 69 Kcals
FAT 1.36 g **SATURATED FAT** 0.50 g
CHOLESTEROL 33.33 mg **FIBER** 0.29 g

1 Preheat the oven to 375°F. Line two baking sheets with non-stick baking paper. Make the filling by beating together the cream cheese and ginger. Chill until required. Sift the flour and instant coffee powder together.

2 Combine the eggs and sugar in a bowl. Beat with a hand-held electric beater until thick and mousse-like (when the beater is lifted a trail should remain on the surface of the mixture for at least 15 seconds.)

3 Carefully add the sifted flour and coffee mixture and gently fold in with a metal spoon, being careful not to knock out any air.

4 Spoon the mixture into a piping bag fitted with a 1-in plain nozzle. Pipe 1½-in rounds on the baking sheets. Bake for 12 minutes. Cool on a wire rack. Sandwich together with the filling.

Oat Crisps

These cookies are very crisp and crunchy—ideal to serve with morning coffee.

Makes 18

INGREDIENTS
1¾ cups rolled oats
½ cup light brown
   sugar
1 egg
4 tbsp sunflower oil
2 tbsp malt extract

malt extract

sunflower oil

*rolled
oats*

*light brown
sugar*

egg

NUTRITIONAL NOTES

PER PORTION:

ENERGY 86 Kcals
FAT 3.59 g **SATURATED FAT** 0.57 g
CHOLESTEROL 10.70 mg **FIBER** 0.66 g

VARIATION

To give these crisp cookies a coarser texture, add ¼ cup finely chopped walnuts or pecans.

1 Preheat the oven to 375°F. Lightly grease two baking sheets. Mix the rolled oats and brown sugar in a bowl, breaking up any lumps in the sugar. Add the egg, sunflower oil and malt extract, mix well, then allow to soak for 15 minutes.

2 Using a teaspoon, place small heaps of the mixture well apart on the prepared baking sheets. Press the heaps into 3-in rounds with the back of a dampened fork.

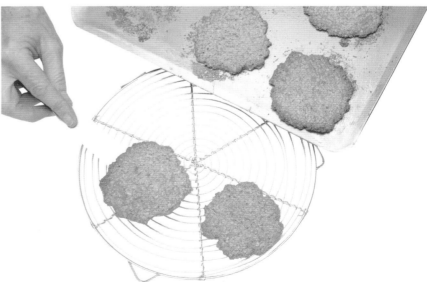

3 Bake the cookies for 10–15 minutes, until golden brown. Let stand to cool for 1 minute, them remove with spatula and cool on a wire rack.

Banana Gingerbread

Bananas make this spicy bread delightfully moist.
The flavor develops over time, so store the
gingerbread for a few days before cutting into
slices, if possible.

Makes 20 slices

INGREDIENTS
2½ cups flour
1 tsp baking soda
4 tsp ground ginger
2 tsp allspice
⅔ cup light brown sugar
4 tbsp sunflower oil
2 tbsp molasses
2 tbsp malt extract
2 eggs
4 tbsp orange juice
3 ripe bananas
⅔ cup raisins or golden raisins

1 Preheat the oven to 350°F. Lightly grease and line an 11 x 7-in shallow baking pan.

2 Sift the flour, baking soda and spices into a mixing bowl. Place the sugar in the sieve over the bowl, add some of the flour mixture and rub through the sieve with a wooden spoon.

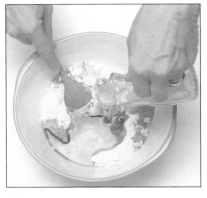

3 Make a well in the center of the dry ingredients and add the oil, molasses, malt extract, eggs and orange juice. Mix thoroughly.

orange
juice

malt
extract   raisins

flour

allspice

light
brown
sugar

eggs

sunflower
oil

baking
soda

ground ginger   bananas   molasses

4 Mash the bananas on a plate. Add the raisins to the gingerbread mixture, then mix in the mashed bananas.

5 Scrape the mixture into the prepared baking pan. Bake for about 35–40 minutes or until the center of the gingerbread springs back when lightly pressed.

6 Let the gingerbread cool in the pan for 5 minutes, then turn out onto a wire rack to cool completely. Transfer to a board and cut into 20 slices to serve.

NUTRITIONAL NOTES
PER PORTION:

ENERGY 148 Kcals
FAT 3.07 g **SATURATED FAT** 0.53 g
CHOLESTEROL 19.30 mg **FIBER** 0.79 g

COOK'S TIP
If your brown sugar is lumpy, mix it with a little flour and it will be easier to sift.

Pear and Raisin Bran Muffins

These tasty muffins are best eaten freshly baked and served warm or cold, on their own or spread with a little low-fat spread, reduced-sugar jam or honey.

NUTRITIONAL NOTES

PER PORTION:

CALORIES 108 PROTEIN 3.40g
FAT 2.68g SATURATED FAT 0.70g
CARBOHYDRATE 18.84g FIBER 2.64g
ADDED SUGAR 4.37g SODIUM 0.15g

Makes 12

INGREDIENTS
⅔ cup all-purpose whole-wheat flour, sifted
½ cup all-purpose white flour, sifted
3 cups bran
1 tablespoon baking powder, sifted
pinch of salt
¼ cup reduced-fat spread
¼ cup light brown sugar
1 egg
scant cup skim milk
½ cup dried pears, chopped
⅓ cup golden raisins

all-purpose whole-wheat flour *all-purpose white flour* **bran**

baking powder **salt** **reduced-fat spread**

light brown sugar **egg** **skim milk**

dried pears **golden raisins**

1 Preheat the oven to 400°F. Lightly grease 12 muffin or deep-cup popover pans or line them with paper baking cups. Mix together the flours, bran, baking powder and salt in a bowl.

2 Gently heat the half-fat spread in a saucepan until melted.

3 Mix together the melted fat, sugar, egg and milk and pour over the dry ingredients.

4 Gently fold the ingredients together, only enough to combine. The mixture should look quite lumpy as over mixing will result in heavy muffins.

5 Fold in the pears and raisins.

COOK'S TIP
For a quick and easy way to chop dried fruit, snip with kitchen scissors.

6 Spoon the mixture into the prepared muffin or popover pans. Bake for 15–20 minutes, until risen and golden brown. Turn out onto a wire rack to cool.

Fruity Muesli Bars

These fruity muesli bars make an appetizing treat for a takeaway snack.

Makes 10–12

INGREDIENTS
8 tablespoons reduced-fat spread
⅓ cup light brown sugar
3 tablespoons light corn syrup
1¼ cups no-added-sugar
  Swiss-style muesli or granola
½ cup rolled oats
1 teaspoon pumpkin pie spice
⅓ cup golden raisins
⅓ cup dried pears, chopped

reduced-fat spread

light brown sugar

light corn syrup

no-added-sugar Swiss-style muesli

rolled oats

pumpkin pie spice

golden raisins

dried pears

1 Preheat the oven to 350°F. Lightly grease a 7 inch square cake pan.

2 Put the reduced-fat spread, sugar and syrup in a saucepan and gently heat, stirring, until melted and blended.

3 Remove the pan from the heat, add the muesli, oats, spice, golden raisins and pears and mix well.

4 Transfer the mixture to the prepared tin and level the surface, pressing down.

5 Bake for 20–30 minutes, until golden brown. Cool slightly in the tin, then mark into bars using a sharp knife.

6 When firm, remove the muesli bars from the tin and cool on a wire rack.

NUTRITIONAL NOTES
PER PORTION:
CALORIES 191 PROTEIN 3.09g
FAT 6.26g SATURATED FAT 1.59g
CARBOHYDRATE 32.57g FIBER 1.66g
ADDED SUGAR 10.14g SODIUM 0.11g

COOK'S TIP
A combination of rolled oats and oatmeal can be used in place of muesli for a delicious change.

Cheese and Pineapple Whole-wheat Scones

These cheese and pineapple scones are delicious eaten freshly baked, warm or cold, with a little low-fat spread or reduced-sugar jam.

NUTRITIONAL NOTES
PER PORTION:

CALORIES 99 PROTEIN 4.22g
FAT 3.62g SATURATED FAT 1.05g
CARBOHYDRATE 13.28g FIBER 1.74g
ADDED SUGAR 1.33g SODIUM 0.06g

Makes 14–16

INGREDIENTS
2 cups self-rising whole-wheat
  flour, sifted
1 teaspoon baking powder, sifted
pinch of salt
3 tablespoons polyunsaturated
  margarine
1 teaspoon mustard powder
¾ cup reduced-fat aged Cheddar
  cheese, finely grated
¼ cup dried pineapple,
  finely chopped
⅔ cup skim milk

self-rising whole-wheat flour

baking powder

salt

mustard powder

polyunsaturated margarine

reduced-fat aged Cheddar cheese

dried pineapple

skim milk

1 Preheat the oven to 425°F. Line a baking sheet with waxed paper. Sift the whole-wheat flour, baking powder and salt into a bowl.

2 Rub in the margarine until the mixture resembles bread crumbs.

3 Fold in the mustard powder, cheese, pineapple and enough milk to make a fairly soft dough.

4 Turn the dough out onto a lightly floured surface and knead lightly. Lightly roll out to ¾ inch thickness.

5 Using a 2-inch plain cutter, stamp out rounds and place them on the prepared baking sheet.

6 Brush the tops with milk and bake for about 10 minutes, until well risen and golden brown. Transfer to a wire rack to cool and serve warm or cold.

COOK'S TIP
For economy, grate the cheese finely so it will go further and you will use less.

Malt Bread

This is a rich and sticky bread. If it lasts long enough to go stale, try toasting it for a delicious variation on taste.

NUTRITIONAL NOTES

PER PORTION:

ENERGY 279 Kcals
FAT 2.06 g **SATURATED FAT** 0.33 g
CHOLESTEROL 0.38 mg **FIBER** 1.79 g

Serves 8

INGREDIENTS
⅔ cup warm skim milk
1 tsp dried yeast
pinch of sugar
3 cups flour
¼ tsp salt
2 tbsp light brown sugar
generous 1 cup golden raisins
1 tbsp sunflower oil
3 tbsp malt extract

FOR THE GLAZE
2 tbsp sugar
2 tbsp water

malt extract

golden raisins

salt

flour

skim milk

light brown sugar

dried yeast

sunflower oil

1 Place the warm milk in a bowl. Sprinkle the yeast on top and add the sugar. Set aside for 30 minutes, until frothy. Sift the flour and salt into a mixing bowl, stir in the brown sugar and golden raisins and make a well in the center.

2 Add the yeast mixture with the oil and malt extract. Gradually incorporate the flour and mix to a soft dough, adding a little extra milk if necessary.

3 Transfer to a floured surface and knead for about 5 minutes, until smooth and elastic. Grease a 1-lb loaf pan.

4 Shape the dough and place it in the prepared pan. Cover with a damp dish towel and set aside in a warm place for 1–2 hours, until well risen. Preheat the oven to 375°F.

5 Bake the loaf for 30–35 minutes, or until it sounds hollow when it is tapped underneath.

6 Meanwhile, prepare the glaze by dissolving the sugar in the water in a small pan. Bring to a boil, stirring, then lower the heat and simmer for 1 minute. Place the bread on a wire rack and brush with the glaze while still hot. Allow the bread to cool before serving.

VARIATION

To make buns, divide the dough into 10 pieces, shape into rounds, leave to rise, then bake for about 15–20 minutes. Brush with the glaze while still hot.

Pear and Raisin Bread

This is an ideal bread to make when pears are plentiful—an excellent use for windfalls.

Serves 6–8

INGREDIENTS
scant ⅓ cup rolled oats
⅓ cup light brown sugar
2 tbsp pear or apple juice
2 tbsp sunflower oil
1 large or 2 small pears
1 cup self-rising flour
⅔ cup golden raisins
½ tsp baking powder
2 tsp allspice
1 egg

small pears
egg
baking powder
sunflower oil
self-rising flour
rolled oats
golden raisins
allspice
light brown sugar
pear juice

NUTRITIONAL NOTES
PER PORTION:

ENERGY 200 Kcals
FAT 4.61 g **SATURATED FAT** 0.79 g
CHOLESTEROL 27.50 mg **FIBER** 1.39 g

1 Preheat the oven to 350°F. Grease and line a 1-lb loaf pan with non-stick baking paper. Put the oats in a bowl with the sugar, pour over the pear and apple juice and oil, mix well and let stand for 15 minutes.

2 Quarter, core and grate the pear(s). Add the oat mixture with the flour, golden raisins, baking powder, allspice and egg, then mix together thoroughly.

3 Spoon the mixture into the prepared loaf pan and level the top. Bake for 50–60 minutes or until a skewer inserted into the center comes out clean.

4 Transfer the bread to a wire rack and peel off the lining paper. Allow to cool completely.

COOK'S TIP
Health food shops sell concentrated pear and apple juice, ready for diluting as required.

Irish Whiskey Cake

This moist rich fruit cake is drizzled with whiskey as soon as it comes out of the oven.

Serves 12

INGREDIENTS
⅔ cup candied cherries
1 cup dark brown sugar
⅔ cup golden raisins
⅔ cup raisins
½ cup dried currants
1¼ cup cold tea
2½ cups self-rising flour, sifted
1 egg
3 tbsp Irish whiskey

golden raisins

currants

sultanas

candied cherries

brown sugar

cold tea

Irish whiskey

self-rising flour

egg

COOK'S TIP

If time is short use hot tea and soak the fruit for just 2 hours.

1 Mix the cherries, sugar, dried fruit and tea in a large bowl. Leave to soak overnight until all the tea has been absorbed into the fruit.

2 Preheat the oven to 350°F. Grease and line a 2½-lb loaf pan. Add the flour, then the egg to the fruit mixture and beat thoroughly until well mixed.

NUTRITIONAL NOTES
PER PORTION:

ENERGY 265 Kcals
FAT 0.88 g **SATURATED FAT** 0.25 g
CHOLESTEROL 16.00 mg **FIBER** 1.48 g

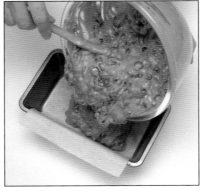

3 Pour the mixture into the prepared pan and bake for 1½ hours or until a skewer into the center of the cake comes out clean.

4 Prick the top of the cake with skewer and drizzle over the whiskey while the cake is still hot. Allow to stand for about 5 minutes, then remove from the pan and cool on a wire rack.

Fruit and Nut Cake

A rich fruit cake that improves over time.

Serves 12–14

INGREDIENTS
1½ cups self-rising whole-wheat flour
1½ cups self-rising flour
2 tsp allspice
1 tbsp apple butter
3 tbsp honey
1 tbsp molasses
6 tbsp sunflower oil
¾ cup orange juice
2 eggs, beaten
4 cups mixed dried fruit
3 tbsp halved almonds
½ cup candied cherries, halved

1 Preheat the oven to 325°F. Grease and line a deep round 8-in cake pan. Secure a band of brown paper around the outside.

mixed dried fruit *honey* *allspice*

molasses

eggs

apple butter

orange juice
halved almonds

self-rising flour

sunflower oil

candied cherries

self-rising whole-wheat flour

2 Sift the flours into a mixing bowl with the allspice and make a well in the center.

NUTRITIONAL NOTES
PER PORTION:

ENERGY 333 Kcals
FAT 8.54 g **SATURATED FAT** 1.12 g
CHOLESTEROL 29.62 mg **FIBER** 3.08 g

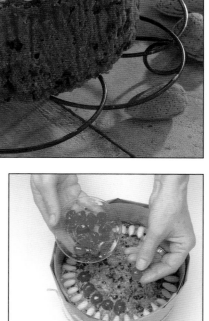

3 Put the apple butter in a small bowl. Gradually stir in the honey and molasses. Add to the dry ingredients with the oil, orange juice, eggs and mixed fruit. Mix thoroughly.

4 Transfer the mixture in the prepared pan and smooth the surface. Arrange the almonds and cherries in a pattern over the top. Stand the pan on a newspaper and bake for 2 hours or until a skewer inserted into the center comes out clean. Transfer to a wire rack until cold, then lift out of the pan and remove the paper.

Spiced Apple Cake

Grated apple and chopped dates give this cake a natural sweetness—omit a bit of the sugar if the fruit is very sweet.

Serves 8

INGREDIENTS
2 cups self-rising whole-wheat flour
1 tsp baking powder
2 tsp ground cinnamon
1 cup chopped dates
½ cup light brown sugar
1 tbsp pear and apple spread
½ cup apple juice
2 eggs
6 tbsp sunflower oil
2 apples, cored and grated
1 tbsp chopped walnuts

ground cinnamon

apple juice *sunflower oil*

self-rising whole-wheat flour

chopped walnuts

chopped dates

baking powder

brown sugar

pear and apple spread

apples

eggs

I Preheat the oven to 350°F. Grease and line a deep round 8-in cake pan. Sift the flour, baking powder and cinnamon into a mixing bowl, then mix in the dates and make a well in the center.

2 Mix the sugar with the pear and apple spread in a small bowl. Gradually stir in the apple juice. Add to the dry ingredients with the eggs, oil and apples. Mix thoroughly.

COOK'S TIP

You do not need to peel the apples – the skin adds fiber, and it softens on cooking.

3 Spoon the mixture into the prepared cake pan. Sprinkle with the walnuts and bake for 60–65 minutes or until a skewer inserted into the center of the cake comes out clean. Transfer to a wire rack, remove the lining paper and allow to cool.

NUTRITIONAL NOTES
PER PORTION:

ENERGY 331 Kcals
FAT 11.41 g **SATURATED FAT** 1.68 g
CHOLESTEROL 48.13 mg **FIBER** 2.50 g

Cinnamon Apple Gâteau

Make this lovely cake for an autumn celebration.

Serves 8

NUTRITIONAL NOTES

PER PORTION:

ENERGY 244 Kcals
FAT 4.05 g **SATURATED FAT** 1.71 g
CHOLESTEROL 77.95 mg **FIBER** 1.50 g

INGREDIENTS
3 eggs
½ cup sugar
¾ cup flour
1 tsp cinnamon

FOR THE FILLING AND TOPPING
4 large apples
4 tbsp honey
1 tbsp water
½ cup golden raisins
½ tsp ground cinnamon
1½ cups low fat cream cheese
4 tbsp reduced-fat fromage frais
2 tsp lemon juice
3 tbsp Apricot Glaze
mint sprigs, to decorate

eggs

apples

flour

reduced-fat fromage frais

lemon

sugar

low fat cream cheese

golden raisins

Apricot Glaze

honey

ground cinnamon

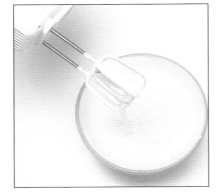

1 Preheat the oven to 375°F. Grease and line a 9-in cake pan. Place the eggs and sugar in a bowl and beat with a hand-held electric beater until thick and mousse-like (when the beater is lifted is lifted, a trail should remain on the surface of the mixture for at least 15 seconds).

2 Sift the flour and cinnamon over the egg mixture and carefully fold in with a large spoon. Pour into the prepared pan and bake for 25–30 minutes or until the cake springs back when lightly pressed. Slide a spatula between the cake and the pan to loosen the edge, then transfer the cake to a wire rack to cool.

3 To make the filling, peel, core and slice three of the apples and put them in a saucepan. Add 2 tbsp of the honey and the water. Cover and cook over low heat for about 10 minutes, until the apples have softened. Add the golden raisins and cinnamon, stir well, replace the lid and allow to cool.

4 Put the cream cheese in a bowl with the remaining honey, the fromage frais and half the lemon juice. Beat until the mixture is smooth.

5 Halve the cake horizontally, place the bottom half on a board and drizzle over any liquid from the apples. Spread with two-thirds of the cheese mixture, then top with the apple filling. Fit the top of the cake in place.

6 Swirl the remaining cheese mixture over the top of the cake. Core and slice the remaining apple, sprinkle with lemon juice and use to decorate the cake. Brush the apples with Apricot Glaze and place mint sprigs on top, to decorate.

Desserts

Pineapple and Peach Upside Down Cake

A tasty combination of pineapple and peaches, this old favorite is delicious served with low-fat custard or ice cream.

COOK'S TIP
Other combinations of canned and dried fruit work just as well, such as apricots and pears or peaches and figs.

Serves 6

INGREDIENTS
5 tablespoons light corn syrup
1 can (8 ounces) pineapple cubes
 in fruit juice
¾ cup dried peaches, chopped
⅔ cup superfine sugar
8 tablespoons reduced-fat spread
1½ cups self-rising
 whole-wheat flour
1 teaspoon baking powder
2 eggs

corn syrup

*pineapple cubes
in fruit juice*

dried peaches

superfine sugar

reduced-fat spread

*self-rising whole-
wheat flour*

eggs

baking powder

NUTRITIONAL NOTES
PER PORTION:

CALORIES 410 PROTEIN 8.36g
FAT 10.69g SATURATED FAT 2.82g
CARBOHYDRATE 74.73g FIBER 4.94g
ADDED SUGAR 37.51g SODIUM 0.21g

1 Preheat the oven to 350°F. Lightly grease a 7-inch, loose-bottomed round cake pan and line the base with nonstick waxed paper.

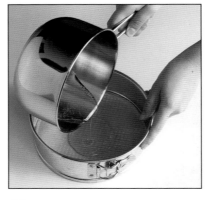

2 Heat the corn syrup gently in a saucepan and pour over the bottom of the pan.

3 Strain the pineapple, reserving 3 tablespoons of the juice.

4 Mix together the pineapple and peaches and scatter them over the syrup layer.

5 Put the sugar, reduced-fat spread, flour, baking powder, eggs and reserved pineapple juice in a bowl and beat together until smooth.

6 Spread the cake mixture evenly over the fruit and level the surface. Bake for about 45 minutes until risen and golden brown. Turn out carefully on to a serving plate and serve hot or cold in slices.

Peach and Raspberry Crumble

A quick and easy tasty dessert, this crumble is good served hot or cold on its own or with low-fat custard.

Serves 4

INGREDIENTS

⅔ cup all-purpose
  whole-wheat flour
¾ cup medium rolled oats
6 tablespoons reduced-fat spread
¼ cup light brown sugar
½ teaspoon ground cinnamon
1 can (14 ounces) peach slices in
  fruit juice
1¼ cups raspberries
2 tablespoons honey

all-purpose whole-wheat flour

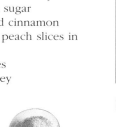
rolled oats

reduced-fat spread

light brown sugar

ground cinnamon

peach slices in fruit juice

raspberries

honey

1 Preheat the oven to 350°F. Put the flour and oats in a bowl and mix together.

2 Rub in the reduced-fat spread until the mixture resembles bread crumbs, then stir in the sugar and cinnamon.

3 Drain the peach slices and reserve the juice.

4 Coarsely chop the peaches and put them in an ovenproof dish, then sprinkle the raspberries on top.

5 Mix together the reserved peach juice and honey, pour over the fruit and stir.

6 Spoon the crumble mixture over the fruit, pressing it down lightly. Bake for about 45 minutes, until golden brown on top. Serve hot or cold.

COOK'S TIP
Use other combinations of fruit, such as apples and blueberries, for a tasty change.

NUTRITIONAL NOTES
PER PORTION:

CALORIES 334 PROTEIN 7.02g
FAT 9.9g SATURATED FAT 2.51g
CARBOHYDRATE 58.57g FIBER 5.22g
ADDED SUGAR 12.66g SODIUM 0.14g

Chocolate, Date and Walnut Cake

Real desserts are not off limits when you're cutting calories or fat—this one stays within the rules! Serve hot, with yogurt or skim-milk custard.

Serves 4

INGREDIENTS
4 tbsp chopped walnuts
2 tbsp chopped dates
2 eggs
1 tsp vanilla extract
2 tbsp sugar
3 tbsp whole-wheat flour
1 tbsp cocoa
2 tbsp skim milk

NUTRITIONAL NOTES
PER PORTION:

ENERGY 185 Kcals **FAT** 8.6 g
SATURATED FAT 1.8 g

skim milk

vanilla essence

whole-wheat flour

sugar

eggs

cocoa powder

walnuts

dates

1 Preheat the oven to 350°F. Grease a 5-cup pudding mold and place a small circle of wax or non-stick baking paper in the base. Mix the walnuts and dates together and then spoon into the pudding mold.

2 Separate the eggs and place the yolks in a bowl, with the vanilla and sugar. Place the bowl over a pan of hot water and whisk until the mixture is thick and pale.

3 Sift the flour and cocoa into the mixture and fold them in with a metal spoon. Stir in the milk, to soften the mixture slightly. Whisk the egg whites until they hold soft peaks and fold them in.

4 Spoon the mixture into the mold and bake for 40–45 minutes or until the cake is well risen and firm to the touch. Run a knife around the cake to loosen it from the mold, and then turn it out and serve immediately.

Fruit and Spice Bread Pudding

An easy-to-make fruity dessert with a hint of spice, which is delicious served either hot or cold.

Serves 4

INGREDIENTS
6 medium slices whole-wheat bread
2 ounces reduced-sugar jam
⅓ cup golden raisins
¼ cup dried apricots, chopped
¼ cup light brown sugar
1 teaspoon pumpkin pie spice
2 eggs
2½ cups skim milk
finely grated rind of 1 lemon

whole-wheat bread slices

reduced-sugar jam

golden raisins

dried apricots

light brown sugar

pumpkin pie spice

eggs

skim milk

lemon

NUTRITIONAL NOTES
PER PORTION:

CALORIES 305 PROTEIN 13.77g
FAT 4.51g SATURATED FAT 1.27g
CARBOHYDRATE 56.38g FIBER 3.75g
ADDED SUGAR 13.47g SODIUM 0.38g

1 Preheat the oven to 325°F. Remove and discard the crusts from the bread. Spread the bread slices with jam and cut into small triangles. Place half the bread triangles in a lightly greased oven-proof dish.

2 Mix together the raisins, apricots, sugar and spice and sprinkle half the fruit mixture over the bread in the dish.

3 Top with the remaining bread triangles and then sprinkle over the remaining fruit mixture.

4 Beat the eggs, milk and lemon rind together and pour over the bread. Set aside for about 30 minutes, to allow the bread to absorb some of the liquid. Bake for 45–60 minutes, until lightly set and golden brown. Serve hot or cold.

Chestnut and Orange Roulade

This moist cake is ideal to serve as a dessert.

Serves 8

INGREDIENTS
3 eggs, separated
½ cup sugar
15½-oz can unsweetened chestnut
   purée
grated rind and juice of 1 orange
confectioner's sugar, for dusting

FOR THE FILLING
1 cup low fat cream cheese
1 tbsp honey
1 orange

eggs

unsweetened chestnut purée

honey

sugar

oranges

low fat cream cheese

COOK'S TIP
Do not beat the egg whites too stiffly or it will be difficult to fold them into the mixture and they will form lumps in the roulade.

NUTRITIONAL NOTES
PER PORTION:

ENERGY 185 Kcals
FAT 4.01 g **SATURATED FAT** 1.47 g
CHOLESTEROL 76.25 mg **FIBER** 1.40 g

1 Preheat the oven to 350°F. Grease a 12 × 8-in Swiss roll pan and line with non-stick baking paper. Beat the egg yolks and sugar in a bowl until thick and creamy.

2 Put the chestnut purée in a separate bowl. Beat in the orange rind and juice, then beat the flavored chestnut purée into the egg mixture.

3 Whisk the egg whites in a grease-free bowl until fairly stiff. Using a metal spoon, stir a generous spoonful of the whites into the chestnut mixture to lighten it, then fold in the rest.

4 Spoon the roulade mixture into the prepared pan and bake for 30 minutes, until firm. Cool for 5 minutes, then cover with a clean damp dish towel and set aside until completely cold.

5 Meanwhile, make the filling. Put the cream cheese in a bowl with the honey. Finely grate the orange rind and add to the bowl. Peel away all the pith from the orange, cut the fruit into segments, chop roughly and set aside. Add any juice to the cheese mixture, then beat until it is smooth. Mix in the chopped orange.

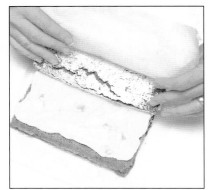

6 Sprinkle a sheet of waxed paper thickly with confectioners' sugar. Carefully turn the roulade out onto the paper, then peel off the lining paper. Spread the filling over the roulade and roll up like a Swiss roll. Transfer to a plate and dust with some more confectioners' sugar.

Tia Maria Gâteau

A feather-light coffee-flavored cake with a creamy liqueur-flavored filling.

NUTRITIONAL NOTES

PER PORTION:

ENERGY 226 Kcals
FAT 3.14 g **SATURATED FAT** 1.17 g
CHOLESTEROL 75.03 mg **FIBER** 0.64 g

Serves 8

INGREDIENTS
¾ cup flour
2 tbsp instant coffee powder
3 eggs
½ cup sugar
coffee beans, to decorate (optional)

FOR THE FILLING
¾ cup low fat cream cheese
1 tbsp honey
1 tbsp Tia Maria
¼ cup preserved ginger,
   roughly chopped

FOR THE ICING
1¾ cups confectioners' sugar, sifted
2 tsp coffee extract
1 tbsp water
1 tsp cocoa powder

1 Preheat the oven to 350°F. Grease and line an 8-in round cake pan. Sift the flour and coffee powder together onto a sheet of waxed paper.

2 Whisk the eggs and sugar in a bowl with a hand-held electric whisk until thick and mousse-like (when the whisk is lifted, a trail should remain on the surface of the mixture for at least 15 seconds).

3 Gently fold in the flour mixture with a metal spoon, being careful not to knock out any air. Transfer the mixture to the prepared pan. Bake the cake for 30–35 minutes or until it springs back when lightly pressed. Transfer to a wire rack and let stand to cool completely.

honey

eggs

coffee extract

coffee essence

low fat cream cheese

coffee powder

flour

ginger

sugar

confectioners' sugar

cocoa powder

Tia Maria

4 Make the filling. Mix the cream cheese with the honey in a bowl. Beat until smooth, then stir in the Tia Maria and chopped ginger.

5 Split the cake in half horizontally and sandwich the two halves together with the Tia Maria filling.

6 Make the icing. In a bowl, mix the icing sugar and coffee essence with enough of the water to make an icing which will coat the back of a wooden spoon. Pour three-quarters of the icing over the cake, spreading it evenly to the edges. Stir the cocoa into the remaining icing until smooth. Spoon into a piping bag fitted with a writing nozzle and pipe the mocha icing over the coffee icing. Decorate with coffee beans, if liked.

VARIATION
To make a Mocha Gâteau, replace the coffee powder with 2 tbsp fat-reduced cocoa powder, sifting it with the flour. Omit the chopped ginger in the filling.

Raspberry Vacherin

Meringue rounds filled with orange-flavored fromage frais and fresh raspberries make a perfect dinner party dessert.

NUTRITIONAL NOTES

PER PORTION:

ENERGY 248 Kcals
FAT 2.22 g **SATURATED FAT** 0.82 g
CHOLESTEROL 4.00 mg **FIBER** 1.06 g

Serves 6

INGREDIENTS
3 egg whites
¾ cup sugar
1 tsp chopped almonds
confectioners' sugar for dusting
    raspberry leaves to decorate

FOR THE FILLING
¾ cup low fat cream cheese
1–2 tbsp honey
1 tbsp Cointreau
½ cup low fat fromage frais
8 oz raspberries

honey

raspberries

low fat fromage frais

eggs

low fat cream cheese

sugar

chopped almonds

Cointreau

COOK'S TIP

When making the meringue, whisk the egg whites until they are so stiff that you can turn the bowl upside-down without them falling out.

1 Preheat the oven to 275°F. Draw an 8-in circle on two pieces of non-stick baking paper. Turn the paper over so the marking is on the underside and use it to line two heavy baking sheets.

2 Beat the egg whites in a grease-free bowl until very stiff, then gradually beat in the sugar to make a stiff meringue mixture.

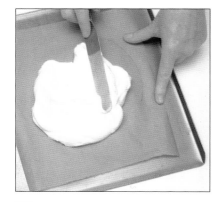

3 Spoon the mixture on to the circles on the prepared baking sheets, spreading the meringue evenly to the edges. Sprinkle one meringue round with the chopped almonds.

4 Bake for 1½–2 hours, then carefully lift the meringue rounds off the baking sheets, peel away the paper and cool on a wire rack.

5 To make the filling, beat the cream cheese with the honey and liquer in a bowl. Fold the fromage frais and raspberries, reserving three of the best for decoration.

6 Place the plain meringue round on a board, spread with the filling and top with the nut-covered round. Dust with confectioners' sugar, transfer to a serving plate and decorate with the reserved raspberries, and a sprig of raspberry leaves, if desired.

Baked Blackberry Cheesecake

This light, low-fat cheesecake is best made with wild blackberries, if they're available, but cultivated ones will do; or substitute other soft fruit, such as raspberries or blueberries.

Serves 5

INGREDIENTS
¾ cup low fat cottage cheese
⅔ cup low fat plain yogurt
1 tbsp all-purpose whole-wheat flour
2 tbsp sugar
1 egg
1 egg white
finely grated rind and juice of
   ½ lemon
2 cups fresh or frozen and thawed
   blackberries

low fat cottage cheese

blackberries

whole-wheat flour

lemon

low fat plain yogurt

eggs

sugar

NUTRITIONAL NOTES
PER PORTION:
ENERGY 111 Kcals **FAT** 3.0 g
SATURATED FAT 1.4 g

COOK'S TIP
If you prefer to use canned blackberries, choose those canned in natural juice and drain the fruit well before adding it to the cheesecake mixture. The juice can be served with the cheesecake, but this will increase the total calories.

1 Preheat the oven to 350°F. Lightly grease a 7-in square cake pan and line the bottom with baking paper.

2 Place the cottage cheese in a food processor and process until smooth. Alternatively, rub it through a sieve, to obtain a smooth mixture.

3 Add the yogurt, flour, sugar, egg and egg white and mix. Add the lemon rind, juice and blackberries, reserving a few for decoration.

4 Tip the mixture into the prepared pan and bake it for 30–35 minutes, or until it's just set. Turn off the oven and leave for a further 30 minutes.

5 Run a knife around the edge of the cheesecake, and then turn it out. Remove the lining paper and place the cheesecake on a warm serving plate.

6 Decorate the cheesecake with the reserved blackberries and serve it warm.

Mango and Amaretti Strudel

Fresh mango and crushed amaretti wrapped in wafer-thin filo pastry make a special treat that is equally delicious made with apricots or plums.

NUTRITIONAL NOTES
Per portion:

CALORIES 239
FAT 8.45 g **SATURATED FAT** 4.43 g
CHOLESTEROL 17.25 mg **FIBER** 3.30 g

Serves 4

INGREDIENTS
1 large mango
grated rind of 1 lemon
2 amaretti cookies
3 tbsp raw sugar
4 tbsp whole-wheat bread crumbs
2 sheets filo pastry, each 19 x 11 in
4 tsp margarine, melted
1 tbsp chopped almonds
confectioner's sugar, for dusting

filo pastry

mango

whole-wheat breadcrumbs

lemon rind

raw sugar

amaretti cookies

soft margarine

chopped almonds

1 Preheat the oven to 375°F. Lightly grease a large baking sheet. Halve, pit and peel the mango. Cut into cubes, then place them in a bowl, and sprinkle with the grated lemon rind.

2 Crush the amaretti cookies, and mix them with the raw sugar and the whole-wheat bread crumbs.

3 Lay one sheet of filo on a flat surface, and brush with a quarter of the melted margarine. Top with the second sheet, brush with one-third of the remaining margarine, then fold both sheets over, to make a rectangle measuring 11 x 9½ in. Brush with half the remaining margarine.

4 Sprinkle the filo with the amaretti mixture, leaving a 2 in border on each long side. Arrange the mango cubes over the top.

5 Roll up the filo from one of the long sides, jelly roll fashion. Lift the strudel onto the baking sheet with the join underneath. Brush with the remaining melted margarine, and sprinkle with the chopped almonds.

6 Bake for 20–25 minutes until golden brown, then transfer to a board. Dust with confectioner's sugar, slice diagonally, and serve warm.

COOK'S TIP
The easiest way to prepare a mango is to cut horizontally through the fruit, keeping the knife blade close to the pit. Repeat on the other side of the pit, and peel off the skin. Remove the remaining skin and flesh from around the pit.

Phyllo and Apricot Purses

Phyllo pastry is very easy to use and is low in fat. Keep a package in the freezer for last minute baking needs.

Makes 12

INGREDIENTS
¾ cup dried apricots
3 tbsp apricot compôte or conserve
3 ameretti cookies, crushed
3 phyllo sheets
4 tsp soft low fat margarine, melted
confectioners' sugar, for dusting

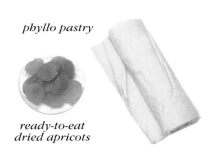

phyllo pastry

ready-to-eat dried apricots

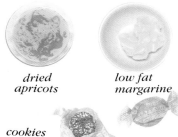

dried apricots

low fat margarine

cookies

COOK'S TIP
The easiest way to crush ameretti cookies to put them in a plastic bag and roll with a rolling pan.

NUTRITIONAL NOTES
PER PORTION:

ENERGY 58 Kcals
FAT 1.85 g **SATURATED FAT** 0.40 g
CHOLESTEROL 0.12 mg **FIBER** 0.74 g

1 Preheat the oven to 350°F. Grease two baking sheets. Chop the apricots, put them in a bowl and stir in the apricot compôte. Add the crushed amaretti cookies and mix well.

2 Cut the phyllo pastry into twenty-four 5-in squares, pile the squares on top of each other and cover with a clean dish towel to prevent the pastry from drying out and becoming brittle.

3 Lay one pastry square on a flat surface, brush lightly with melted margarine and lay another square diagonally on top. Brush the top square with melted margarine. Spoon a small mound of apricot mixture in the center of the pastry, bring up the edges and pinch together in a money-bag shape. Repeat with the remaining phyllo squares and filling to make 12 purses in all.

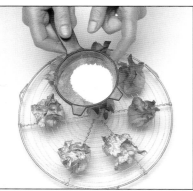

4 Arrange the purses on the prepared baking sheets and bake for 5–8 minutes, until golden brown. Transfer to a wire rack and dust lightly with confectioners' sugar. Serve warm.

Phyllo Scrunchies

Quick and easy to make, these pastries are ideal to serve at any time of day. Eat them warm or they will lose their crispness.

Makes 6

INGREDIENTS
5 apricots or plums
phyllo pastry sheets
4 tsp low fat margarine, melted
⅓ cup brown sugar
2 tbsp sliced almonds
confectioners' sugar, for dusting

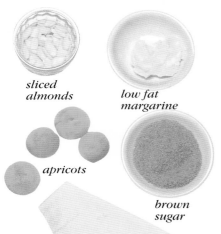

sliced almonds

low fat margarine

apricots

brown sugar

phyllo pastry

COOK'S TIP
Phyllo pastry dried out very quickly. Keep it covered as much as possible with a dry cloth or plastic wrap to limit exposure to the air, or it will become too brittle to use.

NUTRITIONAL NOTES
PER PORTION:

ENERGY 132 Kcals
FAT 4.19 g **SATURATED FAT** 0.63 g
CHOLESTEROL 0 **FIBER** 0.67 g

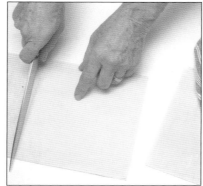

1 Preheat the oven to 375°F. Halve the apricots or plums, remove the pits and slice the fruit. Cut the phyllo pastry into twelve 7-in squares. Pile the squares on top of each other and cover with a clean dish towel to prevent the pastry from drying out.

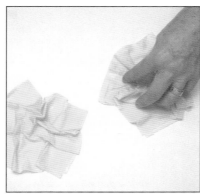

2 Remove one square of phyllo and brush it with melted margarine. Lay a second phyllo on top, then, using your fingers, mold the pastry into folds. Make five more scrunchies in the same way, working quickly so that the pastry does not dry out.

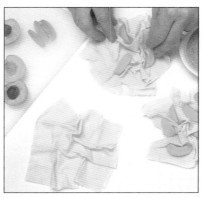

3 Arrange a few slices of fruit in the folds of each scrunchie, then sprinkle generously with the brown sugar and sliced almonds.

4 Place the scrunchies on a baking sheet. Bake for 8–10 minutes, until golden brown, then loosen the scrunchies from the baking sheet with a spatular and transfer to a wire rack. Dust with confectioners' sugar and serve at once.

Brown Sugar Meringues

These light brown meringues are extremely low in fat and are delicious served on their own or sandwiched together with a fresh fruit and soft cheese filling.

Makes about 20

INGREDIENTS
⅔ cup light brown sugar
2 large egg whites
1 tsp finely chopped walnuts

eggs

light brown sugar

walnuts

NUTRITIONAL NOTES
PER PORTION:

CALORIES 30
FAT 0.34 g **SATURATED FAT** 0.04 g
CHOLESTEROL 0 **FIBER** 0.02 g

COOK'S TIP

For a sophisticated filling, mix ½ cup nonfat cream cheese with 1 tbsp confectioner's sugar. Chop 2 slices of fresh pineapple, and add to the mixture. Use to sandwich the meringues together in pairs.

1 Preheat the oven to 325°F. Line two baking sheets with parchment paper. Press the sugar through a metal strainer into a bowl.

2 Whisk the egg whites in a clean bowl until very stiff and dry, then whisk in the sugar, about 1 tbsp at a time, until the meringue is very thick and glossy.

3 Spoon small mounds of the mixture on to the prepared baking sheets.

4 Sprinkle the meringues with the chopped walnuts. Bake for 30 minutes. Cool for 5 minutes on the baking sheets, then leave to cool on a wire rack.

Lemon Lady Fingers

These lady fingers are perfect for serving with fruit salads or light, creamy desserts.

Makes about 20

INGREDIENTS
2 eggs
6 tbsp sugar
grated zest of 1 lemon
½ cup flour, sifted
sugar, for sprinkling

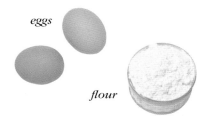

eggs

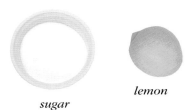

flour

sugar

lemon

VARIATION
To make Spicy Orange Lady Fingers, substitute grated orange rind for the lemon rind and add 1 tsp ground cinnamon with the flour.

1 Preheat the oven to 375°F. Line two baking sheets with non-stick baking paper. Beat the eggs, sugar and lemon rind together with a hand-held electric beater until thick and mousse-like (when the whisk is lifted, a trail should remain on the surface of the mixture for at least 15 seconds). Gently fold in the flour with a large metal spoon using a figure-eight spoon.

2 Place the mixture in a large piping bag fitted with ½-in plain nozzle. Pipe the mixture into finger lengths on the prepared baking sheets.

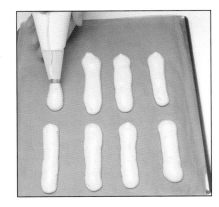

3 Sprinkle the fingers with sugar. Bake for 6–8 minutes, until golden brown, then transfer the lady fingers to a wire rack to cool.

NUTRITIONAL NOTES
PER PORTION:

ENERGY 33 Kcals
FAT 0.57 g **SATURATED FAT** 0.16 g
CHOLESTEROL 19.30 mg **FIBER** 0.08 g

Cherry Crêpes

These pancakes are virtually fat-free and lower in calories and higher in fiber than traditional ones. Serve with a spoonful of low fat plain yogurt.

Serves 4

INGREDIENTS
FOR THE CRÊPES
½ cup flour
⅓ cup whole-wheat flour
pinch of salt
1 egg white
⅔ cup skim milk
⅔ cup water
a little oil for frying

FOR THE FILLING
15-oz can black cherries in juice
1½ tsp arrowroot

skim milk

whole wheat flour

all-purpose flour

black cherries

arrowroot   **egg**

1 Sift the flours and salt into a bowl, adding any bran left in the sifter to the bowl at the end.

2 Make a well in the center of the flour and add the egg white. Gradually beat in the milk and water, whisking hard until all the liquid is incorporated and the batter is smooth and bubbly.

3 Heat a non-stick pan with a small amount of oil until the pan is very hot. Pour in just enough batter to cover the base of the pan, swirling the pan to cover the base evenly.

4 Cook until the crêpe is set and golden, and then turn to cook the other side. Remove to a sheet of paper towel and then cook the remaining batter, to make about eight crêpes.

5 Drain the cherries, reserving the juice. Blend about 2 tbsp of the juice from the can of cherries with the arrowroot in a saucepan. Stir in the rest of the juice. Heat gently, stirring, until boiling. Stir over moderate heat for about 2 minutes, until thickened and clear.

COOK'S TIP

If fresh cherries are in season, cook them gently in enough apple juice just to cover them, and then thicken the juice with arrowroot as in Step 5.

The basic pancakes will freeze very successfully. Layer them with paper towels or wax paper, wrap them in plastic wrap and seal. Freeze for up to six months. Thaw at room temperature.

NUTRITIONAL NOTES

PER PORTION:

ENERGY 165 Kcals **FAT** 3.03 g
SATURATED FAT 0.4 g

6 Add the cherries and stir until thoroughly heated. Spoon the cherries into the pancakes and fold them in quarters.

Blueberry and Orange Crêpe Baskets

Impress your guests with these pretty, fruit-filled crêpes. When blueberries are out of season, replace them with other soft fruit, such as raspberries.

Serves 6

INGREDIENTS
FOR THE CRÊPES
1¼ cups all-purpose flour
pinch salt
2 egg whites
⅞ cup skim milk
⅔ cup orange juice

FOR THE FILLING
4 medium-size oranges
2 cups blueberries

orange juice

oranges

eggs

blueberries

skim milk

NUTRITIONAL NOTES
PER PORTION:

ENERGY 158 Kcals **FAT** 0.85 g
SATURATED FAT 0.08 g

COOK'S TIP
Don't fill the pancake baskets until you're ready to serve them, because they will absorb the fruit juice and begin to soften.

1 Preheat the oven to 400°F. To make the crêpes, sift the flour and salt into a bowl. Make a well in the center of the flour and add the egg whites, milk and orange juice. Whisk hard, until all the liquid has been incorporated and the batter is smooth and bubbly.

2 Lightly grease a heavy or non-stick crêpe pan and heat it until it is very hot. Pour in just enough batter to cover the base of the pan, swirling it to cover the pan evenly.

3 Cook until the crêpe has set and is golden, and then turn it to cook the other side. Remove the crêpe to a sheet of toweling paper, and then cook the remaining batter, to make 6–8 crêpes.

4 Place six small ovenproof bowls or molds on a baking sheet and arrange the crêpes over these. Bake them in the oven for about 10 minutes, until they are crisp and set into shape. Carefully lift the 'baskets' off the molds.

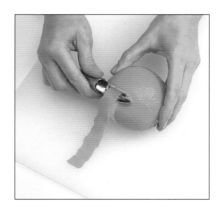

5 Pare a thin piece of orange rind from one orange and cut it in fine strips. Blanch the strips in boiling water for 30 seconds, rinse them in cold water and set them aside. Cut all the peel and white pith from all the oranges.

6 Divide the oranges into segments, catching the juice, combine with the blueberries and warm them gently. Spoon the fruit into the baskets and scatter the shreds of rind over the top. Serve with yogurt or light crème fraîche.

Baked Apples in Honey and Lemon

A classic mix of flavors in a healthy, traditional family dessert. Serve warm, with skim-milk custard.

Serves 4

INGREDIENTS
4 medium-size cooking apples
1 tbsp honey
grated rind and juice of 1 lemon
1 tbsp low-fat spread

honey

cooking apples

lemon

low-fat spread

COOK'S TIP

This recipe can also be cooked in the microwave to save time. Place the apples in a microwave-safe dish and cover them with a lid or pierced plastic wrap. Microwave on FULL POWER (100%) for 9–10 minutes.

1 Preheat the oven to 350°F. Remove the cores from the apples, leaving them whole.

2 With a cannelle or sharp knife, cut lines through the apple skin at intervals and place in an ovenproof dish.

NUTRITIONAL NOTES
PER PORTION:

ENERGY 65 Kcals **FAT** 1.62 g
SATURATED FAT 0.42 g

3 Mix together the honey, lemon rind, juice and low-fat spread.

4 Spoon the mixture into the apples and cover the dish with foil or a lid. Bake for 40–45 minutes, or until the apples are tender. Serve with skim-milk custard.

Grilled Nectarines with Spiced Ricotta

This easy dessert is good at any time of year – use canned peach halves if fresh ones are not available.

Serves 4

INGREDIENTS
4 ripe nectarines or peaches
1 tbsp light brown sugar
½ cup ricotta cheese or fromage
frais
½ tsp ground star anise

nectarines

light brown sugar

ricotta cheese

ground star anise

 Cut the nectarines in half and remove the stones.

2 Arrange the nectarines, cut-side upwards, in a wide flameproof dish or on a baking sheet.

NUTRITIONAL NOTES
PER PORTION:

ENERGY 95 Kcals **FAT** 3.3 g
SATURATED FAT 1.98 g

COOK'S TIP
Star anise has a warm, rich flavor – if you can't get it, try ground cloves or ground allspice instead.

3 Stir the sugar into the ricotta or fromage frais. Using a teaspoon, spoon the mixture into the hollow of each nectarine half.

4 Sprinkle with the star anise. Place under a moderately hot broiler for 6–8 minutes, or until the nectarines are hot and bubbling. Serve warm.

Raisin and Couscous Puddings

Most couscous on the market now is the pre-cooked variety, which needs only a minimum of cooking, but check the package instructions first to make sure. Serve hot, with yogurt or skim milk pudding.

Serves 4

INGREDIENTS
⅓ cup raisins
2 cups apple juice
1 cup couscous
½ tsp allspice

apple juice

couscous

allspice

raisins

NUTRITIONAL NOTES
PER PORTION:
ENERGY 131 Kcals **FAT** 0.46 g
SATURATED FAT 0

1 Lightly grease four 1-cup pudding molds or one 4-cup pudding mold. Place the raisins in a pan and pour in the apple juice.

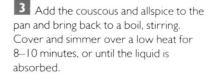

2 Bring the apple juice to a boil, and then cover the pan and let simmer gently for 2–3 minutes, to plump up the fruit. Using a slotted spoon, lift out about half the fruit and place it in the bottom of the bowls.

3 Add the couscous and allspice to the pan and bring back to a boil, stirring. Cover and simmer over a low heat for 8–10 minutes, or until the liquid is absorbed.

4 Spoon the couscous into the molds, spread it level, and then cover the molds tightly with foil. Place the molds in a steamer over boiling water, cover and steam for about 30 minutes. Run a knife around the edges, turn the puddings out carefully and serve immediately.

Orange Yogurt Brûlées

A luxurious treat, but one that is much lower in fat than the classic brûlée, which is made with cream, eggs and large amounts of sugar.

Serves 4

INGREDIENTS
2 medium-size oranges
⅔ cup low fat plain strained yogurt
¼ cup low fat crème fraîche
3 tbsp sugar
2 tbsp light brown sugar

light brown sugar

raw sugar

crème fraîche

oranges

low fat yogurt

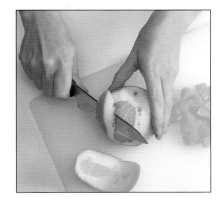

1 With a sharp knife, cut away all the peel and white pith from the oranges and chop the fruit. Or, if there's time, segment the oranges, removing all the membrane.

2 Place the fruit in the bottom of four individual flameproof dishes. Mix together the yogurt and crème fraîche and spoon the mixture over the oranges.

3 Mix together the two sugars and sprinkle them evenly over the tops of the dishes.

4 Place the dishes under a preheated, very hot broiler for 3–4 minutes or until the sugar melts and turns to a rich golden brown. Serve warm or cold.

COOK'S TIP

For an even lighter version, simply use ¾ cup low fat plain yogurt instead of the strained yogurt and crème fraîche.

NUTRITIONAL NOTES
PER PORTION:

ENERGY 147 Kcals **FAT** 2.9 g
SATURATED FAT 1.75 g

Apricot and Banana Compote

This compote is delicious served on its own or with low-fat custard or ice cream. Served for breakfast, it makes a tasty start to the day.

Serves 4

INGREDIENTS
1 cup dried apricots
1¼ cups unsweetened orange juice
⅔ cup unsweetened apple juice
1 teaspoon ground ginger
3 medium bananas, sliced
¼ cup toasted flaked almonds

dried apricots

unsweetened orange juice

unsweetened apple juice

ground ginger

bananas

toasted flaked almonds

1 Put the apricots in a saucepan with the fruit juices and ginger and stir. Cover, bring to the boil and simmer gently for 10 minutes, stirring occasionally.

2 Set aside to cool, leaving the lid on. Once cool, stir in the sliced bananas.

3 Spoon the fruit and juices into a serving dish.

4 Serve immediately, or cover and chill for several hours before serving. Sprinkle with flaked almonds just before serving.

COOK'S TIP
Use other combinations of dried and fresh fruit such as prunes or figs and apples or peaches.

NUTRITIONAL NOTES
PER PORTION:

CALORIES 241 PROTEIN 4.92g
FAT 4.18g SATURATED FAT 0.37g
CARBOHYDRATE 48.98g FIBER 4.91g
ADDED SUGAR 0.00g SODIUM 0.02g

Golden Ginger Compote

Warm, spicy and full of sun-ripened ingredients – this is the perfect winter dessert.

Serves 4

INGREDIENTS
2 cups kumquats
1 ¼ cups dried apricots
2 tbsp raisins
1 ⅔ cups water
1 orange
1 in piece fresh ginger root
4 cardamom pods
4 cloves
2 tbsp honey
1 tbsp slivered almonds, toasted

orange

honey

kumquats

fresh root ginger

dried apricots

slivered almonds

cloves

cardamom pods

raisins

1 Wash the kumquats, and, if they are large, cut them in half. Place them in a pan with the apricots, raisins and water. Bring to a boil.

2 Pare the rind thinly from the orange and add to the pan. Peel and grate the ginger and add to the pan. Lightly crush the cardamom pods and add them to the pan, with the cloves.

NUTRITIONAL NOTES
PER PORTION:

ENERGY 198 Kcals **FAT** 2.94 g
SATURATED FAT 0.22 g

3 Reduce the heat, cover the pan and leave to simmer gently for about 30 minutes, or until the fruit is tender, stirring occasionally.

4 Serve immediately, or cover and chill for several hours before serving. Sprinkle with flaked almonds just before serving.

Winter Fruit Salad

A colorful, refreshing and nutritious fruit salad, which is ideal served with reduced-fat plain yogurt or cream.

Serves 6

INGREDIENTS
1 can (8 ounces) pineapple
  cubes in fruit juice
scant cup freshly
  squeezed orange juice
scant cup unsweetened apple juice
2 tablespoons orange or
  apple liqueur
2 tablespoons honey (optional)
2 oranges, peeled
2 green-skinned apples, chopped
2 pears, chopped
4 plums, pitted and chopped
12 fresh dates, pitted and chopped
½ cup dried apricots
fresh mint sprigs, to garnish

*pineapple cubes
in fruit juice*

*freshly
squeezed
orange juice*

*unsweetened
apple juice*

*orange
or apple
liqueur*

honey

oranges

*green-skinned
apples*

pears

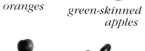
plums

*fresh
dates*

*dried
apricots*

1 Drain the pineapple, reserving the juice. Put the pineapple juice, orange juice, apple juice, liqueur and honey, if using, in a large serving bowl and stir.

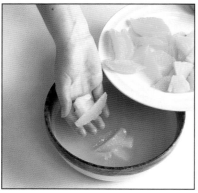

2 Segment the oranges, catching any juice in the bowl, and put the orange segments and pineapple in the fruit juice mixture.

NUTRITIONAL NOTES
PER PORTION:

CALORIES 227 PROTEIN 2.85g
FAT 0.37g SATURATED FAT 0.00g
CARBOHYDRATE 53.68g FIBER 5.34g
ADDED SUGAR 1.33g SODIUM 0.01g

3 Add the apples and pears to the bowl.

4 Stir in the plums, dates and apricots, cover and chill for several hours. Decorate with fresh mint sprigs to serve.

COOK'S TIP
Use other unsweetened fruit juices such as pink grapefruit and pineapple juice in place of the orange and apple juice.

Watermelon, Ginger and Grapefruit Salad

This pretty, pink combination is very light and refreshing for any summer meal.

Serves 4

INGREDIENTS
1 lb/2 cups diced watermelon flesh
2 ruby or pink grapefruit
2 pieces preserved ginger in syrup
2 tbsp preserved ginger syrup

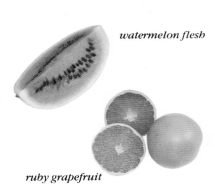
watermelon flesh

ruby grapefruit

preserved ginger in syrup

COOK'S TIP
Toss the fruits gently – grapefruit segments will break up easily and the appearance of the dish will be spoiled.

NUTRITIONAL NOTES
PER PORTION:

ENERGY 20 Kcals **FAT** 0.4 g
SATURATED FAT 0.1 g

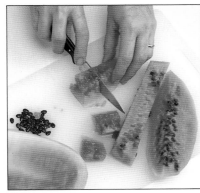

1 Remove any seeds from the watermelon and cut into bite-sized chunks.

2 Using a small sharp knife, cut away all the peel and white pith from the grapefruits and carefully lift out the segments, catching any juice in a bowl.

3 Finely chop the ginger and place in a serving bowl with the melon cubes and grapefruit segments, adding the reserved juice.

4 Spoon over the ginger syrup and toss the fruits lightly to mix evenly. Chill before serving.

Cappuccino Coffee Cups

Coffee-lovers will love this one – and it tastes rich and creamy, even though it's very light.

Serves 4

INGREDIENTS
2 eggs
7.7 oz can low-fat milk
5 tsp instant coffee granules or
   powder
2 tbsp granulated artificial sweetener
2 tsp powdered gelatin
4 tbsp light crème fraîche
extra cocoa powder or ground
   cinnamon, to decorate

evaporated low-fat milk

powdered gelatin

granulated sweetener

instant coffee

eggs

crème fraîche

cocoa powder

VARIATION
Strained plain yogurt can be used instead of crème fraîche, if you prefer.

NUTRITIONAL NOTES
PER PORTION:

ENERGY 131 Kcals **FAT** 6.8 g
SATURATED FAT 2.3 g

1 Separate one egg and reserve the white. Beat the yolk with the whole of the remaining egg.

2 Put the evaporated milk, coffee granules, sweetener and beaten eggs in a pan; whisk until evenly combined.

3 Put the pan over a low heat and stir constantly until the mixture is hot, but not boiling. Cook, stirring constantly, without boiling, until the mixture is slightly thickened and smooth.

4 Remove the pan from the heat. Sprinkle the gelatin over the pan and whisk until the gelatin has completely dissolved.

5 Spoon the coffee custard into four individual dishes or glasses and chill them until set.

6 Whisk the reserved egg white until stiff. Whisk in the crème fraîche and then spoon the mixture over the desserts. Sprinkle with cocoa or cinnamon and serve.

COOK'S TIP
It's important to ensure that the gelatin is completely dissolved before spooning the mixture into the dishes, otherwise the texture will not be smooth.

Figs with Ricotta Cream

Fresh, ripe figs are full of natural sweetness, and need little adornment. This simple recipe makes the most of their beautiful, intense flavor.

Serves 4

INGREDIENTS
4 ripe, fresh figs
½ cup ricotta or cottage cheese
3 tbsp crème fraîche
1 tbsp honey
½ tsp vanilla extract
freshly grated nutmeg, to decorate

vanilla essence

honey

crème fraîche

ricotta cheese

figs

nutmeg

1 Trim the stalks from the figs. Make four cuts through each fig from the stalk-end, cutting them almost through but leaving them joined at the base.

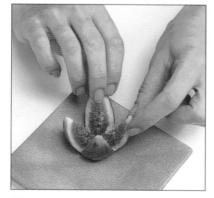

2 Place the figs on serving plates and open them out.

3 Mix together the ricotta or cottage cheese, crème fraîche, honey and vanilla.

4 Spoon a little ricotta cream on to each plate and sprinkle with grated nutmeg to serve.

NUTRITIONAL NOTES

PER PORTION:

ENERGY 99 Kcals **FAT** 5.5 g
SATURATED FAT 3.5 g

Pineapple Wedges with Allspice and Lime

Fresh pineapple is easy to prepare and always looks very festive, so this dish is perfect for easy entertaining.

Serves 4

INGREDIENTS
1 medium-size, ripe pineapple
1 lime
1 tbsp dark brown sugar
1 tsp ground allspice

ground allspice   *pineapple*

brown sugar

lime

1 Cut the pineapple lengthways into quarters and remove the core.

2 Loosen the flesh, by sliding a knife between the flesh and the skin. Cut the flesh into slices, leaving it on the skin.

3 Remove a few shreds of rind from the lime and then squeeze out the juice.

4 Sprinkle the pineapple with the lime juice and rind, sugar and allspice. Serve immediately, or chill for up to an hour.

VARIATION

For a quick hot dish, place the pineapple slices on a baking sheet, sprinkle them with the lime juice, sugar and allspice and place them under a hot broiler for 3–4 minutes, or until golden and bubbling. Sprinkle with shreds of lime zest and serve.

NUTRITIONAL NOTES
PER PORTION:

ENERGY 55 Kcals **FAT** 0.3 g
SATURATED FAT 0.03 g

Raspberry Granola Layer

As well as being a delicious, low-fat, high-fiber dessert, this can also be served for a quick, healthy breakfast.

Serves 4

INGREDIENTS
2¼ cups fresh or frozen and thawed
   raspberries
1 cup low-fat plain yogurt
½ cup granola

raspberries

granola

plain yogurt

NUTRITIONAL NOTES
PER PORTION:

ENERGY 122 Kcals **FAT** 2.7 g
SATURATED FAT 0.4 g

COOK'S TIP

This recipe can be made in advance and stored in the fridge for several hours, or overnight if you're serving it for breakfast.

1 Reserve four raspberries for decoration, and then spoon a few raspberries into four stemmed glasses or glass dishes.

2 Top the raspberries with a spoonful of yogurt in each glass.

3 Sprinkle a layer of granola over the yogurt.

4 Repeat with the raspberries and other ingredients. Top each with a whole raspberry.

Brazilian Coffee Bananas

Rich, lavish and sinful-looking, this dessert
takes only about 2 minutes to make!

Serves 4

INGREDIENTS
4 small ripe bananas
1 tbsp instant coffee granules or
   powder
1 tbsp hot water
2 tbsp dark brown sugar
1⅛ cups strained plain yogurt
1 tbsp toasted slivered almonds

bananas

yogurt

slivered almonds

instant coffee

dark brown sugar

1 Peel and slice one banana and mash
the remaining three with a fork.

2 Dissolve the coffee in the hot water
and stir into the mashed bananas.

3 Spoon a little of the mashed banana
mixture into four serving dishes and
sprinkle with sugar. Top with a spoonful
of yogurt, then repeat until all the
ingredients are used up.

4 Swirl the last layer of yogurt for a
marbled effect. Finish with a few banana
slices and slivered almonds. Serve cold.
Best eaten within about an hour of
making.

VARIATION

For a special occasion, add a dash –
just a dash – of dark rum or brandy
to the bananas for extra richness.
1 tbsp of rum or brandy adds about 30
calories.

NUTRITIONAL NOTES

Per portion:

ENERGY 169 Kcals **FAT** 2.7 g
SATURATED FAT 0.46 g

Minted Raspberry Bavarois

A sophisticated dessert that can be made a day in advance for a special dinner party.

Serves 6

INGREDIENTS
5½ cups fresh or frozen and thawed
    raspberries
2 tbsp confectioners' sugar
2 tbsp lemon juice
1 tbsp finely chopped fresh mint
2 packets powdered gelatin
5 tbsp boiling water
1¼ cups vanilla pudding made with
    skim milk
1⅛ cups low fat plain yogurt
fresh mint sprigs, to decorate

skim-milk pudding

confectioners' sugar

low fat plain yogurt

powdered gelatin

lemon

mint

raspberries

NUTRITIONAL NOTES
PER PORTION:

ENERGY 113 Kcals **FAT** 0.6 g
SATURATED FAT 0.3 g

COOK'S TIP
You can make this dessert using frozen raspberries, which have a good color and flavor. Allow them to thaw at room temperature, and use any juice in the gelatin.

1 Reserve a few raspberries for decoration. Place the raspberries, confectioners' sugar and lemon juice in a food processor and process them until smooth.

2 Press the purée through a sieve to remove the raspberry seeds. Add the mint. You should have about 2½ cups of purée.

3 Sprinkle 1 tsp of the gelatin over 2 tbsp of the boiling water and stir until the gelatin has dissolved. Stir into ⅔ cup of the fruit purée.

4 Pour this gelatin into a 4-cup mold, and leave the mold to chill in the refrigerator until it is just on the point of setting. Tip the mold to swirl the setting gelatin around the sides, and then leave to chill until the gelatin has set completely.

5 Stir the remaining fruit purée into the custard and yogurt. Dissolve the rest of the gelatin in the remaining water and stir it in quickly.

6 Pour the raspberry custard into the mold and let it chill until it has set completely. To serve, dip the mold quickly into hot water and then turn it out and decorate it with the reserved raspberries and the mint sprigs.

Lemon Hearts with Strawberry Sauce

These elegant little hearts are light as air, and they are best made the day before your dinner party—which makes them especially convenient.

Serves 6

INGREDIENTS
FOR THE HEARTS
¾ cup ricotta cheese
⅔ cup crème fraîche or sour cream
1 tbsp granulated artificial sweetener
finely grated rind of ½ lemon
2 tbsp lemon juice
2 tsp powdered gelatin
2 egg whites

FOR THE SAUCE
2 cups fresh or frozen and thawed strawberries
1 tbsp lemon juice

crème fraîche

ricotta cheese

powdered gelatin

lemon

strawberries

eggs

granulated sweetener

1 Beat the low fat ricotta cheese until smooth. Stir in the crème fraîche, sweetener and lemon rind.

2 Place the lemon juice in a small bowl and sprinkle the gelatin over it. Place the bowl over a pan of hot water and stir to dissolve the gelatin completely.

3 Quickly stir the gelatin into the cheese mixture, mixing it in evenly.

4 Beat the egg whites until they form soft peaks. Quickly fold them into the cheese mixture.

5 Spoon the mixture into six lightly oiled, individual heart-shaped molds and chill the molds until set.

VARIATION

These little heart-shaped desserts are the perfect choice for a romantic dinner, but they don't have to be heart-shaped—setting the mixture in individual fluted molds, or even in ordinary teacups.

NUTRITIONAL NOTES

PER PORTION:

ENERGY 112 Kcals **FAT** 8.2 g
SATURATED FAT 5.14 g

6 Place the strawberries and lemon juice in a blender and process until smooth. Pour the sauce onto serving plates and place the turned-out hearts on top. Decorate with slices of strawberry.

Strawberry Rose-petal Pashka

This lighter version of a traditional Russian dessert is ideal for dinner parties – make it a day or two in advance for best results.

Serves 4

INGREDIENTS
1½ cups cottage cheese
¾ cup low-fat plain yogurt
2 tbsp honey
½ tsp rosewater
2½ cups strawberries
handful of scented pink rose petals, to
decorate

clear honey

cottage cheese

rose-water

strawberries

yogurt

NUTRITIONAL NOTES
Per portion:

ENERGY 151 Kcals **FAT** 3.8 g
SATURATED FAT 2.3 g

COOK'S TIP
The flowerpot shape is traditional for pashka, but you could make it in any shape – the small porcelain heart-shaped molds with draining holes usually used for *coeurs à la crème* make a pretty alternative.

1 Drain any free liquid from the cottage cheese and tip the cheese into a sieve. Use a wooden spoon to rub it through the sieve into a bowl.

2 Stir the yogurt, honey and rose-water into the cheese.

3 Roughly chop about half the strawberries and stir them into the cheese mixture.

4 Line a new, clean flowerpot or a sieve with fine cheesecloth and tip the cheese mixture in. Leave it to drain over a bowl for several hours, or overnight.

5 Invert the flowerpot or sieve on to a serving plate, turn out the pashka and remove the cheesecloth.

6 Decorate with the reserved strawberries and rose petals. Serve chilled.

Chocolate Vanilla Timbales

You really can allow yourself the occasional chocolate treat, especially if it's a dessert as light as this one.

Serves 6

INGREDIENTS
FOR THE TIMBALES
1½ cups skim milk
2 tbsp cocoa
2 eggs
1 tsp vanilla extract
3 tbsp granulated artificial sweetener
1 packet powdered gelatin
3 tbsp hot water

FOR THE SAUCE
½ cup low fat plain yogurt, strained
½ tsp vanilla extract
extra cocoa powder, to sprinkle

skim milk

granulated sweetener

vanilla extract

eggs

cocoa powder

powdered gelatin

NUTRITIONAL NOTES
PER PORTION:

ENERGY 81 Kcals **FAT** 3.5 g
SATURATED FAT 0.14 g

1 Place the milk and cocoa in a saucepan and stir until the milk is boiling. Separate the eggs and beat the egg yolks with the vanilla and sweetener in a bowl, until the mixture is pale and smooth. Gradually pour in the chocolate milk, beating well.

2 Return the mixture to the pan and stir constantly over a gentle heat, without boiling, until it's slightly thickened and smooth. Dissolve the gelatin in the hot water and then quickly stir it into the milk mixture. Let it cool until it's on the verge of setting.

3 Whisk the egg whites until they hold soft peaks. Fold the egg whites quickly into the milk mixture. Spoon the timbale mixture into six individual molds and chill them until set.

4 To serve, run a knife around the edge, dip the molds quickly into hot water and turn out the chocolate timbales on to serving plates. For the sauce, stir together the yogurt and vanilla, spoon on to the plates and sprinkle with a little more cocoa powder.

Whole-wheat Bread and Banana Yogurt Ice

Serve this tempting yogurt ice with some fresh fruit, such as strawberries, or with wafer cookies, for a light dessert.

Serves 6

INGREDIENTS
2 cups fresh whole-wheat
  bread crumbs
¼ cup light brown sugar
1¼ cups low-fat cold custard
5 ounces low-fat ricotta cheese
  or low-fat cream cheese
5 ounces plain yogurt
4 bananas, mashed
juice of 1 lemon
¼ cup confectioners' sugar, sifted
¼ cup raisins, chopped
pared lemon rind, to garnish

fresh whole-wheat bread crumbs

light brown sugar

low-fat cold custard

low-fat ricotta cheese

lemon

yogurt

bananas

sugar

raisins

NUTRITIONAL NOTES
PER PORTION:

CALORIES 227 PROTEIN 7.55g
FAT 5.51g SATURATED FAT 2.99g
CARBOHYDRATE 52.27g FIBER 2.01g
ADDED SUGAR 12.77g SODIUM 0.17g

1 Preheat the oven to 400°F. Mix together the bread crumbs and brown sugar and spread the mixture out on a nonstick baking sheet. Bake for about 10 minutes, stirring occasionally, until crisp. Set aside to cool, then break the mixture up into crumbs.

2 Meanwhile, put the custard, ricotta cheese and yogurt in a bowl and mix. Mash the bananas with the lemon juice and add to the custard mixture, mixing well. Fold in the confectioners' sugar.

3 Pour the mixture into a shallow, plastic, freezerproof container and freeze for about 3 hours or until mushy in consistency. Spoon into a chilled bowl and quickly mash with a fork to break down the ice crystals.

4 Add the breadcrumbs and raisins and mix well. Return the mixture to the container, cover and freeze until firm. Transfer to the fridge about 30 minutes before serving, to soften a little. Serve in scoops, decorated with lemon rind.

Summer Fruit Salad Ice Cream

What could be more cooling on a hot summer day than fresh summer fruits, lightly frozen in this irresistible ice?

Serves 6

NUTRITIONAL NOTES
PER PORTION:

ENERGY 70 Kcals **FAT** 2.9 g
SATURATED FAT 0.12 g

COOK'S TIP
Red grape juice has a good flavor and improves the color of the ice, but if it is not available, use cranberry, apple or orange juice instead.

INGREDIENTS
4½ cups mixed soft summer fruit, such as raspberries, strawberries, black currants, red currants, etc.
2 eggs
1 cup low fat plain yogurt
¾ cup red grape juice
1 packet powdered gelatin

red grape juice

powdered gelatin

yogurt

eggs

summer fruits

1 Reserve half the fruit and purée the rest in a food processor, or rub it through a sieve to make a smooth purée.

2 Separate the eggs and whisk the yolks and the yogurt into the fruit purée.

3 Heat the grape juice until it's almost boiling, and then remove it from the heat. Sprinkle the gelatin over the grape juice and stir to dissolve the gelatin completely.

4 Whisk the dissolved gelatin mixture into the fruit purée and then pour the mixture into a freezer container. Freeze until half-frozen and slushy in consistency.

5 Whisk the egg whites until they are stiff. Quickly fold them into the half-frozen mixture.

6 Return to the freezer and freeze until almost firm. Scoop into individual dishes or glasses and add the reserved soft fruits.

Muscat Grape Frappé

The flavor and perfume of the Muscat grape is rarely more enticing than when captured in this icy-cool salad. Because of its alcohol content, this dish is not suitable for young children.

Serves 4

INGREDIENTS
½ bottle Muscat wine, Beaumes de
    Venise, Frontignan, or Rivsaltes
1 lb Muscat grapes

Muscat wine

Muscat grapes

1 Pour the wine into a stainless-steel or enamel tray, add ⅔ cup water and freeze for 3 hours or until completely solid.

2 Remove the seeds from the grapes with a pair of tweezers. If you have time, peel the grapes.

3 Scrape the frozen wine with a tablespoon to make a fine ice. Combine the grapes with the ice and spoon into 4 shallow glasses.

NUTRITIONAL NOTES
PER PORTION:

ENERGY 138 Kcals **FAT** 0.1 g
SATURATED FAT 0

Rhubarb and Orange Granita

Pretty pink rhubarb, with sweet oranges and honey – the perfect sweet ice.

Serves 4

INGREDIENTS
12 oz pink rhubarb
1 medium-size orange
1 tbsp honey
1 tsp powdered gelatin
orange slices, to decorate

honey

powdered gelatin

orange

rhubarb

NUTRITIONAL NOTES
PER PORTION:

ENERGY 70 Kcals **FAT** 2.9 g
SATURATED FAT 0.12 g

COOK'S TIP
Most pink, forced rhubarb is naturally quite sweet, but if yours is not, you can add a little more honey, sugar or artificial sweetener to taste.

1 Trim the rhubarb and slice into 1 in lengths. Place the rhubarb in a pan.

2 Finely grate the rind from the orange and squeeze out the juice. Add about half the orange juice and the grated rind to the rhubarb in the pan and allow to simmer until the rhubarb is just tender. Stir in the honey.

3 Heat the remaining orange juice and stir in the gelatin to dissolve. Stir it into the rhubarb. Pour the whole mixture into a rigid freezer container and freeze it until it's slushy, about 2 hours.

4 Remove the mixture from the freezer and beat it well to break up the ice crystals. Return the granita to the freezer and freeze it again until firm. Allow the granita to soften slightly at room temperature before serving.

Frozen Apple and Blackberry Terrine

Apples and blackberries are a classic autumn combination; they really complement each other. This pretty, three-layered terrine can be frozen, so you can enjoy it at any time of year.

Serves 6

VARIATION

For a quicker version the mixture can be set without the layering. Purée the apples and blackberries together, stir the dissolved gelatin and whisked egg whites into the mixture, turn the whole thing into the pan and leave the mixture to set.

INGREDIENTS
1 lb cooking or eating apples
1¼ cups cider
1 tbsp honey
1 tsp vanilla extract
2 cups fresh or frozen and thawed
  blackberries
1 packet powdered gelatin
2 egg whites
fresh apple slices and blackberries,
  to decorate

cider

vanilla extract

honey

eggs

blackberries

powdered gelatin

1 Peel, core and chop the apples and place them in a pan, with half the cider. Bring the cider to the boil, and then cover the pan and let the apples simmer gently until tender.

2 Tip the apples into a food processor and process them to a smooth purée. Stir in the honey and vanilla. Add half the blackberries to half the apple purée, and then process again until smooth. Sieve to remove the pips.

3 Heat the remaining cider until it's almost boiling, and then sprinkle the gelatine over and stir until the gelatin has completely dissolved. Add half the gelatin to the apple purée and half to the blackberry purée.

4 Leave the purées to cool until almost set. Whisk the egg whites until they are stiff. Quickly fold them into the apple purée. Remove half the purée to another bowl. Stir the remaining whole blackberries into half the apple purée, and then tip this into a 7½-cup loaf pan, packing it down firmly.

5 Top with the blackberry purée and spread it evenly. Finally, add a layer of the apple purée and smooth it evenly. If necessary, freeze each layer until firm before adding the next.

6 Freeze until firm. To serve, allow to stand at room temperature for about 20 minutes to soften, and then serve in slices, decorated with fresh apples and blackberries.

INDEX